Secularizing the Sacred

The Demise of Liturgical Wholeness

A Case Study of Liturgical Minimisation in the Presbyterian Church of Australia

John E. Webster and Ronald S. Laura

University Press of America,® Inc.
Lanham • Boulder • New York • Toronto • Plymouth, UK

Copyright © 2016 by University Press of America,® Inc.
4501 Forbes Boulevard, Suite 200, Lanham, Maryland 20706
UPA Acquisitions Department (301) 459-3366

Unit A, Whitacre Mews, 26-34 Stannary Street,
London SE11 4AB, United Kingdom

All rights reserved
Printed in the United States of America
British Library Cataloguing in Publication Information Available

Library of Congress Control Number: 2016934539
ISBN: 978-0-7618-6761-6 (pbk : alk. paper)—ISBN: 978-0-7618-6762-3 (electronic)

∞™ The paper used in this publication meets the minimum requirements of American National Standard for Information Sciences Permanence of Paper for Printed Library Materials, ANSI/NISO Z39.48-1992.

This book is written in acknowledgement of those
who were influential in my life in the pursuit of Biblical truth.
My grandmother Coral Howard was pivotal in her encouragement of my
decision to enter the ministry of the Christian Church. Her commitment
and her devotion to prayer was always inspirational. Her death in 1967
was indelibly inscribed upon my mind as her simplicity of faith was
expressed in her favourite hymn:

Jesus Thou art everything to me,
All my lasting joys are found in Thee,
Jesus Thou art everything to me.

There were many people over the formative years in the Christian ministry who were gracious but intellectually challenging. Professor Crawford Miller introduced me to the complexities of Philosophical Theology. The philosophy of John Locke and Austin Farrer were of primary interest. Whilst most students could never fathom the inter-relationships of theological reasoning and epistemology in particular, I realised that truth is so vast that an understanding of philosophy /epistemology is critical to the opening up of an existing treasure trove of knowledge ready to benefit a confused and disoriented Church.

History has never been the same to me since I meet Professor John Ramsland. From him I learnt that history is alive and cogent for the present, it is no dead issue. The present can only be appreciated with an understanding of the past and the future can have no destiny unless the wisdom of the past be its guiding principle.

John E. Webster
Easter 2015

Let me first acknowledge my gratitude to the Rev. Dr. John Webster for having invited me to join him in this exciting project. The opportunity to explore with him philosophically and theologically the array of engaging issues on the secularisation of Christian worship has led to the most engaging intellectual journey. Our joint reflection has provided me the opportunity to extend my earlier theories on transformative subjugation and empathetic epistemology to areas of theological discourse which have not previously received sufficient epistemic scrutiny. The result of the analysis will perhaps best be judged by our informed readers, but there is no doubt that we have enormously enjoyed and benefited from the insight from our collaborative ratiocination. It is to be hoped that those who read what we have written will have been encouraged to ask some new and important philosophical questions and perhaps gained enough in novel perspective to answer them differently.

Professor Ronald S. Laura
Easter 2015

Contents

Introduction		1
1	Socio-Political Patterns in Early Presbyterianism in New South Wales	21
2	Defining the Practice of Worship in the Presbyterian Church	35
3	The Climax of Calvinist Liturgical Development in New South Wales	61
4	A Brief History of the Theological Aetiology of Liturgical Minimization	81
5	Minimization since 1977 in the Presbyterian Church of Australia	111
6	Towards an Epistemology of Worship	145
7	Towards a Reconstruction of Theological Education	179
Conclusion		207
Bibliography		213
About the Authors		219

Introduction

In this book we shall argue that the role of theological education in the professional development of clergy for the Presbyterian Church in Australia is at a critical point in its history. Liturgical Minimization which we define as, *the process of removing from a liturgy anything that is theologically unacceptable or anything that is indifferent which has no direct command in holy Scripture,* has been a process that has been evolving in the Presbyterian Church, and in New South Wales in particular, and represents a microcosmic template for understanding a crisis which confronts the Presbyterian Church at the broader macrocosmic level throughout Australia and which impacts on its theology and institutional politics. Liturgical Minimization is the principal theme of this book and it impacts upon theological education because the minimization process is a reflection of how the doctrine of God and the doctrine of the Church are understood, doctrines that should be taught in detail in a student's formative years in College.

We shall show that this crisis in the liturgy of the Presbyterian Church is another example of how "a pattern of conflict" can emerge within the Church whether it emerges in the early colonial Church of the nineteenth century or resurfaces in the twentieth and twenty first centuries, in other forms. We shall also argue that the liturgical minimization process is seriously flawed as it relies upon a scientific methodology that is epistemologically inconsistent with Biblical Christianity. We will argue for a consistent Christian Epistemology which will provide a better means upon which to develop a liturgical practice that is consistent with the Church's Reformed heritage.

The role of theological education is of critical importance as it is the provider of the professional development of clergy for the Presbyterian Church in Australia. A critical assessment and a possible reconstruction of its curriculum will become a necessity.

The crisis which faces the Church has not occurred in a vacuum, not unlike many other public institutions which find it difficult to adjust to a rapidly changing social climate and a major philosophical shift from a modern to a post-modern paradigm. In a very poignant article, Charles Colson, of Watergate fame, points out how accurate George Orwell's *1984* and Aldous Huxley's *Brave New World*, have been. He writes:

> Orwell foresaw a Communist government that would ban books; Huxley foresaw a Western government that wouldn't need to ban them – because no one would read serious books any more. Orwell predicted a society deprived of information; Huxley predicted a society oversaturated by information from the electronic media – until people lost the ability to analyse what they saw and heard. Orwell feared a system that concealed the truth; Huxley feared a system where people stopped caring about truth and cared only about what made them feel good... It is Huxley's book that opens a window on our own society—where the Christian message is not forcibly suppressed; instead it is swamped by triviality.[1]

The crisis the Church faces is serious as the postmodern context in which it struggles to survive is by its very nature antithetical to the religious world view, impacting in turn on its theological teaching and its consequent practices of worship. One serious expression of concern has been voiced that some worship services of the Church seem to be more a reflection of modern pop culture than the doctrinal foundations of the Church that demand a deep reverence and awe of God, characteristic of the Calvinistic mode of worship. N.R. Needham has expressed the construct of contemporary worship in terms of "the human subject—human experiences, feeling and responses—rather than in terms of the divine object, God, the blessed self-revealing Trinity, and his will, word and activity".[2] The crisis the Church faces impacts on the Church's role as a provider of higher education, as the cultural paradigm in which the evangelical faith of the past was explained, proclaimed, and defended has come to an end. With the emergence of a new paradigm, we see that the old wineskins are collapsing. It is not the faith that needs to be changed but the paradigm in which Christianity is communicated.[3] Theological Education is of prime importance to the Church's expression of its theology and worship practices.

Throughout this book we will be developing the idea of Liturgical Minimization as a radical departure from the theology of worship advocated by the protestant reformer John Calvin. We will argue that there has been a radical departure from Calvin's notion of worship in which recognition is given to "God's unspeakable Majesty and Otherness, and the nothingness and simplicity of man". In the service of worship, the worshipper is confronted with the divine transcendence of a Holy God. Calvin's paradigm has given way to a new and disturbing paradigm whereby worship has capitulated to the desires and whims of a culture that is imbued with a postmodern philosophy. We have laboured to explain this paradigm shift and the unfortunate outcomes, by incorporating two fundamental themes: one of which is minor while the other constitutes the major theme of the thesis.

We begin our investigation by providing the minor theme of the thesis, a *pattern of conflict*, in which the major theme of liturgical Minimization is considered. Liturgical Minimization must be placed within the historical context of Australian Presbyterianism as we will labour to show in this minor theme that the founding of Presbyterianism, in New South Wales, by the Rev. Dr John Dunmore Lang, was so turbulent in the harsh political, social and economic environment, that a *pattern of conflict* emerged within the Church, and this characteristic has resurfaced from time to time in its history up to the present day. The evolution of socio-political factors and the associated theological considerations in the developing "patterns of conflict" are often overlooked in favour of expedient resolution. Let us now turn more determinately to the way in which we shall elaborate this task. We do so by briefly outlining the chapters of the thesis.

CHAPTER 1: SOCIO-POLITICAL PATTERNS IN EARLY PRESBYTERIANISM IN NEW SOUTH WALES

We will endeavour to show that the rise of Presbyterianism, especially in the colony of New South Wales, began as the result of Scottish immigration to Australia. The Scots naturally brought with them their passions and ideals of life. Their world view of life focused upon a Biblical interpretation of the whole of life. The influence of the famous Dr Thomas Chalmers was profound. Chalmers held the chair of Divinity at Edinburgh University and was one of the leaders of the Disruption in the Church of Scotland in 1843. Chalmers breathed new life into evangelical Christianity long before he was installed in the prestigious chair at Edinburgh. Stuart Piggin has encapsulated the influence and importance of Chalmers' teaching whilst he was professor of Moral Philosophy at St Andrews University.[4] Chalmers sought to establish a Godly Commonwealth where Education, the Sciences, Commerce, Social welfare and Ethics were all part of a comprehensive Christian world view. There had always been a close connection and commitment between Church and school and it is no surprise that this gave rise to the founding of educational institutions, such as the Australian College, established by the first Presbyterian minister to the Colony, the Rev. Dr John Dunmore Lang. The Scots also brought with them the theological foundations of their Church. The Westminster Confession of Faith and the Larger and Shorter Catechisms were foundational for the Church which they established, reflecting the theology of the Protestant revolt of the sixteenth century.

The Presbyterian Church in N.S.W. began with humble beginnings very early in Australian history. It was in 1809 that an honorary catechist conducted worship according to the customs of the Presbyterian Church. The worship was marked by simplicity and the awe of the presence of the Creator. The fundamentals of worship were expressive of "Reformed Worship" which was grounded in the theology of Jean (John) Calvin, the sixteenth century reformer. For Calvin, a worshipper is confronted with God's unspeakable Majesty and Otherness and the nothingness and simplicity of man.[5] Evelyn Underhill notes that this type of worship is the result of a great religious experience – the impact of the divine transcendence on the awe struck soul – and the efforts towards a response is conditioned by a deep sense of human limitation.

The immigration of the Scots was promoted by John Dunmore Lang, who arrived in Sydney on 23 May 1823. Lang soon concluded that the Church and society had a limited future unless there was a significant immigration of people who could provide expertise in every facet of society and promote the Protestant ascendancy in the Colony. In 1831 he persuaded the British government to assist 140 Scottish workers and their families to settle in Australia, so that they could build a Presbyterian school.[6] The scheme was successful. He urged that monies raised from the sale of crown land should be used to assist immigrants with their expenses. His many visits to his homeland of Scotland resulted in the immigration of free settlers who had expertise in agriculture, commerce, education, medicine, trades and other occupations. Australia was seen as a land of opportunity. Between March 1837 and January 1840, 5,263 Scots migrated to Australia.[7] Lang's commitment to education was soon realised with the building of a school commencing in 1831 and classes commencing in the same year in rented premises. The College was established on the plan of the Belfast College. There was a Principal and four professors teaching English, Mercantile Education, Latin, Greek, Mathematics and Natural Philosophy.[8] The staff of the College came from Glasgow and Edinburgh Universities. James Cameron notes that many of the prominent colonists received their education at this institution.[9] This illustrates how important immigration was for the founding of the Colony as builders and educators were needed to build and establish this important institution, some nineteen years before the founding of the University of Sydney. Such was Lang's influence in immigration policy, the *Sydney Morning Herald* noted in Lang's obituary upon his death on the 8th August 1878, "Posterity will remember Dr. Lang as a hard working, enthusiastic labourer in the cause of free immigration, yeomanry settlement, popular government and national education." Ultimately, the Presbyterian Church became the third largest Christian denomination behind the Anglican and Roman Catholic Churches.

The foundational basis of Presbyterianism was written into the "Enabling Acts" of Parliament in all Australian States soon after federation. Specifically the New South Wales Act says:

> From the twenty Fourth Day of July 1901, the basis of Union and Articles of Agreement set forth in this Schedule to this Act, shall have the full force and effect of law, and except as therein provided, nothing done in accordance with the provisions of the said Basis of Union and Articles of Agreement shall have the effect of divesting the Presbyterian Church of N.S.W., the Presbyterian Church of Victoria, the Presbyterian Church of Queensland, the Presbyterian Church of South Australia, or the Presbyterian Church of Tasmania, or any congregation, body or person, of any property situated within the Colony of NSW or subject to the jurisdiction of that colony, which is or shall be held in trust for any of the Churches, or for any congregation or body in connection therewith.

This Act may be cited as "The Presbyterian Church of Australia Act, 1900".

The Scots brought with them their high educational ideals. The Scots became a dominant force in the founding of the University of Sydney in 1850. The first professors of medicine, chemistry, physics, geology, philosophy, modern literature, education, economics, zoology, veterinary science, agriculture and mathematics were all Scots. The central importance of philosophy in Scotland was reflected in the fact that three Scots held the chair of Philosophy for a total of sixty six years, between 1890 and 1963.

It comes as no surprise that the high value of education was also reflected in Theological Education. The Scottish Theological tradition was embraced by the NSW Presbyterian Church when it appointed its first professor, Andrew Harper from Glasgow. Andrew Harper came with a wealth of academic experience. He trained at New College, Edinburgh, and the University of Berlin. He became the Principal of St. Andrews College, Sydney, and held the chair of Oriental Languages within the Sydney University. The Church in NSW set up its Theological Hall within St. Andrew's College. This arrangement continued by the grace of St Andrews until 1977.

The rules and regulations governing theological education specified that each applicant should be a graduate in another faculty or its equivalent other than theology. The courses of study ideally were to lead to the University's postgraduate Bachelor of Divinity, although a certificate course was also in place for non graduate students.

Theological Education played a very important role in the life of the Church and the broad educational attainments of its ministers. In the twentieth century the Church appointed two outstanding professors who had a great appeal and who were to exercise a powerful influence upon the Church at large. Professor Samuel Angus from Princeton and Professor John McIntyre from Edinburgh brought with them world- class scholarship that had a lasting influence upon the Church's intellectual life.

In 1977 the Uniting Church was formed. This was a union between the Presbyterians, Congregationalists and the Methodists. Not all the Presbyterians entered the union. Broadly speaking there were about 53% of the membership joined the new Uniting Church. The other 47% remained within the continuing Presbyterian Church, as the Articles of Agreement were never withdrawn, so preserving the legal identity of the Church. The formation of the Uniting Church created just another denomination, its ideal of "uniting" various denominations into a single entity was never realised. The remnant of the Presbyterian Church was theologically very conservative, and was anxious to uphold its confessional standards. It was generally thought among the conservative elements of the Church that the theological basis of the Union document was not only deficient but represented a radical departure from the historical foundations of Presbyterianism.

It was primarily the adherence to its Confessional standards that defined the worship practices of the Church as Calvinistic in character. Evelyn Underhill notes that in worship, Calvin sees "God's unspeakable Majesty and Otherness, and the nothingness and simplicity of man". It is in worship that man experiences the "Divine Transcendence on the awe-struck soul".[10] This becomes the bedrock of ideal worship. If the Church's practice of worship is reflective of its historical and theological heritage the practice of worship with its theological foundations becomes an important aspect of Theological Education just as the theory of the practice of education is in any faculty of education. In this chapter we have not only given a brief outline of the founding of Presbyterianism in New South Wales, but we will show the extent to which the commitment of the Church to education has been regarded as a priority. As part of its commitment to education, the Church established a faculty for Theological Education in the eighteen seventies. The establishment of the theological faculty should not be underestimated as it is in the process of Theological Education that the doctrinal basis of the Church is inculcated and given expression in the life and function of the Church. Theological Education is of critical importance for the future direction of the Church, as its theological adherence and practical outworking of its theological perspective is passed on to succeeding generations of clergy. It is therefore necessary to define the practice of worship and its connection with the Church's theological perspective. That is to be teased out in chapter two.

CHAPTER 2: DEFINING THE PRACTICE OF WORSHIP IN THE PRESBYTERIAN CHURCH

It is in chapters two and three that we begin the major theme of this thesis: Liturgical Minimisation.

We will seek to show in this chapter that the practice of worship needs to be "Trinitarian" in which belief systems are given one of their most poignant forms of expression. There are many contemporary and independent Churches whose worship practices give expression to a theological foundation that is vague and lacking in biblical and historical substance. To a "traditionalist" within a mainline denomination, these modal expressions of worship seem chaotic and, from a theological perspective, dysfunctional. This may well be true of any number of independent Churches but it is also true of many congregations within the Presbyterian Church in recent years. This immediately raises serious questions of theological importance. For example, the worship patterns have been changing rapidly especially in the past ten years. It has been suggested by some members of the Church that a hurricane has hit the Church as the old patterns of worship have been torn apart. The worship patterns of the twenty-first century stand in stark contrast to the pre-union Church. The traditional form of worship with its pronounced liturgical and Calvinistic tenor is now retained only by a handful of parishes.

- The solemnity of worship has given way to a jovial atmosphere.
- The sense of God's Majesty and Otherness has given way to a Lutheran idea of worship as liberation and assurance.
- The sense of God's Holiness has dissipated to a shadow of the past.
- In the most part, liturgical forms and symbol are no longer evident, as they are deemed to be unnecessary. Such forms and symbols are viewed by many as a capitulation to Roman Catholicism or as an unnecessary part of Reformed worship practice.
- The Davidic line, "Be still and know that I am God", is replaced by the noise of amplified contemporary band music which leads the singing of chorus type songs instead of hymns.
- Clerical attire of cassock, collars, preaching scarves etc. has given way to lounge suits, sportswear and in some instances even jeans, as being more relevant to modern society.
- It is claimed that the new styles of worship patterns are consistent with "Reformed" and Biblical principles, the focus of which is the "exposition of Scripture" or "Bible talks".

Congregations are encouraged to reject all matters that conflict with the simplicity and evangelical ardour. One writer has coined the phrase "pop gospel Churches", where the worship is characterised by "subjectivity and informality". Worship formats found in *Books of Common Order* or *Books of Common Prayer* are dispensed with and replaced with anything that will appeal to those living in the secular age. Most contemporary worship has now lost what Robert Webber notes as the idea of mystery, "God was the *Terium tremendum"*.[11] The contextualisation of the Church's ministry at the present time may well express an empathic concurrence of the new Spirituality which claims that modern people, (we assume "baby boomers"), feel alienated by institutional authority and dogmatism.

It would seem that the fundamental motive for change in the worship practices of the Presbyterian Church is an earnest desire to be "relevant" in a postmodern world. David Tacey in his book *The Spirituality Revolution*[12] notes that there is a desire currently among young people to be free, and to seek a meaningful spirituality without reference to outside authority or dogma. This seems to be a reaction from the strictures of rationalism which gave little or no place to artistic expression and meaning and purpose in life. There is now the acknowledgement that there is more to human life than being a mere scientific object. If in the context of popular opinion, the changes in the worship practices of the Church have been affected by the idea of relevance, then we would claim that they are flawed, as the authority and the parameters of worship are no longer located in the Scriptures[13] but rather in the authority of the self that expresses itself in the culture of the day. In other words the worship is no longer "Trinitarian". The authority of the Scriptures has been discounted in favour of popular expediency by the very people who claim to uphold the principles of the Reformed Faith. Relevance in this context can only mean the re-categorization of Biblical principle to popular opinions which have little Biblical foundation. This may give the impression among young people that there can be freedom of worship without the strictures of dogma and traditionalism, but such an impression is misleading as the constitution of the Church states categorically that the Church is a doctrinal entity. Adherence to the confessional statements of the Westminster Confession and the Larger and Shorter Catechisms are essential for admission into office in the Church. The idea of "freedom" of worship without reference to doctrinal statements cannot exist for any length of time without causing fragmentation and ultimately self destruction as the two viewpoints are mutually exclusive.

The influence of the Robinson/Knox debate on the doctrine of the Church has also been an important ingredient in promoting a contemporary Christianised spiritual revolution within the Church context, as this view removes traditional institutional authority and relocates the authority in the local fellowship. This is certainly a paradox for both Robinson and Knox, as they belong to the famous traditional institution called the Anglican Church of Australia which is light years away from independency. Nevertheless the spirit of independency that this view promotes has effected enormous change in worship patterns in both the Anglican Diocese of Sydney and the Presbyterian Church of NSW. Considering the profound changes in the liturgical practice, any comparison to the practices of contemporary Pentecostalism shows many similarities. It may well be argued that Pentecostalism and other similar independent type Churches may be more consistent with the premises of popular secular belief:

- They are thoroughly independent in structure.
- They embrace contemporary spirituality in a Christian context.
- There is little commitment to systematics and historical theology.
- There is little evidence of any theology of worship.

This means that change will always be a necessary part of these Churches, as they will always be in a state of flux as there is no serious and detailed theology to govern its life.

If the theology of the Reformed Standards invokes what Underhill calls "God's unspeakable Majesty and Otherness" and if contemporary worship deprecates the awe, majesty and holiness of the Divine, it then can then be asked, "What areas of reformed theology have been under valued or conveniently glossed over in the interest of pragmatism, within the theological education process?".

It will be the burden of this chapter to show that the doctrinal formulations of the Presbyterian Church need not only dictate the parameters of worship, but also express its theology. It will be necessary to provide an outline of a conceptual framework which will reflect the Church's Calvinistic foundations. Providing such a framework gives opportunity to examine any departures from the Calvinistic tradition. It may well be in the contemporary era, if liberties are being invoked for expediency, that the question would need to be asked whether the Calvinistic foundations for worship are being pushed to such extremities that the Calvinistic theological foundations of Presbyterianism are becoming an icon of the past. It could then be argued whether or not such Churches are really "Reformed"!

At this juncture in the research it will be necessary to show that worship needs to be "Trinitarian" in nature. It is this that gives expression to Calvin's theology. Trinitarian worship finds its focus in the priesthood of Christ. Christ by the Spirit enables our participation in the triune life of God. He takes our faults and failures, sanctifies them by his own atoning work on the cross and offers them perfectly to the Father. He gives the perfect worship to God that we fail to give.[14] In this model, worship is not so much our activity as it is the activity of Christ. John Armstrong makes the point that it is disturbing to know that there is no discussion about the doctrine of God in the midst of all the contemporary changes in the Church. He says, "We have actually come to think that the Bible is primarily about us. We then reason that the Church is also about us. Surely the future is also about us. Indeed, everything finally relates to us. We are the consummate *me* generation. God is there for us!"[15] This resonates with Descartes *cognito ergo sum*. A theology of worship that is consistent with the doctrinal formulations of the Presbyterian Church, we submit, has necessarily its focus on Christ. This is the essential focus of John Calvin and the early Church Fathers. It will be argued in a later chapter that this focus shifted in the sixteenth and seventeenth centuries to the focus on the "Word".

CHAPTER 3: THE CLIMAX OF CALVINIST LITURGICAL DEVELOPMENT IN NEW SOUTH WALES

In Chapter 3, special reference will be made to the influence of the Rev. Alan Dougan, principal of St Andrews College within Sydney University, as he sought to preserve the awe, mystery and dignity of Trinitarian worship.

Alan Dougan held the lectureship in "Liturgics" for many years and had enjoyed the reputation as the Church's authority on liturgical practice. He was greatly admired and had considerable influence in the Church at large. Unfortunately, Alan Dougan died over twenty years ago. Considerable work has been given to the collection of writings and papers of Dougan by his Anglican friend the Rev. Robert Willson. It will be shown that the very basis of Dougan's approach was truly Calvinistic and Trinitarian. It stands in stark contrast to much of what passes for Presbyterian worship today that seems to be strongly Zwinglian in character. It is due to the influence of Dougan that the Presbyterian Church in New South Wales reached its high point in Trinitarian liturgical practice.

Dougan was misunderstood by a wide section of the Church and was dubbed a "high churchman". We will show that this attitude which prevailed for many years was unfortunate as it reflected the Church's neglect of John Calvin's theology of worship.

This chapter is unique in that it is the first time that any one has produced a serious article on Dougan's theology of worship since Robert Willson gathered together all known primary resources relating to Dougan's life and ministry. For Dougan, worship was the Church's supreme task.

CHAPTER 4: A BRIEF HISTORY OF THE THEOLOGICAL AETIOLOGY OF LITURGICAL MINIMISATION

It is our intention in this chapter to provide a Historical and Theological Aetiology of "Liturgical Minimization". This provision will reveal the theological polarisations within the Reformed tradition which impinge upon theological education.

It is in this chapter that we define the meaning of "liturgical minimization". We trace the minimisation process from the Reformation period. We argue that the Scots did not approve of everything in the "reformed liturgy" found in the English Prayer Book, and chose to exercise liberties in the usage of the Prayer Book. However there were many Puritans in the English and Scottish Church who believed that the reforms in the liturgy did not go far enough. We make specific reference to the influence of Zwingli, John Knox and the Puritans.

We examine the liturgy of John Knox and show how it was minimized and argue that in its usage the liturgy was not "fixed" and it was not intended to be a mere directory.

In order to show the impact of the minimization process we compare Calvin's Strasbourg liturgy of 1540 with Knox's 1564, Calderwood and Henderson liturgies.

We discuss the radicalisation of the minimization process by the Scottish Parliament and the General Assembly of the Church of Scotland when they approved the *Westminster Directory of Publick Worship*. The Scots regarded the prescribed prayers, set forms and ceremonies of the *English Prayer Book* as an offence.

This chapter also discusses how this minimized liturgy came to be accepted in the Australian Presbyterian Church and contextualised the change in liturgical direction from the rich liturgical heritage and ideals of Alan Dougan to the impoverished liturgical mishmash that is perpetrated upon the contemporary Church.

The final section of this chapter examines the philosophical basis of the minimization process. We argue here that just as theology in the medieval era came to a standstill because of the impregnation of Platonic and Aristotelian ultimate and primary causes, so with the legalising of a minimized liturgy, the theology of worship also becomes frozen, unable to advance due to the imposition of a theologically laden theory of worship. It is what Professor Ronald Laura has elsewhere called the "paralysis of the intellectual imagination".

CHAPTER 5: MINIMISATION SINCE 1977 IN THE PRESBYTERIAN CHURCH OF AUSTRALIA

Chapter 5 discusses liturgical minimization since 1977, the year that Church Union took place. We make an in depth analysis of the revision of the *Book of Common Order*, ordered by the General Assembly of Australia that met in 1991. It is from this analysis that we argue that liturgical minimization since 1977 has been progressing at a rapid rate. The 1985 revision of the *Book of Common Order*, published in 1990, was a revision that adhered to the principles of worship found in the *Scottish Book of Common Order* of 1954. The changes that were to take place in the 1998 revision were so radical that the Assembly approved a resolution that forbade the use of the 1990 publication.

In this chapter we argue that the change in direction in the theology of worship has resulted in:

- the removal of many of the specific "orders of service" from the 1990 version of the *Book of Common Order*, we argue that this change is motivated by the idea that "ministry to people" is the important issue not things such as buildings and memorials;
- the removal of symbols;
- change in architecture;
- and the content of the sacrament of Holy Communion has been changed in favour of a simplified kind of Zwinglianism. All suggestions of "sacramentalism" in the previous *Books of Common Order* were removed.

In all these changes we argue that the liturgical changes are not "neutral", as all liturgies, minimized or not, embody our theology of belief in God, ourselves, redemption and the chief end of human existence.

Our critical analysis is made in the context of the change in the theological direction after Church Union, and the significant role that theological education played in the lead-up to the "minimization" of the Church's liturgy.

The complex causes and influences need to be understood within the context of the Church Union debates of the 1970s and the division that occurred in 1977. One of the complex factors was the revival of Puritan literature. During the late 1960s and all through the 1970s and 1980s the works of Dr Martyn Lloyd Jones were popularised as were the republications of many Puritan works. *The Banner of Truth Trust* journal had a wide circulation among Presbyterian ministers. *Banner of Truth* conferences were held annually receiving widespread patronage. The editor of the journal, the Rev. Iain Murray, who had been the assistant to the famous Martyn Lloyd Jones for some years at the Westminster Chapel London, became an endearing and engaging speaker at these conferences. Murray was a fascinating speaker and his presence guaranteed a crowd. Murray was an authority on the history and theological thought of the Puritans. His publications had a wide appeal and adorned the book shelves of most evangelical Presbyterian ministers. The influence of "Puritan" thought was cemented into the Presbyterian psyche when Iain Murray was inducted into the pastoral charge of Hurstville, in Sydney. This gave great impetus to the Reformed cause in Australia.

"Theological Education" became a major factor in the complexity of change. The theological college is the cradle wherein the new generation of ministers is nurtured. It is our conviction that there is a real connection between the theological college and the current practice of worship in the Church.

When Church Union became a reality in 1977, theological education as the pre-union Church had known it in N.S.W. was swept away. A new process of theological education had to be formulated. To this end the Presbyterian Theological Institute was born. The name was to change in the 1980s to the Presbyterian Theological Centre, which was to reflect the Church's commitment to theological studies and research. The Church, through its new College, implemented a multi-strand course of studies. Students would elect one of the following strands:

- A diploma course which met the criteria for ordination.
- A B.Th. degree through Moore Theological College, an Anglican foundation within the Diocese of Sydney.
- A postgraduate B.D. from Sydney University, or the Melbourne College of Divinity.

The theological emphasis of the Moore College course was Biblical and Evangelical in its thrust, but there was a concern among some Presbyterians as Presbyterian students were being exposed to the peculiar doctrine of the Church promoted by the Knox/Robinson regime. Drs Broughton Knox and Donald Robinson, both well- known international scholars, had developed a distinctive doctrine of the Church, which is basically congregational in nature. Knox and Robinson argued that the Greek word for Church, *ekklesia*, means no more and no less than "assembly" and in the New Testament it is only used for

- Local assemblies of Christians on earth
- The great assembly of all believers in continuous session in heaven.[16]

This challenging doctrine of the Church is an oddity coming as it does from within the Anglican Church. Using this doctrine as a premise meant that the term "Anglican Church" is a misnomer as no earth-bound association other than local congregation may be called the "Church." This spirit of "independency" fits very well with the Puritanism expounded by John Owen, a Puritan with strong independent convictions. This particular view gives understanding to the "independency" of many of the younger ministers within the Presbyterian Church. It also gives a rational understanding to the view that "office" does not matter.

This was not the only concern, as there were issues in respect to the sacraments. It is our intention to show that the theology of the sacraments was not that of Calvin but rather that of the theology akin to Zwinglianism. This outlook tends to promote the view that worship is something we do, rather than engaging in the perfect worship of Christ before the Father, which is more in keeping with a Trinitarian viewpoint. By way of contrast the Zwinglian view sees the Holy Communion as a memorial supper. This stands in contrast to the strong sacramental overtones of Calvin's view of the sacrament. This Zwinglian teaching has had an enormous influence within the Presbyterian Church. It gives explanation to the resistance or the horror of using set forms as outlined in the *Book of Common Order*. Orders of liturgy in the *Book of Common Order* preserve the Calvinistic view of the sacraments.

Not only were many ministers trained at Moore College but up to 2005 many of the lecturers at the Presbyterian Theological Centre were also trained at that institution. It can only be assumed from a theological and educational perspective there is a natural continuity that co-exists between the two colleges, even though there is liberty of opinion in theological matters.

CHAPTER 6: TOWARDS AN EPISTEMOLOGY OF WORSHIP

We argue that the underlying epistemology of the "minimization process" is faulty. We have therefore titled the chapter "Towards an Epistemology of Worship".

In chapter five we expound the view that the rich liturgical Calvinist tradition expressed in the *Book of Common Order* of 1929 and 1954 as well as the "provisional" *Worship Book* of 1991, was displaced in favour of a through going Zwinglianism. The revised *Worship Book* of 1998 saw revolutionary changes in the liturgy of the Church, in which symbols were removed together with large sections of the liturgical content. We also argue that the change in the liturgical perspective was generated largely due to the theological perspective of those who were in sympathy with the mien of Moore Theological College. We also argue that the influence of Dr Broughton Knox, in particular, was very evident among those who sought liturgical change. Critical to Knox's theological perspective was the notion of "Propositional Revelation."

The publication of the *Worship Book* of 1998 signalled far reaching consequences. Ten years on, "worship" in most Presbyterian Churches has degenerated to the point where the beauty of the Calvinistic forms that sustained the idea of the majesty and holiness of God, has largely disappeared. Special services of the Church, such as ordination and induction of ministers into pastoral charges, the ordination of elders and the celebration of Holy Communion and other services were always conducted according to the set forms contained in the *Books of Common Order*. In this way the dignity and the theology of worship was preserved. In recent time this practice has all but disappeared. Special services are now conducted without the aid and guide of set forms. It is at this point that we want to argue that there exists a serious philosophical explanation as to why the current liturgical minimisation has had such a detrimental impact upon the Church. We wish to argue that the contemporary liturgical outcomes to which we have alluded admit of a richer theological force, when they are understood in terms of philosophical principles of the Enlightenment which covertly served to inform them.

We are arguing in this chapter that it is essential to develop a Christian Epistemology. Foundational to our argument is the theology of Cornelius Van Til. This contemporary theologian, John Frame, claims that Van Til's contribution is comparable in magnitude to that of Immanuel Kant in non-Christian philosophy. The foundation of Van Til's system and its most persuasive principle is the rejection of the autonomy of man, since Christian thinking, like all of the Christian life, is subject to God's lordship. Van Til specifically rejects the traditional epistemic methodology as it is offered in Thomas Aquinas in its Catholic form and in Joseph Butler in its protestant form, as it is based upon "the assumption that man has some measure of autonomy, that in the space-time world is in some measure contingent and that man must create for himself his own epistemology in an ultimate sense."[17]

From Van Til's perspective we argue that the framers of the *1998 Worship Book* are caught in a time warp. While upholding a Reformed theology, they seek a reconstruction of the liturgy by arguing univocally, and in doing so, they superimpose a secular epistemology upon the interpretation of the Scriptures. Their conclusions become highly reductionist.

CHAPTER 7 TOWARDS A RECONSTRUCTION OF THEOLOGICAL EDUCATION

Chapter 7 argues for the Reconstruction of Theological Education. Nineteenth century rationalism found itself in a philosophical straightjacket after David Hume brought philosophy of the day to a logical conclusion. Reid and Stewart, fellow Scots, chose to reject the rational conclusions of Hume and to launch out into "Common Sense" philosophy. Perhaps a similar movement needs to occur today sustained by the recognition that the destruction of the Church's heritage has occurred because of a reductionist epistemology with its blood child the Regulative Principle.[18] The Regulative Principle is actualised as an efficient tool of analysis only within a through-going paradigm of modern thought with its attendant characteristics of individualism, rationalism and factualism. Outside of this paradigm the outcomes are too diverse to provide meaningful insights for community. In other words it becomes a tool for personal opinion.

We will argue that it is of paramount importance to opt for a reconstruction of theological education. The need is great as the principles of theological education are locked into a methodology that has not progressed for hundreds of years. We argue that priority is given to scientific knowledge and it is this form of knowledge upon which western culture relies to promote "value" of power and control. This particular form of knowledge has been institutionalised in our educational institutions. "It is our insatiable appetite for power that drives us to a form of knowledge which covertly stipulates that the only knowledge worth having is that which allows us to reorder the world and our relationships to each other in ways that suit our own ends and presumed interests, no matter how selfish or destructive those ends and interests are."[19] Such is the influence of this epistemology of power that "it has become an elemental facet of our physical existence".[20] The nature of the epistemology of power and subjugation is necessarily divorced from belief in a creator God and takes for granted that the space and time world is immanent in itself and man is the ultimate interpreter of the world. This particular form of knowledge has been institutionalised in our schools and is shaped by our obsession with power. Laura elsewhere writes that "western culture has lured generations of school children into the false belief that scientific knowledge and the technologies deriving from it are the ultimate tools of social and even personal salvation".[21] We submit that the technologization of nature linked to this type of epistemology is so entrenched in our educational institutions that society thinks now that it cannot survive without such technology. It follows then that if the epistemology of power is the fundamental organising principle underpinning the institution of Church it also shapes the philosophical directions even of our theological institutions. In common parlance it is a matter of students carrying their baggage to whatever institution they decide to enter, be it a university or a theological institution.

We will therefore argue that in the reconstruction of theological education, the theories of R.S. Laura and C. Van Til, can be joined to form a powerful philosophical alliance capable of generating a distinctive epistemology.

Ideally, this could be achieved if the students for the ministry were required to study the history of philosophy over a period of two years with specific studies in epistemology at year three or four. This would expose a student to the development of the systems of rationalism and the corresponding trends in theology. To omit such studies is to deny a student of theology the essential background that explains why certain theologies developed as they did. The traditional understanding of the Roman Catholic Church's view of the Mass, for example, can only be understood in terms of the Aristotelian metaphysic which is foundational to the specific doctrine. The Reformers could be critical of Thomas Aquinas and the theory of the mass only because of the collapse of the Aristotelian metaphysic which no longer provided an adequate explanation of reality. In other words there was a major shift in the paradigm which had far reaching consequences not only for theology but also for the progress of scientific endeavour. The reconstruction which would refocus the Church on the "Centrality of Christ" would raise a number of issues:

- The rationalist epistemic needs to be shown that it is inadequate as an interpretive tool in theological education. Science has accepted the fact that the rise of quantum mechanics has been forced to take the human subject into theoretical account in the development of its explanations. The rationalist approach forces an unnecessary distinction between subject –object. It is precisely this distinction that regulates beauty, art, mystery and the idea of the holy, moral and spiritual responsibility as being unimportant. It is in this environment that dogmatism prevails. This means that the "Reformed Theological Perspective" can be enforced by the Regulative Principle, and for some within the denomination it can dominate, subjugate and suppress every other theological perspective. It is fascinating to note that John Calvin in the 16th century saw that theology beginning with actuality cannot abstract itself from the subject – object relation as theological science starts with the knowledge of God and the knowledge of ourselves because they are already found together in a profound mutuality
- The spirit of "empathy" in the pursuit of theological education needs to be acknowledged. The idea of empathetic connectivity in theological education must be to educate "the sensibilities of moral and spiritual conscience". In the words of Koestler, it is the "stepping out of one's skin, as it were, and putting oneself into the skin of the other".[22] This would only be made possible by embracing the "Centrality of Christ" as the interpretive principle with all its flexibility and common sense, unencumbered with the epistemic rational of the Enlightenment.
- The recovery of the doctrines of God, the Church and the Sacraments, by expressing them in terms of the centrality of Christ.

Until the above occurs the Presbyterian Church will continue to lean towards Congregationalism and continue to deny its Calvinistic heritage. Until a reconstruction takes place the practice of worship will continue in what Evelyn Underhill describes as Free Church worship. She offers this description:

- The small company of keen believers ready to press the teaching of the Gospel to its logical conclusions: ruthlessly rejecting all that conflicts with evangelical ardour and simplicity, demanding personal consecration, downright costly conversion of the whole life to God's purpose, repudiating all substitutes for the offering of the self. It restores to their original position of importance the charismatic and prophetic characteristics of primitive Christianity: and hence is suspicious of set forms, and demands a spontaneous worship which shall be the devotional expression of a personal and subjective relation to God. The responsibility and capacity of each soul, the priesthood of all believers, the universal call to sanctity, are the central truths governing real Free Church worship.[23]

This is a brilliant summation of what Free Church worship is, but it is a very apt description of what some sections of the Presbyterian Church in New South Wales have embraced and ruthlessly apply in the contemporary era.

Although Calvin would not disagree with the transformed nature of human life bearing the Godliness and holiness of Christ, he would object to modern rational thought that obliterates the mystery and awe of a Holy God in the life of the Church and especially in the celebration of the sacraments. The present Church is something less than its Calvinistic heritage would demand. Whilst saying this, it is true to say that there are pockets of resistance that seek to preserve the theological and liturgical heritage of Calvin.

Most of the issues contained in this dissertation are not new. What is new is the attempt to provide a more comprehensive perspective in which to assess the theological, socio-political and educational complexities which serve to advance our understanding of the crises of worship patterns within the Presbyterian Churches in New South Wales in the twenty-first century.

NOTES

1. Charles Colson, *Burden of Truth* (Illinois: Tyndale House, 1997), 79.
2. N.R. Needham, in P.G. Ryken edit., *Give Praise to God* (New Jersey: P&R, 2003), 407.
3. Robert E. Webber, *The Younger Evangelicals* (Michigan: Baker Books, 2002), 15.
4. Stuart Piggin, *St. Andrews Seven* (Edinburgh: Banner of Truth Trust, 1995).
5. Evelyn Underhill, *Worship* (London: Collins, 1936), 287.
6. A. Gilchrist and G. Powell, *John Dunmore Lang, Australian Pioneer Republican* (Melbourne: New Melbourne Press, 1999), 71.
7. Iain Murray, *Australian Christian Life from 1788* (Edinburgh: Edinburgh Banner of Truth Trust, 1988), 113.
8. Gilchrist and Powell, *John Dunmore Lang*, 89.
9. James Cameron, *Centenary History of the Presbyterian Church in N.S.W.* (Sydney: Angus & Robertson, 1905), 6.
10. Underhill, *Worship*, 286–87.
11. Robert E. Webber, *Ancient Future Faith* (Grand Rapids: Baker Books, 1999), 14–17.
12. David Tacey, *The Spirituality Revolution* (Sydney: Harper Collins, 2003).
13. It is written into the constitution of the Presbyterian Church that "the Scriptures of the Old and New Testament is the supreme rule of faith and practice".
14. James Torrance, *Worship, Community and the Triune God* (Illinois: Intervarsity Press, 1966), 20.

15. John Armstrong, edit., *Reformation and Revival* (Illinois: Carol Stream, Illinois), Vol. 10 No 3.
16. See Kevin Giles, *What on Earth is the Church?* (Blackburn Australia: Dove, 1995), 13–14.
17. C.Van Til, *My Credo in Jerusalem and Athens* (Phillipsburg: Presbyterian and Reformed Publishing, 1980), 10–11.
18. It could be said that the work of R.S. Laura and C. Van Til are possibly the modern counterparts of Reid and Stewart. Both are seeking a new way forward to overcome the perils of transformative subjugation. Both see that there is a greater dimension to truth than the strict adherence to an empiricist methodology. To pursue this point further here would be extraneous to the central argument of this book. See John Wisdom, *Paradox and Discovery* (Oxford: Basil Blackwell, 1965); John Wisdom, *Philosophy and Psycho- Analysis* (Oxford: Basil Blackwell, 1957).
19. R. Laura, T. Marchant & S. Smith, *The New Social Disease* (Maryland: University Press of America, 2008), 6–7.
20. Laura, Marchant & Smith, *The New Social*, 7.
21. R. S. Laura & M. Cotton, *Empathetic Education* (Philadelphia: Falmer Press, 1999), 2–3.
22. R. Laura & M. Cotton, *Empathic Education*, 163–67.
23. Underhill, *Worship*, 299.

Chapter One

Socio-Political Patterns in Early Presbyterianism in New South Wales

The introduction of this study claimed that "radical changes in the theological direction of the Presbyterian Church have impacted significantly on the practice of worship". Our initial idea was to look at the practice of worship from the 1970s to the present. However, to tease out the practice of worship in the modern Australian Presbyterian Church, it is necessary to interpret the relevant issues in the context of the historical foundations of Scottish Presbyterianism, along with the social and political challenges confronting the British Colony of New South Wales in the early nineteenth century. Every denomination in any country has its own story of its founding in a colonial era. Such stories often impinge on the practices and attitudes for decades to come. This is true for those denominations that have experienced some form of what we have in this book called, 'liturgical minimization'.

Careful reflection on the first sixty years of Presbyterian history in the colony of Australia will show that in the practice of Church life, be it in the provision of education, missionary activity, policy on immigration, or relations with other denominations, there were issues which caused violent disagreement, hostile debate, and eventually schism. The early foundational years were by no means peaceful and harmonious. The modern day controversies and debates, whether they be the issues relating to Church Union in 1977, the heresy hunts of Professor Samuel Angus in the 1940s or those of Dr Peter Cameron in the 1990s, would seem, to be in keeping with the turbulent nature of the politics which has long threatened the stability of the Presbyterian Church. While there are many researchers who have found it tempting to embrace this view in its entirety, we submit that it is a temptation to be resisted. Another dimension of the problem has to do with the intransigent dispositions of the so-called 'founding fathers' of Presbyterian ministry in Australia. In the colonial era, for example, the source of much of the conflict was basically the direct result of the theological adamancy of Rev. Dr. John Dunmore Lang, who was the first Presbyterian minister to arrive in the colony in 1823. Lang was known to be argumentative, easily provoked, dogmatically rigid, and so egotistical that if he did not get his own way, disposed to treating anyone who dared to challenge his views with contempt.[1]

Lang was soon involved in vitriolic debate with anyone in the Presbyterian community whose Biblical and administrative views differed from his own. The community soon became theologically polarised, and a deep schism inevitably emerged which divided the Church into various theologically warring parties. This polarization within the Church is easily observed between Lang and the Rev. Dr. John McGarvie a committed 'moderate' whereas Lang was a committed 'evangelical' following a ridged form of Puritanism.[2] Both men were powerful figures within the colonial Church with its various fractions.

It comes as no surprise that given these deep divisions within the foundations of the Presbyterian community, significant disparities were to develop in future worship practices of the early Presbyterian Church, often reflecting the different liturgical dispositions of ministerial leadership. Within the context of the modern era of Australian Presbyterianism, there still exists an array of diverse approaches to the place of liturgy in the currently existing modalities of worship within the denomination. It is tempting to conclude that such radically different approaches to worship are simply manifestations of worship that fit the pattern of ferment and debate that continues to characterise the biographical identity of the Church. It is salutary to remind ourselves, however, that modern liturgical debate has been open and well-controlled within the Presbyterian General Assembly. The problem is that some of the current practices of worship clearly appear to deny the once accepted liturgical traditions and assumptions of Presbyterianism as expressed in the books of Common Order. This will be discussed in detail in a later chapter in this book. Although change within the Church is to be expected, the sociocultural departure from the theological foundations of Presbyterian orientation has become so radical that we may have lost our identity, rather than just matured it.

The chaotic worship practices which have in recent times infested the Presbyterian Church have their origin more in the pop-culture peculiar to post-moderns and postmodernism. One consequence of this shift of vision is that all practices and assumptions are not only questioned , but also cavalierly dispensed with, if such assumptions and practices do not coincide with the personal opinion of the Minister in charge, whose approach to keeping the pews full often involves adopting elements of the current pop culture largely to entertain the congregation, rather than to help them develop their religious/

spiritual sensibilities and deepen their understanding of righteousness. The Church, that is to say, should shine within the community as a lighthouse to project and illuminate the Christian values which help people to find the best in themselves and in others, and to learn to cultivate authentically loving relationships which are self transforming. Instead, what is happening is that the Sacredness of the Church is thus Secularised to accommodate many of the very sociocultural attitudes and entailed behaviours which the Church was from the outset intended to reflect upon and challenge. Instead of standing strong to propagate Christian values within the Church community, we are allowing the Church to be corrupted by uncritically integrating the dominant values of the wider culture in which we live simply because they are 'dominant', and popular. Part of the problem is, as intimated above, that the Church embraces the values of pop-culture to make itself more popular, but in so doing commodifies the sacred values which define its identity as a benchmark and the hallmark of righteous living are eroded.

However, whilst the Paradox of Secularising the Sacred and Sacralising the Secular has seriously diminished the integrity of the Church, and its capacity to preserve the noble values for which it once stood, there are also problems in respect to theological interpretation. As the book progresses, many of these issues will be expounded.

Throughout the colonial foundational years and beyond, it was difficult to determine the authoritative voice of the Presbyterian Church. This is largely due to the nature of the Presbyterian form of Church government, and as we averred earlier, the strong personalities who were in leadership positions at that moment in time. We shall argue that the task of establishing a Presbyterian Church in a new colony under the leadership of the Rev. Dr John Dunmore Lang was not at all easy for several reasons independently of his feisty persona. In fairness to him, and in appreciation of his foundational achievement, it is important to bear in mind that he was all alone; began his venture with no Presbytery, and he was far from the stable social and prestigious educational environment that he had grown up with in Scotland.

Lang was the first Presbyterian minister in New South Wales who visited Britain on nine occasions, seeking government support for colonial education, endeavoring to recruit clergy and school masters for the new colony, while also promoting migration to Australia. While en route to Britain between 1833 and 1834, he wrote *"An Historical and Statistical Account of New South Wales"*.[3] Over the period of a long parliamentary career he witnessed the achievement of almost all his political aims. These included : the end of transportation, the separation of Victoria and of Queensland, the introduction of responsible and democratic government, radical land reform, national education and the abolition of state aid to religion.[4] It was only the establishment of a republican state eluded him. Although he achieved more in Australia's development than most, his achievements came at the price of severe turbulence, division and disharmony within the Church and much personal heart ache.

It is useful at this point to understand that the turbulent beginnings of Presbyterianism in the new colony cannot be appreciated without empathetic reference to the initial ineptitude of the young John Dunmore Lang, who was born in August 1799, and was merely 23 years of age when he arrived in Sydney, though resolutely committed to establishing a Church in a penal colony, no less.[5] Lang was well educated, graduating from Glasgow University with an M.A., and later a D.D. in 1825, ordained by the Presbytery of Irvine in Scotland in 1822, with the purpose of "forming a Church of the Presbyterian persuasion in Sydney, New South Wales, in connection with the Church of Scotland". Lang was accompanied by several free settlers whose numbers were growing rapidly in the colony. It is difficult to know whether Lang or the Presbytery of Irvine understood the extent of the demands and implications that would arise in the Antipodes. Inasmuch as the establishment of a Church within a penal community should be understood in the wider context of the sociopolitical and other demographic dimensions of the frontier situation, Lang was confronted with a much more challenging task than he had anticipated. The difficulties involved were also exacerbated by the fact that the severe isolation experienced by Lang during his early years made him feel that once the Scottish Presbytery ordained him, they simply sent him off to Australia and promptly forgot him. Whether the problem of Lang's protracted isolation and disconnection from his Scottish Presbyterian mentors was deliberate on their part is unlikely, but difficult to resolve retrospectively. The lack of interaction was more likely due to the huge distance between Australia and Scotland and the difficulty in bridging the communication gap. At worst, the lack of interaction on the part of the Scottish Presbytery was more likely to reduce to a case of "out of sight, out of mind".

What seems clear, however, is that upon Lang's arrival, he found that there was no Church education system in place, and he was convinced anyway that the moral and spiritual standards of the penal colony in which he found himself were repugnant. Lang noted that, "in August 1807 there were in the colony 395 men and 1035 concubines, 807 legitimate children and 1025 illegitimate children". In terms of actually building a physical Church, Lang was confronted with the problem that there was a critical shortage of tradesmen, and it was doubtful that the quality of their workmanship would be satisfactory.

Not long after his arrival, Lang explicitly and colourfully laments the state of the colonial society in which he finds himself living:

> The climate is delightful, the country is highly productive, but its people – O generation of vipers! Will they never be warned to flee from the wrath to

come? I scorn to be the pensioner of thieves and adulterers. I shall stay here only till I get our Scots Kirk finished and till I can leave the place honourably.[6]

It appears that the moral and spiritual situation had changed little since Governor Bligh's 1810 report about its decadence to the House of Commons. It is surprising that Lang could be so critical so early in his ministry and so soon after his arrival in the colony. The question arises whether he knew the content of the Bligh and Bigge Report to the House of Commons before he left for Australia. Did he, for example know that John Thomas Bigge received a royal commission in January 1819 to investigate all laws, regulations and usages of the colonial settlement, notably those affecting civil administration, management of convicts, development of the courts, the Church, trade, revenue and natural resources? Lord Bathurst suggested to Bigge to oppose the compassionate policies of Governor Macquarie toward convicts. It was further suggested that transportation should be made an object of real terror. His authority went as far as reporting the confidences of the private or public lives of servants of the Crown and of leading citizens and officials. Macquarie had converted New South Wales from a rebellion-torn, open air penitentiary to a settlement of some substance. Macquarie's humane policy was to readmit emancipated convicts to society without regard for their past. The economy needed their labour and their skills. To Bigge such an attitude was incompatible with the Tory concept of the criminal law. He opposed Macquarie vehemently.[7] Since Bigge submitted the first of three reports on 19 June 1822 and the others on the 21 February 1823 and the 13 March 1823, J.D. Lang would not have been aware of them nor would he have understood the implications or the future policy of the Tory Government as he sailed from Britain on the 14 October 1822. Given the slowness of communications in those days, it is highly unlikely that there was any opportunity for the Presbytery of Irvine and J.D. Lang to have become aware of the report. Besides, there is always a time lapse between receiving a report and the study and consideration of the contents by a parliamentary committee. Had Lang and the presbytery been aware of the reports, it is likely that he may never have sailed to Australia. Had that transpired, then the relationship between Church and State in Australia may have been very different as there would have been less opposition to Anglican hegemony. Nevertheless, Lang must have been full of missionary zeal as he left the shores of Great Britain.

The task of establishing a responsible society with a sound economy seemed immense. It required the expertise of qualified teachers and skilled artisans who were willing to play their part; but as with most young men of that age, in many cases they lacked experience of the world. As we have earlier observed, Lang was well educated, young, dynamic and enthusiastic.

Angus Edmonds the convenor of the John Dunmore Lang Bicentenary Committee concluded that though Lang was involved in a wide range of interests, "his ineffective management, and his propensity for disputation, was more a planner than a practical man: new states, new communities, and new colleges were his visions. By urging such measures steadily, he blazed the way for other men to follow and achieve them."[8]

LANG'S WORLD VIEW

Despite his laments on the moral and spiritual aspects of colonial society that he noticed initially, he nevertheless had an enormous impact on the developing colony. An understanding of Lang's motives in both the ministry and politics in the colony can be explained more fully by considering the foundations of his theology together with the distinctive worldview of Biblical Christianity. He was a minister of the Church of Scotland and embraced the "evangelical party" within the national Church. Barry Bridges explained it this way: "the evangelicals regarded themselves as the true heirs of John Knox's Reformation ...They believed in full participation of the laity in the affairs of the Church and in filling a vacant pulpit by a call from a congregation ... Most initiatives in social and mission affairs and concern for expatriates in the colonies came from evangelicals."[9] Lang embraced the worldview of the Rev Dr Thomas Chalmers. Chalmers was a famous figure in Scottish Church history, as he held the prestigious chair of Theology at Edinburgh University and was also the leader of the Free Church movement. Chalmers initiated and spearheaded the split in the Church of Scotland in 1843, largely over government interference in the life of the Church. Patronage became a key issue. Most evangelicals identified themselves by walking out with Chalmers to form the "Free Church of Scotland". He ultimately established the 'New College', which has since formally become part of Edinburgh University. When Lang was a student at Glasgow University, Chalmers was ministering in Glasgow, at first at the Tron Church. He then established a new parish known as St Johns, where he implemented many new ideas.[10] The new work was an outstanding success. Lang sat under the spell of Chalmers every Sunday. It was Chalmers who embraced the notion of the "Godly Commonwealth". He therefore did not make a distinction between the spiritual and the material. Rather, he applied Christianity to social issues such as economics and poor relief, the needs of the working class, ethics, science and technological change. It was his conviction that through the Gospel of Jesus Christ, society as a whole, as well as men, were to be renovated. All aspects of life were parts of a greater whole.[11]

Lang devoted himself to Chalmers "Grand Design". Appreciation of this point makes it easier to understand why Lang was so immersed in community life, as the community was his mission field and his labours were for the social good of Australia. He believed that the community was in dire need of renovation. The social historian, Mark Hutchinson has summed up Chalmers' influence upon the young Lang:

> Lang obviously imbibed a great deal of the pre 1823 Chalmers programme during his career at University, including Chalmers' integration of activism,
> Biblical social concern, and a renewal of Knox's vision of a Godly Commonwealth, built on a revived national parochial structure with emphases on poor relief, education, and ministry to the whole of life. The most thoroughgoing prototype of this sort of worldly Calvinistic evangelism was in full swing in the St. John's parish of Glasgow when Lang left for Australia, and Chalmers left for St. Andrews University.[12]

Ideals are one thing, but the implementation of them is quite another. In his pursuit of his version of a "Godly Commonwealth" in Australia, Lang was a raspy person. He was frequently inept and possessed a destructive type of oratory.[13] These fundamental defects in his character only aided and abetted those who opposed his policies and actions. His many accomplishments were at the high cost of the peace and unity of the colonial Presbytery, along with partly disenfranchising the powerfully placed Church of England. Lang soon discovered that in the colony there was a minority of Presbyterians with no Church, who were dominated by an Anglican administration and outnumbered by Irish Catholics.

THE BUILDING OF SCOTS CHURCH

Deficiencies in Lang's character became even more manifest when he began building Scots Church in 1824, in part with private subscription monies which were insufficient, thereby creating a considerable deficit. The Colonial government had been assisting The Church of England and Roman Catholic Church to erect their buildings, so Lang applied to the Governor of NSW for public funds to help with the building programme. The governor Sir Thomas Brisbane refused the request.

From this moment on Lang's lack of judgement and immaturity became a serious handicap when interacting with government officialdom.

It has been suggested that Brisbane decided to decline Lang's request due to certain financial constraints of the period which had put significant pressure on government spending. Lang regarded this as a form of religious discrimination, inasmuch as the government had continuously been expending vast sums of money on the Anglican cause. To avoid the matter of religious inequity getting out of hand Brisbane passed the matter on to Major Frederick Goulburn, the colonial secretary, to provide a "polite refusal". At the time Goulburn was the secretary and registrar of the Records for New South Wales and was publicly associated with Brisbane's new arrangements for land grants and convict re absorption into the community, commissariat matters, and the law courts.[14] Mark Hutchinson notes that Goulburn had no love of Presbyterians whom he regarded as "tub thumpers" (*sic*) and this was particularly so with people such as John Dunmore Lang. In his reply Goulburn, under the signature of Governor Brisbane suggested that the Presbyterians adopt the principle of toleration as seen in the Church of England. It is under this principle of toleration and the financial support of private subscriptions that the Colonial Government supported the erection of a Catholic Chapel. It was further suggested that if the Presbyterians followed the example of the Roman Catholics who put into practice the proposal of instructing people to fear God and to honour the King and seek to 'keep the unity of the spirit in the land of peace', the Colonial Government would support the erection of a Church building.

Hutchison asserts that in four short passages, Goulburn supported Anglican Hegemony, placed Presbyterians on the same level as Catholics, attacked Lang and William Wemyss personally, and accused the colony's Presbyterian community generally of hypocrisy. But this also meant that Lang became more involved in colonial politics.[15] Lang replied to Governor Brisbane in the following way:

> Your Excellency states that toleration is one of the glories of the Church of England. I beg leave to remind Your Excellency that toleration is the glory of the British constitution, not of the Church of England. Your Excellency knows that Scotsmen are not reduced to the necessity of being thankful to the Church of England for toleration, or of asking for toleration as a boon from the Church of England. Sir, Scotsmen are free born. Their civil and religious liberties were won for them by the swords of their forefathers and they are a degenerate race if in every situation they do not vindicate their right to both. Their case is widely different from that of English Dissenters, but even the Dissenters enjoy toleration as a civil right which the Church of England neither can give nor take away. Your Excellency is aware, moreover, that by the Articles of Union the same privileges and the same rights were secured to the Scottish nation in all the British colonies as to the English. And in other colonies of the British Empire, this provision has been understood to secure not merely the toleration but the encouragement and support also of ministers of the Scottish National Church, where they are required.[16]

This response caused such great offence at Government House that the Governor withdrew his personal financial support to the erection of Scots Church. This had dire consequences for both Scots Church and Lang. Lang writes:

> The action of the Governor acted as a sentence of proscription against me and the work in which I was embarked. For the military officers, with few exceptions, forsook my ministry. Private individuals of respectability who

were dependent on Government acknowledged that they could not come to Scots Church for fear of losing their bread.

A merchant of the first character in the colony, on being asked why he did not go to Scots Church as usual, replied that he did not choose to go there now as the Government had set their face against it and were determined to put it down.[17]

D.W.A. Baker considers that the way in which Lang handled this altercation established a "pattern of conflict" from which Lang never escaped. Baker writes: "Lang could never shut his eyes and ears to rudeness or imagined slights, he could never avoid forcible methods of gaining victories nor suffer fools or knaves gladly. He always sought to carry his points by damaging rather than by conciliating his opponents".[18]

Given Lang's ineptitude, rudeness, violent language and his strong vilifying spirit, Lang's leadership of the Presbyterian Church was all but guaranteed continued trouble with both the government and with the constituents of his own Church. The *pattern of conflict which Lang unwittingly unfolded gave rise to a sea of discord in which Lang would eventually drown.*

EDUCATION

Both Lang and the leaders of the Church of England agreed that the establishment of educational facilities were a necessity. However there was little else they agreed upon, and distrust became common place. Another example of Lang's negotiation ineptitude is as follows: Lang met with the new Church of England appointee Archdeacon Broughton and promised him that he would support the establishment of a school in which the clergy of other denominations would be admitted to its general management. Lang preferred to do this than to support the establishment of a school under the leadership of Laurence Halloran. It was considered that Halloran's school would become too secular. Lang was advised by Alexander McLeay, the colonial secretary, that it was the intention to establish a school on strict Anglican lines—no other clergy would be permitted to share in the administration of it. Instead, Lang gave his support to the founding of the Sydney College. This proved fruitless as internal strife created unease and public support rapidly waned. This meant that if the Archdeacon's plans came to fruition, then the Anglicans would have a monopoly on education.

Lang turned his attention to establishing his own school. To this end he went to Scotland and organised tradesmen to help build the Colony College and convinced a number of school masters to come teach classes. Broughton considered that these plans were a breach of trust and he was "distinctly irked by Lang's ability, not only to build and operate a College but also to return to the colony with new ministers, when publicly funded Anglicans seemed to be unable to meet the desperate need for clergy".[19] So education became the issue which caused a serious rift between these two capable men, who viewed each other with suspicion and distrust. This was a sad outcome, as the two denominations were in the main unified in doctrine. Although the two denominations held to either the Westminster Confession of Faith in the case of the Presbyterians, or the Thirty Nine Articles in the case of the Church of England, they were both Calvinistic documents. Unfortunately, both denominations in Great Britain were national Churches, in the sense that the Anglican Church was based in English culture, and the Presbyterian Church in the culture of Scotland. It was, therefore, always going to be difficult to have common recognition by an English appointed administration in the colony of New South Wales. The twin difficulties of ineptitude and a destructive oratory are clearly evident in the saga of the establishment of the Scots Church and the founding of the first school.

CHURCH STRUCTURE

The decidedly argumentive and vitriolic spirit of Lang was also evident in his dealings within the Church. It was not long before William Wemyss, who was the Deputy Commissary General and a member of Scots Church, fell out with Lang due to his contemptuous disposition. The tension caused by Lang grew so intensely that by 1832 the Colony's Legislative Council actually censured Lang. This badly impaired his credibility and served to diminish the public's financial support for Lang's projects.

On 14th December 1832 the Presbytery of New South Wales was constituted with four ministers. Lang was not impressed with the make up of the Presbytery as several members were too fond of the bottle and verged on being alcoholics. Others were flung to distant and remote parts of the states and were either in poor health, or had the reputation of being lazy.

In 1836 Lang again visited Britain to encourage immigration especially among destitute highlanders and to recruit clergy so as to out vote the backsliders and drunkards in the Presbytery. It was during Lang's absence that the Presbytery chose to meet in September 1837. It was this meeting that set the stage for a nasty falling-out between Lang and the Presbytery. Cameron summarizes the resolutions and their importance:

> During the absence of Dr. Lang, the Presbytery had applied to the Legislative Council for a Temporalities Act, which was passed on the 9th September 1837. It is entitled *An Act to regulate the temporal affairs of Presbyterian Churches and Chapels connected with the Church of Scotland in the Colony of NSW.*[20]

Cameron notes that the Presbytery met again on the 2 November and processed three calls: one from Singleton in favour of the Rev. I. Hetherington, one from Goulburn in favour of Rev. W. Hamilton, and one from Illawarra in favour of Rev. J. Tait. The importance of these two meetings of the Presbytery was that the Presbytery had now become entrenched in a position of power and administered authority. The Presbyterian Church, represented by the Presbytery, had received legal recognition, and the Presbytery became invested with the sole authority to certify for the payment of State salaries to ministers of the Presbyterian Church.

This action of the Presbytery meant that John Dunmore Lang was stripped of much of the authority that he had formerly held. He now had to submit to the authority of the Presbytery.

In December of the same year Lang returned from his trip to Britain with another eight ministers and four probationers. He was furious with the Presbytery's actions during his absence and in particular the *Temporalities Act*. His anger was such that all who disagreed with him he considered to be dishonourable Christians. Gilchrist and Powell in their notes on Lang's reaction write: "Lang was an eloquent man at any time but when it came to invective he was a genius".[21] Lang published a pamphlet stating that the *Temporalities Act* was designed to bind the Church in fetters of iron for all time.[22] In another pamphlet he declares the content of a letter to Lord John Russell, who was the Principal Secretary of State for the State of the Colonies, in which he suggests that the Presbyterian Church *Temporalities Act* be overturned.[23] Without one word or any reference to the Presbytery, Lang was acting independently and contrary to the Presbyterian form of government. Concerning the decisions of Presbytery, he singles out the Rev. Dr John McGarvie the Moderator of the Presbytery and his principal helper since 1826 and in whose care was the Scots Church during Lang's absence saying:

> In my absence the Rev John McGarvie, Moderator of Presbytery applied to the Legislative Council to pass an act to be called *The Presbyterian Church Temporalities Act* which was to change completely the character of the Church from what it had been before I left the colony—I refused, along with a majority who had come out with me, to re-enter it.[24]

The significant point here is that while the Presbytery was scattered from one end of the country to the other and unable to meet, Lang was in control. When he returned to the colony the Church was a constitutional entity and no longer a Church under the sole direction of himself. Lang was just one of a number of members of a Church Court and he no longer had any authority. The voice of the Church was no longer located in Lang, but in the resolutions of the Presbytery.

Lang was to have none of this, so the first schism occurred. Lang constituted his own Presbytery, calling it the Synod of New South Wales. It was constituted with four ministers on the 11 December 1837, as a rival institution to the Presbytery formed in 1832. Cameron notes that the essential difference between the two rival groups was that the Synod of NSW was the final court of appeal i.e. no Church under its jurisdiction could appeal any matter to a higher court in Scotland. However, Lang was expelled by his new Presbytery in 1838 for 'schism'. Lang's vitriol and bitterness was made very public as he used the press to air his grievances. This schism lasted till 1840 when a union was effected. This bad spirit continued. The new Presbytery in 1842 admonished Lang to pay more attention to the resolutions of the Church Courts. Lang responded in a sermon in which he denounced the Synod of Australia as a mere synagogue of Satan.

James Forbes writing in 1846 about the 1837 period said: "it has ever appeared to us one of the most mysterious permissions of Divine Providence that the founding of an infant Church in an infant colony should have fallen into such hands."

The story of the Presbyterian Church in the colony during the nineteenth century was a story of turbulence and dispute. Although Lang was possibly his own worst enemy ,and despite his argumentative personality, he achieved so much for the benefit of the colony in particular and for Australia in general. Historians may just wonder how the colony would have developed socially had it not been for a highly assertive and courageous personality such as Lang's. Importantly, Lang realized that there was no real future for the colony without migration of free settlers who could provide the expertise to develop social coherence, education, rural industries, manufacturing industries and adventure capital to secure the wool and mining industries. He was an activist who got things done despite his vindictive disposition. It should be remembered that so many of the disputes were in the context of a struggling Church that was hampered from the beginning, being cut off from the security and the moral and the financial support of the established Church in Scotland. There were two sides to many of these disputes.

It is unfortunate that Lang fell out with so many well-intentioned people who dared to disagree with him. His slanderous language used to discredit and disarm his opponents paved the way for unnecessary litigation. The heated disputes over matters of Church government, the urgent need for education, immigration and theological issues cemented into the Church a culture of conflict which was to have a lasting and disruptive impact upon the Presbyterian Church in future years. While it is easy to focus on Lang's ineptitude at negotiation, and although there were many in the colony who had little time for him, he nevertheless was a champion of many causes which paved the way for others to follow.

Despite the turmoil of the early Colonial era the practice of Christian worship followed the pathway of the dispositions of ministerial leadership.

With the increasing numbers of ministers arriving from Scotland diversity of theological opinion and Church practice could only increase. Chapter four of this book will show that with the passing of several Acts by the Church of Scotland from 1694 to 1856 *The Directory of Public Worship* with its minimized liturgical approach, and the lack of liturgical forms had become well accepted in Scottish Church practice. Up to 1865 fifty three ministers arrived in Australia from Scotland: 30 came from the Church of Scotland, 20 from the Free Church of Scotland, 2 from the United Presbyterian Church and 1 from an independent Church. With little opportunity for serious theological reflection minimized liturgical practices were to influence the Australian Church for decades to come. Changing theological opinion of future ministers in the decades to come was inevitable and would be reflected in worship practice. Ministers of the Colonial era would never have imagined that in the twenty first century would see serious liturgical debate which would look back to John Calvin's Strasbourg liturgy as a basis for liturgical reform.

NOTES

1. R.S. Ward, Rev. Dr. John Dunmore Lang 1799- 1878 Turbulent Presbyterian Leader, www.knoxpcea.org.au/php?view,retrieved 14th January 2016
2. R.S. Ward, A Short History of the Church of Scotland (Melbourne: New Melbourne Press, 2015.), 87-88
3. Revised editions appeared in 1837, 1852, 1875.
4. H.S. Matthew & B. Harrison, Edit., *The Oxford Dictionary of National Biography* (Oxford: Oxford University Press, 2004), Vol. 32, 461–62.
5. The New South Wales Parliamentary Service provides the following summary of Lang and his service as a politician: Clergyman. Educated for the Ministry at Largs Parish School and University of Glasgow, where he won many scholarships and prizes. (MA 1820 and D.D. 1825). Arrived in Sydney in May 1823 as the first Presbyterian Minister in NSW. Founded Scots Church in Sydney where he was minister from 1826 until 1878, although stripped of executive functions. Sponsor of Morton Bay and Port Phillip separation movements. Strong opponent of transportation. Leading republican in early 1850s. A leader of radical movement 1840s to early 1860s. Struggled for better schools. Advocated home rule for Ireland and attacked Roman Catholicism. The Parliamentary Service also supplies the details of his service to the colony: Member of the NSW Legislative Council 1/6/1843 to 1/11/1847; Member of the NSW Legislative Council 1/7/1850 to 30/6/1851; Member of the NSW Legislative Council 1/10/1851 to 1/10/1851, 1/8/1854 to 29/2/185 and 14/6/1859 to 15/11/1869; Member for Sydney West 14/6/1859 to 10/11/1860, 12/12/1860 to 10/11/1864 and 24/11/1864 to 15/11/1869—a total of a little less than 28 years.
6. Baker & Powell, 31.
7. *Australian Dictionary of Biography* (Clayton: Melbourne University Press, 1983), Vol. 1, 99-101.
8. Gilchrist & Powell, *John Dunmore Laing*, 8.
9. Barry Bridges, *Ministry in Scotland in the First Half of the Nineteenth Century*, Private Paper in Ferguson Library, Sydney.
10. See John Roxborogh, "The Legacy of Thomas Chalmers", *International Bulletin of Missionary Research*, 23 (4) October 1999: 173–76.

11. See Piggin & Roxborogh, *The Saint Andrew's Seven*, Ch. 1; also J. Webster, "Thomas Chalmers, Science and Scottish Evangelical Movement", MA(Hons) Thesis, University of Wollongong, 1989.

12. M. Hutchinson, *Iron in our Blood* (Sydney: Ferguson Publications and the Centre for the Study of Australian Christianity, 2001), 22.

13. Example, the "Synagogue of Satan" speech, in Gilchrist & Powell, *John Dunmore Lang*, 122–27.

14. *Australian Dictionary of Biography*, Vol. 1, 463–64.

15. Hutchinson, *Iron in our Blood*, 28.

16. Gilchrist & Powell, *John Dunmore Laing*, 48.

17. Gilchrist & Powell, *John Dunmore Laing*, 49.

18. Baker, *Days of Wrath*, 48.

19. Hutchinson, *Iron in Our Blood*, 36-37.

20. Cameron, *Centenary History*, 7.

21. Gilchrist & Powell, *John Dunmore Laing*, 123.

22. J. D. Lang, *The Dead Fly in the Apothecary's Ointment* (Sydney: 1861).

23. J. D. Lang, *Lord John Russell*, January 1840; the same request is found in a letter in pamphlet form, *Rt Honourable H. Labouchere*, July 1839.

24. Gilchrist & Powell, *John Dunmore Laing*, 122–23.

Chapter Two

Defining the Practice of Worship in the Presbyterian Church

In chapter one, we have laboured to show that the structure of Presbyterianism tends to promote argument and debate. As with any system of Church government, various theological factions and forceful personalities are able to upset the Church's equilibrium. The global Presbyterian Church, particularly in Scotland, has suffered so many such traumas in its history that it has fractured into several groups, only to reunite years later when the theological equilibrium has been restored. History has shown that such reunions never mend the whole fracture, and a small group usually stays out of the reunion. The idea of *a pattern of conflict* will always be present in the Church where cultural, philosophical and theological change occurs. So long as there is a mutual concern for the stability of the Church in theological debate, *the pattern of conflict* can be healthy and fruitful.

In New South Wales, and elsewhere, the concept of Presbyterian worship has been subjected to the pressure of change since the formation of the Uniting Church of Australia. Worship services in New South Wales, in particular, are very different from what they were before the Union in 1977. It would seem that little attention has been given to the theology of worship.

It is the burden of this chapter to show that since the Presbyterian Church holds to a Calvinistic theology, this same theology is able to provide profound insights into the current crisis of worship, as John Calvin himself experienced a major crisis in worship practices while he was in both Strasbourg and Geneva. The radical theological and philosophical changes which took place during the Protestant Reformation in Europe demanded a complete restructure of worship practices. Calvin provided the theological leadership to resolve the serious crisis of the time.

It would be a monumental misunderstanding of the theology of Calvin if modern practitioners believed that there was no plausible link between theology and worship. This chapter will seek to define what Calvinism is, so as to provide a contextual balance. We will then tease out Calvin's inextricable links between worship and doctrine.

In this and the next chapter we will provide a contextual balance and observe the climax of Calvinistic worship in the Presbyterian Church in New South Wales. Liturgical minimization will then be more readily defined by contrast. It is the contrast of "what used to be" and "what now is".

The practice of Presbyterian worship is determined by the adherence to theological presuppositions. The practice of worship necessarily becomes a theological barometer which indicates the leaders understanding of the Church's history and philosophical and theological foundations. It is also reflective of the theological educative process where candidates for the ministry are trained in a whole range of theological disciplines. These should include systematics and historical theology with specific reference to the theology of John Calvin, the study of which provides the theological foundations of the practice of ministry, particularly that of public worship. The Presbyterian Church belongs to that grouping of Churches known as *Reformed*, which is by definition Calvinistic in its theological context. The most famous of the Calvinistic statements of the Reformed Faith in the English speaking world is the Westminster Confession of Faith, as are the Thirty-Nine Articles of the Church of England. This being so, it is of paramount importance that the theology of John Calvin is understood as well as the way in which it expresses itself in practical applications of the Church's ministry. The failure to understand the theological and philosophical foundations of the Church will be made manifest in the longer term in the practice of ministry, long after the candidate has fulfilled the academic requirements for ordination.

There are several words in the Bible that are translated as worship. The Hebrew word *abodah* and the Greek word *latreia* indicate "labour" or "service". These two words refer to the service to God that is carried out by the priests in the tabernacle and the temple in the Old Testament. Worship is something that is done, that is something that we do and in which we participate. There are two other words that are also translated as worship: the Hebrew word *Shachah* and the Greek word *proskuneo*. These two words literally mean "bowing" or "bending". These words in the context of worship imply homage that is honouring the worth of someone else. Robert Rayburn shows that *latreuein* is used for worship in passages such as Acts 7:42, 24:14, Philip. 3: 3 and Heb.10: 2. Rayburn notes that the original meaning of the word was simply "to serve as a slave serves his master or a hired servant his employer".[1] This means that in worship we seek to please not ourselves but

God. It is therefore imperative to understand the doctrine of God for without it, worship will become all about us and what satisfies our particular needs.

To labour in service implies special relationships in which we see ourselves subservient to one whom we adore and honour. This is fundamental to our understanding of worship; the way we engage in public worship and the content of the worship is dependent upon a theological perspective or lack of it. The constitution of the Presbyterian Church embraces the Calvinistic documents, the Westminster Confession of Faith and the Larger and Shorter catechisms as its understanding of its theological foundations. The practice of worship needs therefore to be contextualised within this theological framework. These theological documents were framed in the seventeenth century and were expressive of the theology of John Calvin. It is Calvin above all others during the reformation period had the greatest influence in the establishment of the Reformed Church. *The Oxford Dictionary of the Christian Church* comments that Calvin's influence was that of "an ecclesiastical statesman, a religious controversialist, an educationalist, author and his theological insights, his exegetical talents, his knowledge of languages, his precision and his clear pithy style, made him the most influential writer among the reformers".[2]

In order to provide an adequate definition of Presbyterian worship and its theological presuppositions, it is essential to understand Calvinism as a world view and its role in worship.

Abraham Kuyper sees Calvinism as the highest form of development reached by the religious and political principle in the sixteenth century.[3] Calvinism provides a unified life system of principles that are rooted in the past so as to fill the present with confidence for the future. Kuyper argues that Calvinism fulfils all the requirements to make it a successful general life system. He sees that there are three fundamental relations that make up all human life: (1) Our relation to *God*. (2) Our relation to *man*. (3) Our relation to the *world*.

In respect to (1) Kuyper understands that our relationship to God is imperative. Without God as the source of our existence or as Tillich would have said the source of our being, movements in history which deny God as the creator and who sustains life, are movements that are always partial and transient, and have no real permanence. The success of Paganism, Islam, and Romanism as life systems is because all three have their starting point in God.

Paganism should be more adequately defined before we proceed any further. Paganism should be used in a very broad sense which goes beyond the popular definition of the worship of foreign gods of wood and stone. Within the definition we include the content of the terms humanism, naturalism and atheism which are terms which express a belief system which denies the priority of God or the complete denial of God as Christians would understand the term, in favour of a belief system which advocates the sufficiency of man's mind as a unifying universal which explains the meaning and purpose of life. The most complete expression of this view is found in Julian Huxley's book *Religion without Revelation*. Norman Geisler shows that this work of Huxley's is built on the evolutionary philosophy of Charles Darwin, the evolutionary philosophy of Herbert Spencer and the evolutionary ethics of his grandfather Thomas H. Huxley.[4] Kuyper argues this way: Paganism assumes and worships God *in the creature*. This he says is true of the lowest Animism as well as the highest Buddhism. Paganism does not rise to the conception of the independent existence of a God beyond and above the creature. In this system there is a definite interpretation of the relation of the infinite to the finite, and to this it owed its power to produce a finished form of human society.

Similarly this is also true of *Islam*. Kuyper notes that Islam *isolates God from the creature,* so as "to avoid all commingling with the creature".[5]

In a similar fashion he argues that in Romanism "the papal tiara, the hierarchy, the mass are but the outcome of the one fundamental thought: viz., that God enters into fellowship with the creature by means of a mystic middle link, which is the Church; not as a mystic organism, but as a visible and tangible institution". In this system the Church stands between God and the world.[6]

Kuyper now argues that Calvinism fulfils this first requirement as a life system in a similar but in a very profound way. Calvinism does not seek God in the creature as does Paganism neither does it isolate God from the creature as in Islam. Calvinism does not posit an intermediate communion between God and the creature as does Romanism; rather it proclaims the idea that God stands in "high majesty above the creature and God enters into immediate fellowship with the creature, as God the Holy Spirit."[7] This means that the Calvinists spiritual life from the very beginning rests entirely upon God himself and not on the actions of man. As Kuyper says "the Deo Soli Gloria" was not the starting point but the result which gave a "guarantee from eternity to eternity, to our inner self a direct and immediate communion with the living God". Kuyper makes the claim that Calvin was unique in that Calvin's theology lay in the general cosmological principle of the sovereignty of God which enabled it to impress a life system both inside and outside the Church. Luther on the other hand, had his starting point in the special soteriological principle of a justifying faith.[8] This seriously limited the Lutherans to change either the social or the political life of a nation.

The second fundamental condition which must be met for Calvinism to become a life system is the *relation of man to man*.

Every life system weakens or accentuates the many differences that exist within the realm of mankind. These are differences in the created order; the biological differences between male and female, is a case in point. There is also a multitude of differences between men, in their various gifts and talents. These differences also extend to the social order of society where differences for example are, the social standing between the rich and the poor, or between those who hold public office and those who do not. Kuyper sees important outcomes of man's relation to man in the principal life systems discussed under the relationship of man to God.

In Paganism, God dwells *in* the creature, so in terms of men's relationship to one another, this means that there is a divine superiority which is exhibited in whatever is high among men.[9] In this way, Kuyper argues, "its demigods, hero-worship and finally its sacrifices upon the altar of Divus Augustus". On the other hand, that which is deemed lower is considered godless and gives rise "to the systems of caste, as in India and Egypt and slavery everywhere else, thereby placing one man under a base subjection to his fellow man". The determinative factor which divides what is high and what is low is contingent upon the whims of man's imagination and rational thought. In other words the final reference point of all interpretation of life rests solely upon man himself. Kuyper notes that under Islam, dreams of its paradise of *houries* (from a Persian word signifying "black-eye") usurp public authority, by which the woman is the slave of man even as the unbeliever (Kafir) is the slave of the Moslem. Social distinctions in Islam tend to be absolute.

In his argument Kuyper notes that Romanism, which embraces a Christian world view, overcomes the absolute character of social distinctions and renders them relative in order to interpret every relation of man to man hierarchically. Just as there is a hierarchy among the angels of God and a hierarchy in God's Church there is also a hierarchy among men, which leads to an aristocratic interpretation of life. Kuyper also sees the impact of modernism on man's relations with man. He sees modernism as the philosophy of life which is void of God. He illustrates this modern movement with Voltaire who sought to exclude God from human life. This godless philosophy depends on naturalism for its building blocks and it has itself become a life system. He further sees that this system is in mortal combat with Christianity where principle must be fought with principle. This godless system cannot be underestimated as a philosophy of life. It possesses a comprehensive and far-reaching influence. In this system all differences are abolished and every distinction is located on the same level, as it "kills life by placing it under the ban of uniformity. One type must answer for all, one uniform, one position and one and the same development of life; and whatever goes beyond and above it, is looked upon as an insult to the common consciousness".[10]

Calvinism stands in stark contrast to all these life systems as it offers a unique philosophy of man's relation to man. Kuyper rightly sees that since human life is located before the sovereign creator God, it follows that, all men or women, rich or poor, weak or strong, dull or talented, as creatures of God, and as lost sinners, have no claim whatever to lord over one another, and that we stand as equals before God, and consequently equal as man to man" . . . Therefore Calvinism condemns "not merely all open slavery and systems of caste, but also all covert slavery of woman and of the poor; it is opposed to all hierarchy among men; it tolerates no aristocracy save such as is able, either in person or in family, by the grace of God, to exhibit superiority of character or talent, and to show that it does not claim this superiority for self-aggrandizement or ambitious pride, but for the sake of spending it in the service of God. So Calvinism was bound to find its utterance in the democratic interpretation of life; to proclaim liberty of nations; and not to rest until, both politically and socially every man, simply because he is man, should be recognised, respected and dealt with as a creature created after the Divine likeness.[11]

The third fundamental of a life system is the relation between *individuals and the world*. Man's attitude toward the world now becomes of critical importance. Kuyper argues that Paganism places *too high* an estimate upon the world and tends to lose itself in it. Opposite to this is the view of Islam which places *too low* an estimate upon the world as it seeks the visionary world of a sensual paradise. These two views are in contrast to the Christian view that was dominant during the Middle Ages under Romanism. The hierarchical view of man's relation to man, established by Romanism, created an antithesis between the world and Christendom. Under this structure, the Church and its ministry were sanctified and the world outside the Church was under the influence of demons and demonical powers. This meant, according to Kuyper, that the whole social fabric of a Christian country had to be controlled and influenced by the Church, "the magistrate had to be appointed and confessionally bound; art and science had to be placed under ecclesiastical encouragement and censure; trade and commerce had to be bound to the Church by the tie of guilds; and from the cradle to the grave, family life was to be placed under ecclesiastical guardianship".[12]

This view of the Medieval Church was pursued with relentless logic, especially when the Church experienced opposition from the early protestant reformers. It explains the intense ecclesiastical and political opposition to Luther's famous declaration at Wittenberg and the theological implications of Calvin's theology. The very foundations of the Roman Church were being challenged and if the Church, with its interpretative structure, was to survive then reformational thinking had to be overturned and made void in any way possible.

Despite the suffering and hardship caused by what seemed to be incongruous behaviour of the Church in its pursuit of eradicating the influence of the reformers it was, nevertheless, motivated, by the ideal of saving and Christianizing the world.

In stark contrast to this third fundamental element of a life system, John Calvin brought a complete change in the conception of the world. Not only did Calvin emphasise the image of God in man but he saw that creation was divine and was not inherently evil. As man was subjected to particular grace for salvation, the world was subject to common grace which maintained the life of the world. This view meant that the dominating control of every aspect of life under Romanism was relinquished. Kuyper argues the change in this way:

> Thus the Church receded in order to be neither more nor less than the congregation of believers, and in every department the life of the world was not emancipated from God, but from the dominion of the Church. Thus domestic life regained its independence, trade and commerce realised their strength in liberty, art and science were set free from every ecclesiastical bond and restored to their own inspirations, and man began to understand the subjection of all nature with its hidden forces and treasures to himself as a holy duty, imposed upon him by the original ordinances of Paradise: "Have dominion over them". Henceforth the curse should no longer rest upon the world itself, but upon that which is *sinful* in it, and instead of monastic *flight* from the world the duty is now emphasized of serving God *in* the world, in every position in life. To praise God in the Church and serve Him in the world became the inspiring impulse, and, in the Church, strength was to be gathered by which to resist temptation and sin in the world.[13]

Calvinism became a formidable life system which had a beneficial impact upon Church and society. It was able to overcome the philosophical problems associated with the failure of identifying nature with God on the one hand and a tendency to locate God out of the world on the other. Drawing a marked distinction between the Creator and creature, Calvinism liberated both man and society from the control of the Church which during the Middle Ages saw, as intimated earlier, everything outside the Church's control, as the domain of the demonic. The change in the philosophical and theological outlook with its distinction of particular and common grace liberated man and his relationship to others; it also liberated the Church to be the Church in terms of its spiritual mission, and it also liberated society from the traditional Aristotelian outlook thereby enabling science to develop and progress. In essence the change in the philosophical outlook impacted on every facet of life.

In essence, as Calvinism fulfils the three fundamental relational requirements of man's existence, it admits of classification as a great life system. It is a unique system of life preserving the dignity of man and unmasking the potentialities and possibilities of the created order.

The distinguishing feature of Calvinism has its foundation in its formative principle. It cannot be understood in its distinction of difference with Lutheranism. It cannot be said that the spirit of Calvinism is located in the doctrines of Predestination and Justification by Faith alone, as is commonly thought. The famous Princeton scholar B.B. Warfield notes that Predestination is not the foundation stone of Calvinism; rather Predestination is the outcome of a complete dependence upon the free mercy of a saving God. Without Predestination this complete dependence cannot be maintained. In keeping with Kuyper, Warfield argues that Calvinism in contrast to Lutheranism is a matter of principle, not individual doctrines which both parties hold in common. Warfield's argument is as follows:

> Lutheranism, the product of a poignant sense of sin, born from the throes of a guilt-burdened soul which cannot be stilled until it finds peace in God's decree of justification, is apt to rest in this peace; while Calvinism, the product of an overwhelming vision of God, born from the reflection in the heart of man of the majesty of a God who will not give His glory to another, cannot pause until it places the scheme of salvation itself in relation to a complete world-view, in which it becomes subsidiary to the glory of the Lord God Almighty. Calvinism asks with Lutheranism, indeed, that most poignant of all questions, What shall I do to be saved? And answers it as Lutheranism answers it. But the great question which presses upon it is, How shall God be glorified?[14]

Calvinism in contrast to Lutheranism is not a philosophy of difference rather it is the nature of the very foundations of Calvinism which enables it to become a world view which encounters every aspect of life, it begins, it centres, it ends with the vision of God in His glory: and it sets itself before all things to render to God His rights in every sphere of life-activity.

Conceptualising Calvinism in this three point outline shows that it is a distinctive world view which embraces man's relation to God, man's relation to each other and man's relationship to the world, which is itself forged out of the doctrine of God sovereignty. It means that the practice of worship becomes a critical aspect of Christian devotion. Given that the reformational era was a turbulent progressive renunciation of the principles of Romanism in respect to man's relation to God, to man and the world, the medieval practice of worship with its notion of the "real presence", expressed in terms of an Aristotelian metaphysic and the Church's adherence to a view of the world in which it sees itself as a matrix between God and every aspect of man's life, then the practice of worship was immediately challenged. Under Calvin's notion of the glory of God, medieval worship became all but irrelevant. What was the meaning of the mass without the philosophical metaphysic of Aristotle? What was the meaning of the Church gathered when Romanism accepted the Church as an institution, responsible for the salvation of the world? Or what was to be the status of worship when the hierarchical notion of man's relation to man was challenged by the reformers? Under such a notion the priest necessarily becomes an intermediary between God and man.

The worshipping public under this system became Godly spectators. In contrast, the foundational system of Calvin located the Church in people not in an institution. Thus worship was a function which expressed the glory of God. Evelyn Underhill rightly interpreted Calvinistic worship in terms of "God's unspeakable Majesty and Otherness and the nothingness and simplicity of man" It is in worship that man experiences the "Divine Transcendence on the awestruck soul".[15] . Worship for Calvin was a serious matter. It was unthinkable to approach worship in a laissez-faire fashion. The Biblical notion of God's sovereignty and the emphasis on the creator/creature distinction demanded a spirit of humility in worship in which man experienced the transcendence of the Almighty God. John T Dyck points out that for Calvin "piety" is essential for worship. Piety is reverence joined with the love of God. Until men recognize that they owe everything to God, that they are nourished by his fatherly care, that he is the Author of their very good, that they should seek nothing beyond him–they will never yield him willing service.[16] Worship was to be governed by God's requirements. Any notion of worship which focused on self-satisfaction rather than on obedience and submission to his authority in worship was unacceptable and by definition regarded as idolatrous. T. F. Torrance rightly comments that Calvin never divorced the doctrine of Christ from the doctrine of the Church. This was the fundamental error of Rome and it impacted on the worship of the Church.[17] Calvin argues that the unity of the Church is both physical and spiritual. He likens the external form of the Church to the body and the worship and doctrine of the Church to the soul. So, true unity involves both the government and doctrine. It is doctrine that regulates the worship of God, just as the soul regulated the functions of the body. Doctrine always has primacy over the body. To separate the two is to fall into the error of the Anabaptists. Calvin makes a special point in noting that the whole substance of Christianity is found and is comprehended in terms of how "God is duly worshipped and the source from which salvation is to be obtained".[18] From this foundation all other parts of Christianity are to be comprehended. It seems so strange that in the practice of the contemporary Church which claims theological adherence to Calvin's theology, so little is known of the unity of doctrine and worship. The common perception among ministers of the Presbyterian Church at the present time is that doctrine is of paramount importance, in that most ministers regard adherence to a Calvinistic theology as being the touchstone of being "reformed". This being so, it would appear that worship is rarely considered as being as important and has little place in theological discussion. We would suggest that there is only a small minority of Presbyterian ministers in New South Wales who would know that Calvin linked doctrine and worship together. This naturally raises the question whether the Church has unintentionally embraced some of the practices of the Anabaptists!

Volume two of the *Tracts and Treatises* is a primary source of Calvin's theology of worship, as it deals with the soul of the Church, i.e. with doctrine and worship. Calvin's understanding of doctrine and worship is located in his Christology. This is foundational. The whole perception of worship in the Middle Ages came under intense scrutiny with Calvin's assertion that the two natures of Christ, His Divinity and His Humanness, were distinct and separate from each other. From this emerged Calvin's distinctive three-fold nature of Christ's ministry, namely as Prophet, Priest and King. If Christ's mediatorship and Priesthood were a function of His Humanness or manhood, as well as His virtues of Deity, then all other human and priestly functions of common man are immediately abolished. Worship no longer depends upon any form of human mediation or human priesthood. Worship is therefore all about Jesus Christ. Without union with Christ through faith, worship cannot be a function of self or what we perform, it is on the contrary engaging in the worship of Christ Himself. Calvin argues at some length to explain the separate nature of Christ's Divinity and Humanness. He argues from specific biblical references in his Institutes:

> When, manifest in the flesh, he is called the Son of David and Abraham . . . made in the seed of David, according to the flesh" (Rom. 1:3.) He then points to other key texts which emphasises the distinction, "God sent his Son, born of a woman, born under law, to redeem those under the law" (Gal.4:4.) The Epistle to the Hebrews figures prominently, "he had to be made like his brothers in every way, in order that he might become a merciful and faithful high priest in the service of God. (Heb. 2:17.)[19]

In passages such as these, the humanness of Christ is stressed as an essential function of the atonement. Any attempt to explain away the humanness of Christ as did Marcion is met with devastating ridicule. Whilst emphasising the human nature of Christ, Calvin sees the necessity of his Divinity working side by side with his Humanness to affect an atoning sacrifice. Calvin points to two principal passages,

> Therefore, just as sin entered the world through one man, and death through sin, and in this way death came to all men, because all sinned . . . consequently, just as the result of one trespass was condemnation for all men, so also the result of one act of righteousness was justification that brings life for all men". (Rom. 5:12–18.) The other passage is 1Corth. 15:47. "The first man was of the dust of the earth and the second man from heaven." Calvin argues that Christ possessed two natures, one human, one divine, "For although the boundless essence of the Word was united with human nature into one person, we have no idea of any enclosing. The Son of God descended miraculously from heaven, yet without abandoning heaven; was pleased to be conceived miraculously in the virgin's womb, to live on earth and hang on a cross and yet always filled the world as from the beginning.[20]

This unique Christology was not something new, thought out by the reformer. This Christology was hammered out by the Church Fathers at Chalcedon. In *The Tome of Leo*, the bishop of Rome 440–461 writes: "God is believed to be both Almighty and Father; it follows that the Son is shown to be co-eternal with him, differing in no respect from the Father. For he was born God of God, Almighty of Almighty, co-eternal of eternal . . . not divided in essence".[21]

Leo continues to argue that: "the properties of each nature and substance were preserved entire, and came together to form one person. . . . and so, to fulfil the conditions of our healing, the man Jesus Christ, one and the same mediator between God and man, was able to die in respect of the one, unable to die in respect of the other".

Perhaps the most famous of all the statements formulated by the Church Fathers which was embraced by Calvin was that which was formulated by the Council of Chalcedon in 451:

> Therefore, following the Holy Fathers, we all with one accord teach men to acknowledge one and the same Son, our Lord Jesus Christ, at once complete in Godhead and complete in manhood, truly God and truly man, consisting also of a reasonable soul and body; of one substance ὁμοούσιος with the Father as regards his Godhead, and at the same time of one substance with us as regards his manhood; like us in all respects, apart from sin; as regards his Godhead, begotten of the Father before the ages, but yet regards his manhood begotten, in the last days, for us men and for our salvation, of Mary the Virgin, the God bearer Φέοτοκος one and the same Christ, Son, Lord, Only –begotten, recognized in two natures, without confusion, without change, without division, without separation; the distinction of natures being in no way annulled by the union, but rather the characteristics of each nature being preserved and coming together to form one person and subsistence πόστάσις , not as parted or separated into two persons, but one and the same Son and Only-begotten God the Word, Lord Jesus Christ; even as the prophets from earliest times spoke of him, and our Lord Jesus Christ himself taught us, and the creed of the Fathers has handed down to us.[22]

The argument that Calvin advances rigidly follows the argument of the Church Fathers quoted above. The advance that Calvin made from the theology of the Fathers was the three fold ministry of Christ, namely the office of Prophet, Priest and King. In the Chalcedon definition Christ had two wills; the human nature of Christ was hypostatised in the Logos, the Son of God; and to view Christ in the flesh was to see God, and not just man. All the agreements were restated by Calvin. Whilst this Christology was restated by Calvin, it became "Calvinistic" due to the fact that the theology of the Fathers was now restated in the context of the Christ in His three fold office of Prophet, Priest and King. The uniqueness of the three-fold office of Christ quite naturally became associated with Calvin. The theology of the three-fold office is founded upon, and belongs to the Church Fathers and became associated with and accepted as Calvinism because of its contextualization.

Calvin, being committed to the reform of the Church in terms of doctrine and worship was anxious to express worship as an outcome of doctrine. It is evident that his Christology is expressed in his liturgy of the Lord's Supper. The great prayer, coming after the Apostles Creed, gives expression to the Christology of the Fathers and our worship is that of Christ due to our union with him. It is a renunciation of the self and the worship is all of Christ, and the nothingness of man. For example:

> Wherefore, O Lord, renouncing ourselves and abandoning all other hope, we flee to this precious covenant by which our Lord Jesus Christ, offering his own body to thee in sacrifice, has reconciled us to thee. Look, therefore, O Lord, not on us but on the face of Christ, that by his intercession thy anger may be appeased, and thy face may shine forth upon us for our joy and salvation, and receive us to be henceforth guided and governed by thy Holy Spirit, who may regenerate us to a better life, . . .[23]

It is due to the humanity of Christ, who has made atonement and has become our mediator before God. In this part of the Great prayer, Calvin expresses man's humble thanks and utter dependence upon Christ's work on the Cross and his perfect intercession to the Father. T.F. Torrance puts it well: "He bears the Word in our name before the Father, and prays for us and in our name, but in the Lord's Prayer He puts his own prayer into our unclean mouth that we, on the ground of His obedience and His prayer, may pray with Him, "Our Father who art in heaven."

It is in the same way that the prayer of Christ in chapter 17 of John's Gospel is to be regarded in relation to the Holy Communion, for in that prayer added to His vicarious passion He first presents Himself before the face of the Father, and then He presents us to the Father as included in Himself, "Behold me and the servants whom Thou hast given me".[24] It is here at this point that Torrance makes comment on Calvin's Chief Foundations of Worship.

CALVIN'S CHIEF FOUNDATIONS OF WORSHIP

So far, Calvin's Christology cannot be ignored as a prerequisite of worship, as doctrine regulated the due worship of God. In defining worship, Calvin uses the term "Chief foundation" of worship, it is "to acknowledge Him to be, as He is, the only source of all virtue, justice, holiness, wisdom, truth, power, goodness, mercy, life and salvation". It is from this biblical view of God that Calvin arrives at the *how of worship*. It is this definition of God that gives rise to "prayer, praise and thanksgiving" as these bring Glory to Him.

To this he links Adoration which acknowledges our reverence to His greatness, and "self abasement" which renews the mind as the worshipper renounces the world and the flesh; this is an indication of obedience and devotion to His will. If Prayer, Praise and Thanksgiving together with Adoration and Self Abasement, constitute the building blocks of the how of worship then the worship needs structure. It is here that Calvin insists upon "Ceremonies". This term is not used in the sense of the Medieval worship practices where there was a ritual for a multitude of religious ideas. Rather it is a means of "providing opportunity of the body and soul being exercised". It is necessary, as Calvin sees it, to worship in this way for two important reasons. The first reason is that it is in this way that we "establish His (God's) authority; the second reason is not to "follow our own pleasure", as to do so is to be left at liberty to go astray.[25] The how of worship is principally grounded in the acknowledgement of who God is and that He is the source of our salvation.[26] It is the doctrine of God that gives rise to the concept of Prayer, Praise and Thanksgiving. In order not to be misunderstood Calvin insists that prayer is more than just making requests. It is in prayer that due glory is given to God where the participant feels "that God is the only being to whom he ought to flee".[27] If Prayer, Praise and Thanksgiving form the essential prerequisite of worship, then, as Calvin insists, adoration, ceremonies and self abasement must accompany it. By adoration he means "our reverence due to his greatness and Excellency". Ceremonies are not defined in terms of Church practice during the Medieval era, rather they are "helps or instruments" subservient to the doctrine of God. Ceremonies are not to be an invention of man rather they are to be justified according to Biblical principle. Calvin continues to argue that enhancing Prayer, Praise and Thanksgiving, ceremonies offer structure and encouragement in worship. The mind of the worshipper will be renewed in the Word of God, when there is the "renunciation" of worldly practices (self abasement) and it submits to God in "obedience and devotedness".

It is in these terms that true worship is engaged. Simply put, worship is expressed in Prayer, Praise and Thanksgiving in a genuine spirit of adoration, self abasement with structure (ceremony) that assists in the worship engagement.

The engagement of Calvin's view of worship by the twenty-first century Church would overcome many of the issues within the "worship wars" of the present day. The friction which exists among many groups within the modern era is due to the failure of recognising Calvin's essential linkage of doctrine and worship. Calvinists give liturgical expression to the Creator–creature distinction. There is a vast gulf which separates God from His creation means that God alone in His infinite and independent existence stands in contrast to our finiteness and dependence. This alone would restrain the notions of individualism, self-reliance and assertiveness that our culture demands, all of which find expression in the contemporary worship services. In contrast, an expression of a Calvinistic outlook would demand humility and self-denial as the chief characteristics of our worship.[28] We assert that much of the worship conflict in the Church today arises out of the failure to maintain the Creator and creature distinction whereby God's knowledge is reduced to man's level of knowledge, which violates the Biblical statement, "My thoughts are not as your thoughts" (Isaiah 55:8). At best the current situation is due to an ignorance of Calvin's theology of worship or at worst it is the contemporary common view that theology does not matter. The foregoing fundamental Biblical principles of worship constitute a regulative principle for Calvinistic governance of worship. This is somewhat different from the popular view of the twenty first century which demands logical reductionism of the various distinctions made by the Puritans.

If the first issue in understanding the worship of God is Christology, then Calvin's next issue is the *knowledge of our salvation*. This is found in three stages: The first stage is the stage in which we understand our "individual wretchedness, fills us with despondency as if we were spiritually dead". It is this depravity which causes "distrust, rebellion against God, pride, avarice, lust . . . making us averse to all rectitude and justice".[29] It is this recognition of one's own worthlessness and knowing that such a state results in eternal death, the soul cries out to the God of Mercy for relief.

The second stage in the knowledge of our salvation can only become operative when the first stage is fully recognised. Being "animated by the knowledge of Christ", relief becomes possible. Christ's work upon the Cross provides the possibility of hope and salvation for lost humanity. Calvin argues that it is in the recognition that Christ is the "only priest who reconciles us to the Father and His death as the only sacrifice by which sin is expiated, the divine justice satisfied and a true and perfect righteousness acquired".[30] This in the history of theology became known as the *imputed righteousness of Christ*. God the Father sees in us those who embrace and follow Christ, the perfect righteousness of Christ rather than our own sinful wretchedness. It is for this reason that the *union with Christ* is so important in Reformed theology.

The third step closely follows the first and second steps: it is a logical progression. Understanding that our salvation can only proceed upon a Biblical Christology, recognises that the salvation secured is by the *Grace of God*, and when instructed in the Grace of God and the fruits of His death and resurrection, there is the confidence and assurance of Salvation. There is no need to be filled with uncertainty and doubt in respect to this Salvation. To support his argument he quotes Romans 5:2: "Through Him we have obtained access to this grace in which we stand and we rejoice in our hope of sharing the glory of God."

Calvin argues that it is essential that the above two points must not be separated. They both go hand in hand and cement together his concept that worship and doctrine are inseparable. To separate these two essentials, asserts Calvin "we may glory in the name of Christian, but our profession is empty and vain".[31]

Proceeding upon these two essential principles, Calvin then proceeds to link the administration of the sacraments with the government of the Church. The natural inclination is to link the sacraments with worship as they are an essential part of the worship activity. Though a part of the worship activity they are nevertheless linked to government as these two entities were instituted for the perseveration of worship and doctrine as already discussed. Calvin claims that if doctrine is corrupted, as it was in the Middle Ages, through the influence of the Schoolmen, then the power and utility of the sacraments are rendered useless. The theory of the Mass is a case in point. The fundamental philosophy to explain the real presence of Christ in the Eucharist is the philosophy of Aristotle in respect to matter. It is only through this philosophical foundation that transubstantiation could be supported. Remove this foundation and the meaning of the Mass collapses. Using the Aristotelian metaphysic to secure the utmost objectivity and reality of the presence of Christ in the sacrament was to render it into something that it was not. It was by this philosophy the reformers were able to accuse Rome of re-crucifying Christ and so encouraging the idea that worshippers were consuming the actual body and blood of Christ. This could not be supported by the teaching of the New Testament. The doctrine struggles to explain the Real Presence with an inadequate metaphysic simply because in scholastic philosophy special properties belong to the accidents not to the substance. This means of course that the presence of Christ is not locally present, but this was not the way it was popularly understood.[32] Consequently, using this metaphysic there was always the danger of the sacrament becoming in the popular mind magical and mechanical. The celebration of the sacrament could only promote ritualism and a substitute for the essential union with Christ through saving faith.

The import of T.F. Torrance's statement that Calvin's theology was never divorced from the worship of the Church, which was quoted earlier in this chapter, can now be seen. Under the influence of reforming doctrine the whole notion of worship changed in root and limb. The sacrament of Holy Communion changed radically as the Aristotelian metaphysic of the Mass was discarded as being unbiblical. As part of the reform, the accepted pageantry of the Mass was also discarded in favour of a more simplified ceremony which was consistent with the new, but Biblical Christology. The implication of Calvin's Christology was that the worshipper's union with Christ, engaging in Christ's worship to the Father, means that the Real Presence is through the saving faith of the believer; any other kind of presence, any local or special presence would be less real and certainly less intimate. Calvin insists that the sacrament must always be associated with the Word as it continually reminds us of our union and participation in Christ's worship.

Fundamental to Calvin's understanding of the Eucharist is that it consists of the Word and the external sign.[33] The word is that which is preached that gives understanding to the visible signs. Calvin adopts and quotes from Augustine in respect to the sacramental word. "Let the word be added to the element and it will become a sacrament ... this is the word of faith which we preach: by which doubtless baptism also, in order that it may be able to cleanse, is consecrated". The preached word becomes efficacious in the sacrament, not because it is spoken but because it is believed. Using this notion of Augustine, Calvin sees the sacrament as a visible word. For Calvin the sacraments, because of their links with the word, impart upon the believer as the means of increasing and confirming the faith. It is for these reasons that within the Reformed Churches the word must be preached each time the sacraments are celebrated. They never stand alone. The efficaciousness of the sacrament depends not on the actions of man but upon the action of the Holy Spirit whose energy penetrates the heart, stirs up the affections and procures access for the sacraments into our souls.[34] Calvin also upholds Augustine's distinction between the sacrament and the matter of the sacrament. This distinction depends upon the Spirit which makes the sacrament efficacious. Without the Spirit the elements of the sacrament loses all virtue. "The cup of the Lord was poison to Judas, not because he received what was evil, but being wicked he wickedly received what was good."[35]

Calvin therefore concludes that the "office of the sacrament differs not from the word of God; and this is to hold forth and offer Christ to us, and, in him, the treasures of heavenly grace". He further claims that the sacrament presents Christ clearly. Baptism "testifies that we are washed and purified; the Supper of the Eucharist that we are redeemed".[36]

It may therefore be seen that Calvinism not only became a life system but it also provided the theological basis for the majority of the Churches of the reformation. The influence of Calvinism cannot be underestimated. Some scholars have shown that Calvinism influenced not only theology but also politics, science, economics and the arts. Calvinism had an enormous impact in England especially among some of the early martyrs such as Cranmer, Latimer and Ridley. The rise of the Puritans has its genesis in a logical expression of Calvinism. It was in Scotland that Calvinism found its most consistent expression, especially under the leadership of John Knox. In the context of this book it can be legitimately asked how this Calvinism came to Australian shores? The simple answer is that it was imported.

It was the Scottish Presbyterians who embraced the Westminster Confession of Faith and the Larger and Shorter Catechisms as an expression of their Calvinistic faith, who brought their Calvinistic faith to Australian shores. The first congregation of Scottish settlers had built a stone Church on the banks of the Hawkesbury River calling it Ebenezer. These people were exposed to Calvinistic theology as James Mein, a catechist, led worship each week with the reading of Scripture, prayers and the reading of a sermon from one of the Puritans. The first Presbyterian minister to arrive in Australia, the Rev. Dr John Dunmore Lang, whose life and work is treated in Chapter one, had embraced the Calvinism of the influential Thomas Chalmers.

It would therefore be reasonable to define the notion of worship for the Presbyterian Church in terms of the rich theological heritage of Calvinism. It necessarily includes the notion of God's sovereignty, expressing a strong Biblical (Calvinistic) Christology, which humbles a man to see himself as a depraved creature, who is wholly dependent upon the Grace and Mercy of God for hope and salvation. Man's response must necessarily be in terms of Prayer, Praise and Thanksgiving. John T. Dyck shows that for Calvin worship begins with a sound understanding of who God is. Dyck notes that the *Institutes* declares the foundation of worship, "it is to acknowledge Him to be, as He is, the only source of all virtue, justice, holiness, wisdom, truth, power, goodness, mercy, life and salvation. The more we know about God, the more cause we have to love and worship Him. When we thus know him to be self–existent and self–sufficient, we will ascribe and render to Him the glory of all that is good, to seek all things in Him alone, and in every want have recourse to Him alone."[37]

To reduce worship to a simple and profound definition is therefore a mammoth task. It must be recognised that the theological starting point of worship will influence any definition, as worship is dependent upon a belief system about God. This necessarily implies a supernaturalism. A Pagan view of worship will obviously be very different as it locates its gods in nature. At the very basic level, worship for the Christian means God and the priority of God[38]. Presbyterian worship must embrace the absolute sense of the Holy, Majestic, Creator God, whose love and mercy embraces the sinner and energises the worshipper by the sovereign action of the Holy Spirit, failing to do so is to deny the rich theological heritage of Calvin. Man in his natural depraved state is totally dependent on the Words of God to bring salvation and peace. Underhill captured the essence of Calvinistic worship and hence Presbyterian worship when she defined it in terms of "Gods unspeakable Majesty and Otherness, and the nothingness and simplicity of man . . . the religious experience is in terms of the divine transcendence on the awe struck soul and the effort towards a response which is conditioned by the deep sense of creaturely limitation".[39]

Perhaps the clearest definition which embraces the theology of Calvin is that of William Temple,[40]

> to worship is to quicken the consciousness by the holiness of God, to feed the mind with the truth of God, to purge the imagination by the beauty of God, to open the heart to the love of God, to devote the will to the purpose of God.[41]

In this definition the foremost characteristics are the attributes of God and the purposes of God. The attributes and purposes of God impact upon the simplicity of man by the quickening of the consciousness, feeding of the mind and the purging of the imagination. Encapsulated here is a well defined practice of genuine Christianity. It may well seem strange that such a Calvinistic definition which so adequately defines Presbyterian worship should come from the pen of an Anglican Archbishop. It is not so strange when it is acknowledged that the system of theology embraced by the *Thirty Nine Articles* of the Anglican Church is Calvinistic. The difference between the Anglican and Presbyterian approach to worship is not so much as to its essence as to the politics of uniformity. The Anglican insistence on the Prayer Book has serious limitations in the freedoms of worship. The Presbyterians on the other hand have the *Book of Common Order* which is recommended as a guide to public worship. The Presbyterian has the freedom to use any liturgy in the book of Common Order verbatim or use them in a way which will suit the occasion within the general parameters of the theology so expressed. Unfortunately in practice, the outcome can be quite different. It has come to our attention that many of our younger ministers do not possess a *Book of Common Order* and given that there is little awareness of Calvin's insistence of the link between Doctrine and Worship, the outcome is chaos and confusion. The situation is little different to that which existed in ancient Israel when there was no political authority, *in those days Israel had no king; everyone did as he saw fit*. Judges 21:25. Relevance to the culture of the present day becomes the operative principle, that is, doctrine is removed from the Doctrine/Worship equation.

It is now necessary to see how Calvin translated his theology of worship into a practical liturgy. Fundamentally a liturgy of worship for Calvin is the solemn acknowledgement of God's sovereignty. His liturgy for worship evolved through several editions where many of the traditional parts of accepted historic liturgical practice were omitted, not for sound theological or exegetical reasons but due to the extremes of the day. Nevertheless the aim was to restore a liturgy of worship, which embraced the simplicity and the theological propriety of the sacraments of the ancient Church of the Apostles, Martyrs and Holy Fathers. This is made clear by the preface to the Sunday Morning Service in the Strasburg editors of his La Forme 1545.[42] Calvin writes:

> we begin with confession of our sins, adding verses from the Law and the Gospel(i.e. words of absolution), . . . and after we are assured that, as Jesus Christ has righteousness and life in Himself, and that, as He lives for the sake

of the Father, we are justified in Him and live a new life in same Jesus Christ, . . . continue with psalms, hymns of praise, the reading of the Gospel, the confession of our faith (i.e. the Apostles Creed) , and the holy oblations and offerings And quickened and stirred by the reading and preaching of the Gospel and the confession of our faith, it follows that we must pray for the salvation of all men, for the life of Christ should be greatly enkindled within us. Now the life of Christ consists in this, namely, to seek and to save that which is lost; fittingly, then we pray for all men. And because we receive Jesus Christ truly in the Sacrament, we worship Him in spirit and truth; and receive the Eucharist with great reverence, concluding the whole mystery with praise and thanksgiving. This, therefore, is the whole order and reason for its administration in this manner; and it agrees also with the administration in the ancient Church of the Apostles, martyrs, and holy Fathers.

This is the primitive simplicity which Calvin sees as consistent with ancient practice. This should be the basic model for weekly worship. In his Institutes, Calvin urges that the sacrament "might be celebrated in the most becoming manner very frequently, at least once a week"[43] In this same section he repudiated the idea of infrequent celebrations of the sacrament by labelling the idea as an invention of the devil.

The evolution of Calvin's forms is clearly seen in the work of W.D. Maxwell.[44]

The Strasbourg liturgy of 1537 is a liturgy that was in place prior to Calvin's arrival in the city in 1538. It was the form used by Bucer,[45] at a time when the sacrament was forbidden by the German magistrates. This policy changed after Calvin arrived to minister to the French congregation. Bucer's liturgy became the basis on which Calvin was to build his own liturgy. Maxwell has reprinted the actual words of Bucer's liturgy of 1537-1539.

Maxwell points out that this reprinted form is not complete with "the prolix alternative prayers", but rather the parts that later became important in the Calvinian and Scottish rites and services.[46]

This rite had its own evolution due to the extremism of the day. Maxwell points out that it was in this period that most of the versicles and responses disappeared and the worship lost its antiphonal character. The extremism of the period that led to these omissions is regrettable. Maxwell points out the extremism of the day led to the unnecessary impoverishment of the liturgy. The *Gloria in excelsis* and the *Kyries* were dropped or made optional in favour of metrical Psalms and hymns, the *Sursum Corda*, the Prefaces, the *Sanctus* and *Benedictus qui venit* became unfashionable, all due to the extremism of the day. These rich liturgical ornaments as Maxwell calls them were replaced by general prayers of thanksgiving for the atoning work of Christ. Such exclusions were an unnecessary departure from a tradition almost as old as the Church itself.[47] C.W. Baird[48] notes that when Calvin arrived in Geneva in 1536 the worship at St Peters cathedral had no structure, as the whole liturgy had been abolished. The iconoclasts of the day had ensured that every reminder of Medieval Catholicism was destroyed. In its wake popular prejudice was ready to pounce on any resumption of the repudiated forms. The uniqueness of Calvin was that amid the turmoil of Reform he could discriminate impartially between the substance and the super additions of many of the Roman practices. The imposition of extreme popular prejudice prevented Calvin from reinstituting good worship practices which were thrown out simply because they were associated with medieval Catholicism. During the Sunday morning service in Geneva, immediately after the prayers of confession and supplication there would naturally come a declaration of forgiveness, but as Baird shows the prejudices of the time prevented the insertion of this traditional feature.[49] This rite became important as it is from this rite that the normal practice of morning worship in Reformed Churches is derived, where there is a separation of the liturgy of the Word and the Eucharist. This practice has become the norm in the contemporary Church scene, both in the Reformed/Presbyterian and the Evangelical Churches. The disturbing feature of this is that the extremism of the sixteenth century liturgical practice has carried over to the modern period and has become a tradition which is deemed Biblical and which, if modified to restore any of the excluded historical parts of the liturgy is viewed with grave suspicion.

Maxwell notes that there are three points that should be observed in the liturgy of the "Upper Room":

- The intercessions are at the beginning of the Consecration prayer.
- The Words of Institution have been removed from the Prayer of Consecration and they now stand alone as a warrant.
- The elements are received standing or kneeling after communicants have gone forward to the Holy Table. One minister stands at the north end of the Holy Table and gives the Bread and the assistant minister stand at the South end to administer the Cup. The communicants formed a continuous line down the central nave, coming slowly forward to receive the bread first, then the Wine, then returning to their places.

This practice of distribution is today completely foreign to the Reformed/Presbyterian Churches, and if ever implemented would cause considerable unrest.

Calvin considered that Bucer's liturgy was a model which conformed to the practice of the ancient Church. Under the influence of Calvin the liturgy continued to evolve. He introduced a long paraphrase version of the Lord's Prayer and the Decalogue in metre, and at the end of each verse the *Kyrie Eleison* was sung. He also introduced the *Dunc Dimittis* at the conclusion of the service. The Genevan service of 1542 onwards was a much more simplified version of the Strasbourg liturgy principally due to the extreme opinions of the magistracy, who insisted that the liturgy be as simple as possible. Maxwell claimed that the Strasbourg rite is a better indication of Calvin's thinking.[50] Calvin's ideal was to restore not only the centrality of the preached word but also to restore weekly communion. Calvin's ministry was a ministry of Word and Sacrament and the minister's function was to preach and teach the Word and to administer the Sacraments every week. He could not agree with Zwingli, who in keeping with the practice of Bucer separated the Eucharist from the normal weekly service of worship. The sacrament is an extension of the Word and is not to be disassociated from it or celebrated without the words of institution. This is the conclusion of John McNeil, an eminent Calvin scholar.[51]

It is in the Eucharist that Christ offers himself to us with all his blessing and we receive Him in faith.[52] Calvin renounces the idea that the eating of the flesh of Christ and the drinking of his blood is nothing more that believing in Christ himself. Partaking of the body and blood of Christ is done by faith, so that the eating and drinking is the effect of the fruit of faith. The Lord is pleased by calling Himself the bread of life, not only to teach that our salvation is treasured up in the faith of His death and resurrection, but also, by virtue of true communion with him, His life passes into us and becomes ours, just as bread when taken for food gives vigour to the body. Our minds may not comprehend the mystery but let faith conceive that the Spirit truly unites things separated by space. The sacred communion of flesh and blood by which Christ transfuses his life into us, just as if it penetrated our bones and marrow, he testifies and seals in the Supper; and that not by presenting a vain or empty sign that by there exerting an efficacy of the Spirit by which he fulfils what he promises. Calvin concludes that in the mystery of the Supper by symbols of bread and wine Christ, his body and his blood, are truly exhibited to us, that in them he fulfilled all obedience, in order to procure righteousness for us and being made partakers of his substance, we might feel the result of this fact in the participation of all His blessings.[53] Having renounced transubstantiation, this is how he explains the "real presence".

This is a far different perception from the Zwinglian[54] view of the sacrament which sees that the Holy Supper as a mere memorial. At this point it is useful to note in passing that there is a real connection between Zwingli and John Knox which explains the transmission of the Zwinglian view into protestant Scotland and at a later time to Australia. Maxwell quotes E. Doumergue (not available in English) who summarises the impact of Calvin's rite:

> Those who were present at the services have told us that often they could not keep back the tears of their emotion and joy. Singings and prayers, adoration and edification, confession and absolution of sins, acts both formal and sponta-

neous: all the essential elements of worship were there. And, perhaps not less important, they were united in an organism that was very simple, yet supple and strong. Calvin is, in fact, of all the Reformers the one who most steadfastly rejected the division of worship into two parts . . . The Calvinian cultus is one.[55]

Earlier in this chapter it was argued that Calvinism became a life system due to his doctrine of God. His whole theology rested upon the "vision of God in His Glory: and it set itself before all things to render to God His rights in every sphere of life activity". This included worship and it was Calvin's conviction that worship could not be separated from doctrine. Having located his theology of worship in Christology, man's worship could be no idle or frivolous matter. Worship was to be governed by God's requirements and not man's perception of what it should be. Culture could never become the interpretive principle. The structure of worship was to be governed by Godly principle, enabling man's worship to be in union with the worship of Christ, as the worship of Christ is perfectly acceptable to the Father. It is this which should constitute the basis of Presbyterian worship. To do otherwise is to reduce the liturgy of Godly worship to the whims of the idols of man's heart.

Within the Presbyterian Church in New South Wales there is little awareness of Calvin's linkage of worship and doctrine Worship in the most part has become a construct that satisfies the whims of popular culture so that it may be perceived to be relevant. The suggested liturgies of the *Book of Common Order* are deemed by many irrelevant and not suitable for the current culture. All that is deemed necessary is the "faithful preaching of the Word". This situation is very similar to that which existed in Geneva in 1536 and the situation that developed in the Free Church in Scotland after the Disruption in 1843. In other words there was a lack of theological consistency or a failure to appreciate Calvin's theology of worship. Consequently *worship* has provided another means of conflict within the Presbyterian Church in New South Wales. Chapter one of this book provided material which leads to the conclusion that the Church has been plagued with conflict from its very inception in 1823. Worship is just another issue that keeps conflict alive. The nature of the change in worship patterns will be dealt with in greater detail in another chapter where it will be shown that Calvin's warning that the danger of separating doctrine from worship has gone unheeded. What passes for Presbyterian worship today is what seems relevant to sinful man. This usually means the embrace of a pop culture as the governing principle, rather than Calvin's broad based Regulative Principle which imposes Biblical Trinitarian worship where man participates in the worship of Christ whose worship alone is perfect before the Father. This Calvinist view of worship demands that which pleases God the Father, rather than that which pleases man. This regulative principle of Calvin is a far cry from today's version in which it is used as a tool to justify a strict rational approach of the Puritans which is iconoclastic in nature. Calvin's worship reform was a struggle between what was Biblical and necessary in the worship forms and practices which had accrued over the centuries, and the extreme prejudices against everything that was associated with the medieval Church. Calvin's work proceeded on a consistent theological base in which he saw the seeds of destruction if sound theology was separated from worship. The eager pursuit of reforming worship practices resulted in worship forms which were stripped of the sense of beauty and holiness in favour of simplicity which was thought to be consistent with early New Testament Church practice. Calvin understood only too clearly that any separation of a precise theology and worship would lead to idolatrous worship. This was the problem in the medieval Church. Whilst Calvin possessed wisdom and discernment in these matters, although hampered by extreme prejudice, this was not the case with many of the other reformers and their followers. All too often the liturgy was left shapeless and formless.

The real issue within Presbyterian Churches in the twentieth century says Donald Macleod is to re-establish the priority of worship (as the Body of Christ taking visible form) that reflects the peculiar genius of its faith.[56] The fact is that the whole man, his heart, mind and will, is involved in the act of worship. To worship God who is the "wholly other", full of Grace and Truth, who is clothed in Majesty and Holiness, who has come to us in transcendent glory, demands a special kind of worship which embraces the whole man. Neville Clark has understood this well when he says, that the worship must "ever be Trinitarian in tone, Christological in pattern, centred on Word and Sacrament; corporate, congregational, embodied; awesome, exultant, ordered, and free".[57] The Presbyterian Church in New South Wales today can only benefit from looking back to the work of Calvin and seeking answers which restore the linkage of doctrine and worship and the restoration of wholeness to the liturgy. This concept of worship cannot be underestimated, as worship is the great presupposition of mission. It was from the worship of the Church gathered in the New Testament that the early Church went out on its mission to change the world. To put it another way, meaningful evangelism must begin with worship, a worship that is Trinitarian, Christological and focused on Word and Sacrament.

NOTES

1. Robert G. Rayburn, *O Come Let us Worship* (Grand Rapids: Baker Book House, 1980), 23–24.
2. F.L. Cross, *The Oxford Dictionary of the Christian Church*, 220.
3. Abraham Kuyper, *Lectures on Calvinism* (Grand Rapids: Eerdmans 1975), 14; see also, James Orr, *The Christian View of God and the World* (1891) Reprint (Grand Rapids: Kregel Pub. 1989).

4. Norman L. Geisler, *Is Man the Measure* (Grand Rapids: Baker Book House 1983), 7–11.
5. Kuyper, *Lectures* 20.
6. Kuyper, *Lectures* 21.
7. Kuyper, *Lectures* 21.
8. Kuyper, *Lectures* 22.
9. Kuyper, *Lectures* 26.
10. Kuyper, *Lectures* 27.
11. Kuyper, *Lectures,* 27.
12. Kuyper, *Lectures,* 29.
13. Kuyper, *Lectures* 30.
14. B.B. Warfield, *Calvin & Augustine,*(Philadelphia: P&R Publishing 1956), 292.
15. Underhill, *Worship*, 287.
16. John T. Dyck, *WRS Journal* 16:1 (February2009), 33–40.
17. T.F. Torrance, ed., *John Calvin's Tracts and Treatises* (Michigan: Eerdmans 1958), Vol. 1, vii; see also Chapter 7 of H.R. Mackintosh, *The Person of Jesus Christ* (Edinburgh: T.&T Clark, 1956). Here Mackintosh traces the history of Christology of the Reformation Church.
18. Torrance, *Tracts and* Treatises, 126.
19. John Calvin, *Institutes of the Christian Religion* (London: James Clark 1962), Vol. 1, 409.
20. Calvin, *Institutes*, 414.
21. Leo, Bishop of Rome (440 -461) Sec.2. Henry Bettenson, *Documents of the Christian Church*, (London: Oxford University Press, 1964) 70.
22. Council of Chalceddon, Actio V. Mansi, vii 116f Bettenson, 73. This quote is in larger print so as to accommodate the printing of the Greek words.
23. Torrance *Tracts and Treatises*, Vol.2, 109.
24. Torrance *Tracts and Treatises*, xxvii–xxviii.
25. Torrance, *Tracts and Treatises*, Vol. 1, 128; Calvin defines in a more detailed way what he means by terms such as prayer, adoration ceremonies, self abasement etc. 130–32.
26. Torrance, *Tracts and Treatises*, Vol.1, 127.
27. Torrance, *Tracts and Treatises*, Vol.1, 130.
28. D.G. Hart and J.R. Muether, *With Reverence and Awe*, (Phillipsburg P &R Publishing 2002), 14.
29. Hart and Muether, *With Reverence and Awe*, 133–34.
30. Hart and Muether, *With Reverence and Awe*, 134.
31. Hart and Muether, *With Reverence and Awe*, 126.
32. See Dom Gregory Dix, *The Shape of the Liturgy* (Westminster: Dacre Press, 1949), 621; also D.M. Baillie, *Theology of The Sacraments* (London: Faber & Faber, 1965).
33. Calvin, *Institutes*, Book 4, Ch. 14, Sec. 4.
34. Calvin, *Institutes*, Sec. 9.
35. Calvin, *Institutes*, Sec. 15.
36. Calvin, *Institutes*, Sec. 17 & 22.
37. John T. Dyck, *WRS Journal* 16:1 (February 2009), 33–40.
38. Underhill, *Worship*, 16.
39. Underhill, *Worship*, 287.
40. William Temple (1881–1944) Archbishop of Canterbury. As Archbishop of York he became prominent in national life through his lively concern with social, economic and international questions. He gave whole-hearted support to the Faith and Order and Life and Work Movement and to the Oecumenical Movement. His short time as Archbishop of Canterbury was marked by World War 2 and sickness.
41. William Temple, *The Hope of a New World*. Cited by D.P. Hustad, *Church Music in the Evangelical Tradition* (Illinois: Hope Publishing, 1981), 78.
42. The French version of the preface is found in W Maxwell, *John Knox Genevan Service Book* 1556 (London: Faith Press, 1965), 35. This is also translated into English by Maxwell in his *Outline of Christian Worship* (London: Oxford University Press, 1963), 116.
43. Calvin, *Institutes*, Bk 4, Ch. 17, Sec. 43.

44. Maxwell, *Outline of Christian Worship*.
45. Martin Bucer (1491-1551) German Reformer. In 1523 he publicly preached Lutheranism. Attempted to mediate between Luther and Zwingli Became the leader of the Reformed Church's in Switzerland. His theology of the Eucharist was closer to Zwingli's position. In 1549 he went to England and had an important influence on Thomas Cranmer who became Regius professor of Divinity at Cambridge.
46. Maxwell, *Outline of Worship*, 101.
47. Maxwell, *Outline Worship*, 100.
48. C. W. Baird, *The Presbyterian Liturgies* (Grand Rapids: Baker Books, 1957).
49. Baird, *Presbyterian Liturgies*, 21.
50. Maxwell, *Outline Worship*, 115.
51. John T. McNeill, *History and Character of Calvinism*,(London: Oxford University Press, 1954), 219.
52. Calvin, *Institutes*, Bk 4, Ch.7, Sec. 5.
53. Calvin, *Institutes*, Sec. 10–11.
54. Ulrich Zwingli (1484–1531) Swiss Reformer. The beginning of the Reformation in Switzerland was over when Zwingli's lectures on the New Testament in 1519. He attacked the doctrines of Purgatory, invocation of the Saints, and Monasticism. He viewed the Eucharist in purely symbolic terms. His disagreements with Luther were so deep that unity among the Protestant forces was impossible.
55. See W.D. Maxwell, *Outline of Christian Worship*, 119.
56. Donald Macleod, *Presbyterian Worship* (Virginia: John Knox Press, 1965), 1.
57. Neville Clark, *Call to Worship* (London: SCM Press, 1960) 37–38.

Chapter Three

The Climax of Calvinist Liturgical Development in New South Wales

In Chapter two, it was argued that John Calvin's liturgical practice can only be seen in the light of the doctrines of the Church, and the doctrine of Word and Sacrament. These doctrines were heavily dependent on his Christology. It was because of his Christology that he held to a high view of the Word. Since his view of the Word was "high", his view of the Church and the Sacraments were also "high". His liturgical framework sought to bring out the mystery of Christ coming to sinful mankind, to dwell with them, to feed them, without at any point giving up His sovereign freedom. To understand Calvin's high view of the Eucharist, it cannot be seen in terms of sacerdotalism in which man offers a Eucharistic sacrifice to God, rather than the once for all sacrifice which Christ has already offered, which is efficacious for eternity. Calvin's Christology clearly shows the essential nature of Christ's atoning sacrifice. Our knowledge of God in worship is dependent on this high view of Christ's atoning death and resurrection. Worshippers are privileged to share in the worship of Christ only by the Grace and mercy of God, through the sovereign action of the Holy Spirit. Worship is not what we do so much as it is our engagement in the worship of Christ before the heavenly Father. That is the defining principle of worship in the Presbyterian Church given its distinctive Christology.

It is critical to understand the concept of worship in Calvin as it explains the theological premises of worship in the thought of the Rev. A.A. Dougan who was the only liturgical scholar in the New South Wales Presbyterian Church up to the time of his death in 1982. There were others who were interested in liturgical studies, but it was Dougan who rose to prominence, as he was a well known identity in the Church, as he was a skilful preacher, lecturer in liturgical studies in the Presbyterian Theological Hall, and the editor of a national journal *Life and Work,* a bulletin of the Church Service Society within the Presbyterian Church of Australia. He was also the Principal of St Andrew's College within the University of Sydney. The General Assembly expressed its confidence and regard for him when it elected him as State Moderator in 1956. He was the youngest person ever to be elected to that prestigious office; he was only 47 years of age. He distinguished himself in his research into several of the pioneering clergy which was published in the *Australian Dictionary of Biography.* Respect for him in academic circles was recognised when he served on the Sydney University Senate.[1] Sad to say there has been no other liturgical scholar of distinction that has graced the New South Wales Presbyterian Church since.

The Rev. Robert Willson has written a resume of Dougan's life for publication in the Australian Dictionary of Biography, but a brief resume is published in the *Presbyterian Review.*[2] Allan Dougan completed his B.A. at the University of Sydney in 1929. He studied Philosophy under the famous atheist Scot, Professor John Anderson. According to the St Andrew's College Magazine, Dougan's degree was made up of studies in Philosophy, Latin, Anthropology and English Literature.[3] He entered the Theological Hall for the Presbyterian Church where he won the Mitchell Prize upon the completion of the Theological Course. He was ordained and inducted into the pastoral charge of Balranald in the far south west of New South Wales in 1933. It was at Balranald that Dougan became friends with Bishop Reginald Halse, later the Archbishop of Brisbane. In 1936 he took up a three year ministry at Blayney and this was followed by a 17 year ministry at Bathurst. It was in Bathurst that he was elected as State Moderator in 1956. It was from Bathurst that he was appointed the Principal of St Andrew's College succeeding Principal John McIntyre who returned to Scotland and ultimately became a world famous theologian at The University of Edinburgh. It was at St Andrew's that he remained until retirement in 1975.

It was in 1965 that one of the present authors, Dr. John Webster became a student of the ministry within the Presbyterian Church. He studied the optional unit in Liturgics, lectured by Alan Dougan. Very few students elected to do this course, and there was little interest on the part of all the other students to learn the history and theology of the Church's liturgical tradition. In effect the attitude on the students' part in treating liturgy as unimportant and the College's policy of relegating liturgical studies as "optional" only helped to set into concrete the idea of liturgical minimization.

Historically, the doctrine of worship during Calvin's time at Strasbourg and Geneva was of crucial importance, as it stands in stark contrast to the disinterestedness of most clergy within the Presbyterian Church. Michael Horton observes that one reason for this contrast is that most evangelicals today are Zwinglians. Zwingli reformed the worship service in Zurich by replacing the Mass with the medieval Prone service, which was a preaching service. Horton shows how Zwingli preaching service became the model for much of Protestantism.[4] While Horton may well be correct, it should not be the case for Calvinist Presbyterians, but sadly, it has been influential as it is consistent with the consumer/marketing approach to Church life that has become popular in the contemporary context.

In this chapter it will be shown that Dougan's High Churchmanship was not formulated upon the views of the High Anglicans or the peculiarities of Romanism or even as a substitute for evangelicalism during a theological liberal era. Rather, his high view was grounded in the thought of John Calvin, and with a genuine "catholic" perspective.[5] It was from this perspective Alan Dougan was greatly misunderstood and the Church was much poorer for it. Dougan represents the pinnacle of Presbyterian liturgical tradition during the twentieth century, by maximising Calvin's theology of worship, whereas a process of minimisation of the Church's liturgy could only invite liturgical chaos and the deprecation of Calvin's theology of worship.

Sifting through Dougan's collected writings[6] it is evident that there has been a painstaking effort put into the collection of these papers and articles.

As previously mentioned Dougan was a "high" Churchman, and his liturgical views were not appreciated by most of clergy in the Church at that time. Robert Willison tells the story of how his views were held in contempt by some clergy:

> In 1948 the distinguished Scottish theologian, Professor John Baillie, visited Australia on a lecture tour and it was advertised as speaking in the Assembly Hall. Alan decided that he would like to drive down to Sydney to hear him and he invited the Anglican Rector of Carcoar to come too. They sat in the front row and had a great time. Afterwards it was announced that Professor Baillie would be in the back room to meet people and Alan and his friend waited their turn to see him. One of the clergy, George Cowie, saw Dougan. He was always having a shot at Dougan's ritualistic tendencies and said in a loud mocking voice: 'Well, if it isn't the Bishop of Bathurst come to pay his respects'! Baillie overheard this and took it seriously. He jumped to his feet and said how honoured he was that the Bishop of Bathurst, who was in the news over the so called 'Red Book heresy' case at the time, had come to hear him. Dougan was stunned and could not do anything except stammer: 'May I introduce the Rector of Carcoar, Professor', 'Of course,' said Baillie, 'You have your chaplain with you.' And he asked the rector if he was the Bishop's driver. So Alan said that Baillie went back to Scotland thinking that the notorious Bishop of Bathurst had come to hear him. By the way the Bishop's name was Arnold Lomas Wylde, known to his critics as 'Arnold Highmass Wylde!'[7]

There is little evidence of any development of Dougan's theological and liturgical practices whilst he was minister at Balranald. He was too busy putting things in order and establishing a viable ministry in a country town where people didn't care very much whether they had a minister or not.

Arriving in the parish he found that the Church had a long vacancy of some ten years. Goats inhabited the Church building. The Church car was on bricks in the garage, stripped, and the Manse was let to the local barber. He was advised that the parish could not afford a minister and besides they did not want one, and he should go back to Sydney. Such was his start to the ordained Ministry! It was not long before he endeared himself to the local community and he soon gathered a growing worship community. In the three years of ministry he was noted as a regular contributor to the local newspaper, the "Riverina Recorder". It was during three years ministry at Blayney and the seventeen years at Bathurst that the serious matters of theology and liturgical practice captivated his eager mind. The *New South Wales Presbyterian* contains a report that Dougan was elected to the executive of the Church Service Society.[8] This Society was formed in 1936 and the General Assembly of 1938 gave recognition to its work and commended its work to all ministers and elders. The object of the Society was expressed in six points of study:

a. The liturgies and service books – ancient and modern – of the Christian Church, and especially of the Church as reformed.
b. The Standards and Confessions of the Presbyterian Church.
c. The Catholic and Apostolic Heritage of the Reformed Church.
d. The principles of Public Worship.
e. The arrangements and furnishing of the Sanctuary.
f. The Church's Praise.

With the study of these six points it was hoped that there would be an encouragement of an adequate, orderly and reverent expression of the corporate acts of Divine Worship.

In the same article Kinmont refers to the comments of the Moderator General of the Presbyterian Church of Australia, Dr McKenzie, "Here then lay one of the tasks of the Church Service Society, in seeking to help men to express the deep consciousness that they have of the reality of the unseen world". The Society must seek to emphasise the mystical, intangible realities of the faith. Dr McKenzie was all too conscious that the warm glow of an inner experience could be dissipated by the cold reasoning of an extreme intellectualism and the reality of those things that are shown through the sacraments and the services of the Church missed.

At this point in the Church's history there occurred an interesting confluence. The formation of the Church Service Society and Dougan's active membership coincided with The Ecumenical Movement. It is a commonly held perception that the ecumenical movement drove the liturgical movement within the Presbyterian Church in New South Wales. It may well have been an influence but the reappraisal of the Church's liturgy would have happened anyway because of the barrenness of the liturgical practice of the Church which arose from the acceptance of the *Directory of Public Worship.*

Dougan's embrace of Calvin's doctrinal understanding of the Church and the Godhead fitted in with his notion of Catholicity in that the Church exists only in Christ and the life of the Church exists only in the ingrafting of Christ. This concept will be explained later in this chapter. The Ecumenical movement was spurred on by resolution 50 of the 1948 Lambeth Conference:

> The conference believes that it is the duty of the Church to bear united witness to God's redeeming grace in Jesus Christ, to do battle against the powers of evil, and to seek the glory of God in all things. It therefore appeals to Christians in all Communions, whatever the differences which may separate them in Church order and doctrine, to join in Christian action in all parts of the world irrespective of political party for the application of the principles of the Christian religion to all departments of national and international life.[9]

The same conference also resolved to welcome the formation of the World Council of Churches. Resolution 76 declares:

> The Conference cordially welcomes the formation of the Word Council of Churches and desires to place on record its deep appreciation of the valuable services already rendered to the cause of Christian Unity by the officers and members of its Provisional Committee, and sends its good wishes to the Council for its first Assembly in Amsterdam and prays that God may Guide and direct all its deliberations. The Conference hopes that the results of the Assembly in Amsterdam may be made widely known throughout the Anglican Communion, and that an active interest in the World Council of Churches may be encouraged in all dioceses and parishes.[10]

The Ecumenical movement soon made an impact on Presbyterianism through the Church of Scotland. In an extract from a Joint Report on the Relations between the Church of England and the Church of Scotland in 1951 it was generally thought that meaningful progress could be made in resolving issues which had caused separation and bitterness over centuries. The Report says among other things:

> ... the Conference recognises the sovereign freedom of Divine grace within the history of the Church; and takes its starting point not from any pronouncement on the validity of Orders on either side, but from consideration of what should belong to the fullness of the Church in that ultimate unity which we are called to seek by our Lord's command and in dependence upon the guidance of the Holy Spirit. ... The long term policy would have as its presupposition the conviction that Our Lord's will for His Church is full unity, and that such unity must involve in the end not only agreement as to the truth in Christ, but also a ministry or ministries universally recognised, freedom to interchange ministries, and fullness of sacramental communion throughout Christendom.[11]

From the Reformed theological perspective, such resolutions offered a continuing process of reform in sacramental unity based on what appeared to be a reformational premise. Dougan must have felt elated at the prospect of continuing reform especially when the Church of Scotland, a few years later in 1940, revised its *Book of Common Order* in which the liturgy for Holy Communion had been radically revised to include so many of the component parts which had previously been excluded. At the risk of putting words in Dougan's mouth this was "catholicity" at work.

If there was any excitement, it was short lived. By May 1952 in a Report bearing the title, "Relations between the Church of England and the Church of Scotland", item 5a declares:

> That this house . . . is of the opinion (a) that duly accredited Ministers of the Church of Scotland may be permitted by a Bishop to preach in an Anglican Church at services other than Holy Communion, when in the Bishop's judgement, the giving of such permission would set forward the ideal of Christian union, which generally approved at the Lambeth Conferences of 1920 and 1930. Such permission should be exceptional and without prejudice to the normal maintenance of the recognised rules of Church order. (b) that Ministers of the Church of England may accept an invitation to preach in Churches of the Church of Scotland, subject, in accordance with ecclesiastical usage, to the consent of the appropriate bishop of the Episcopal Church in Scotland.[12]

From this extract there was no level playing field. In this statement, Ministers of the Church of Scotland were limited in their ministry as they could only preach in Anglican Churches upon the permission of the Bishop and there was no permission to celebrate the sacraments.

In 1953 the Report to the General Assembly of the Church of Scotland indicated a failure of "catholicity":

> It seems plain to the Committee that progress is not likely to be made in the long term policy unless the conferring parties penetrate beyond questions of valid ministries and sacraments and discuss together the fundamental theological problems of the nature of the Church itself.[13]

This was a serious blow for the ecumenical movement in the Church of Scotland and also for all Presbyterian Churches that had specific relations with the Scottish Church as the demands of the ecumenical movement became restrictive and one-sided as the Church of England refused to negotiate on the theological issues of the Doctrine of the Church. This outcome makes nonsense the lofty but meaningless rhetoric and the ideals of catholicity of the Lambeth Conference in 1948 which called for unity. The ecumenical experiment came to its finality in 1957. Professor Ian Henderson sums up the difficulties in response to the *Bishops Report* which was tabled at the General Assembly of the Church of Scotland and it came as a bombshell, the reason being that the Church had not realised the extent to which the ecumenical party had a stranglehold upon the Church. The Anglicans had conceded all but nothing but the Church of Scotland had to concede everything. Bishops, duly consecrated into the apostolic succession were to be permanent moderators of Presbyteries. This says Henderson was a naked reality of power which was contrary to the Presbyterian constitution of the Church of Scotland written into legislation of the Treaty of Union in 1707.[14] Henderson argues that the Report was an exercise in "diplomatic ineptitude" and its authors ignorant of the sociological factors. The proposals of the *Bishops Report* were rejected by the General Assembly. Henderson comments on the debate on the matter in the General Assembly. It revealed a curious ignorance of the Church of Scotland constitution on which one might have expected the Ecumenical party chiefs to be able to illuminate their Anglican friends. One basic feature of the constitution of the Church of Scotland is the Barrier Act which goes back to 1697. This act lays down that all changes in doctrine and constitution must secure not only a majority in the General Assembly but also be approved by a majority of the Presbyteries in the Church.[15] Had this ecumenical experiment worked itself out differently and the Church of Scotland acceded to all the proposals of the *Bishops Report* and the *Barrier Act* procedure had been successful and the Scottish Parliament changed the Church's constitution, the Church of Scotland would be so Anglicanised that its real authority would reside in the Bishops. For the purposes of this book, this would sweep away the whole process of liturgical minimization in favour of a maximised liturgy of the English *Prayer Book*.

This then was the historical background to the rising prominence of Allan Dougan's liturgical convictions.

Dougan's membership of the Church Service Society motivated him to be more than a passive member. It wasn't long before Dougan submitted an article on "Worship" to the New South Wales Presbyterian.[16] This article proved to be a defining moment in Dougan's ministry as it was the beginning of a lifetime of serious study in the historical and theological aspects of Presbyterian worship. In this article he makes observations on the book *An Outline of Christian Worship* by Dr W. D. Maxwell. In this article Dougan gives expression to his commitment to a Calvinistic theology. He sees clearly that Presbyterian worship has its theological foundation in Calvinism. Calvin based his morning service on the Eucharist and had no desire to reduce the sacrament to a shadow Eucharist or a *missa sicca* – a service which culminates in the prayer of thanksgiving and intercession which is followed by the lections and a sermon. Dougan affirmed Calvin's view that the Eucharist should be celebrated with the preaching of the Word every Sunday, as Calvin saw the Eucharist as a sermon in action. In another article Dougan expressed this thought in this way, "the Eucharist is the unveiling in time, again and again of the Divine Love perpetually given for the sin of the world".[17]

Calvin's work become indispensable for Dougan, as he says, "the Reformers based their services on the Eucharist, but one need not deduce from this that they desired the sacrament or its shadow to be the chief worship of the Church". It is to be remembered that Calvin considered the infrequent celebration of the Eucharist as an invention of the devil. Dougan took Calvin's view of worship to heart. During his time as principal of St Andrew's College he conducted worship every Sunday in the College Chapel in which he followed the Church Lectionary and administered the Eucharist. This practice alone marked him out as a High Churchman or Ritualist. What was generally viewed as innovative on the part of Dougan was in fact consistent with Reformed practice by Calvin. Worship was for Dougan so profound and so important that he says that "The Church's supreme task is worship". It is as though God says, "on My Day it is your task to gather together to express for me the things that are of worth eternally". The Church calls for Sunday October 28th 1945, as she called every Lord's day for twenty centuries, "O come, let us worship".[18] This particular view of worship is that of John Calvin. In his article on the Origins of Presbyterian Worship, he dismisses two commonly held views:

1. The order of service in the Reformed Church had its roots in the Medieval "Prone" service. Dougan argues as does Maxwell[19] that the Prone was a short vernacular service inserted in the Mass and said from the pulpit. It consisted of the Lord's Prayer, Sermon, Bidding Prayers, the Apostles' Creed and sometimes an Exhortation before the prayer of Consecration. Using the argument of Maxwell, Dougan sees similarities between the Prone and the Reformed Service; the claim is an extravagance, unwarranted, by the facts of history. As Horton points out, Zwingli adopts this view. It was the Mass minimised. All the essential elements of the medieval service were removed except for the Prone.
2. Dougan disagrees with Maxwell who claims that the Reformed Service has its roots in the English Book of Common Prayer, particularly in the Mattins and evensong formats. Dougan nevertheless agrees with Maxwell's argument, that by the last part of the eighteenth century the worship in the Scottish Church had sunk to its lowest point and the original form was lost. During the mid-nineteenth century innovators such as Dr Robert Lee of Greyfriars Church in Edinburgh turned to the only service book in English for their models, and that was the English *Book of Common Prayer*. If Reformed worship was based on Mattins and Evensong services then the worship in the Reformed Church is fundamentally the "daily office" of the Church of England. Although, like the Prone, there are many similarities between the Reformed Service and the daily office, Dougan points out that Calvin still located

his service in the Eucharist. He argues that even if the Reformed service were based on the Book of Common Prayer the Scottish influence is seen in the elevation of the Sermon. Dougan concludes that it would be better to re-emphasise our belief in the Word as sacramental, than to turn the weekly worship into a "shadow Eucharist", that is a service without its essentials.

In chapter two of this book it was noted that the separation of the liturgy of the Word and Eucharist which occurred in Geneva was due to the extreme prejudices of the day, which prevented Calvin from creating a genuine Reformed liturgy. What was permissible in Geneva became the normal practice of worship in the Reformed Churches. This is a disappointment as Calvin's liturgical format is best seen in his Strasbourg liturgy.

It is interesting to note that Dougan expresses the view that mere duplication of forms does not revive the true spirit of worship. It is here that the openness of Dougan is revealed. Mere duplication can never provide the spiritual dynamic and meaning in Calvinistic worship. Dougan sees that the duplication process is a mistake on Maxwell's part, as well as the mistake of the Anglo–Catholics. It is better to realise the necessity of form and strive to produce a form, reasonable, beautiful, a true expression of our Reformed heritage and intelligible to our modern thought.

Beneath the trappings of Dougan's High Churchmanship is a fundamental adherence to Calvinistic thought. It is unfortunate that Alan Dougan did not commit his theological and liturgical views into book form. All we have is a vast collection of newspaper articles and articles in a number of Journals. The Rev. Robert Willison who was a student of Dougan and personal friend has collected all Journal and newspaper entries and bound them into three volumes which are now located in the Ferguson Memorial Library, Sydney.[20] There is sufficient evidence, as already suggested in this chapter, that Dougan was a Calvinist and his liturgical practice was in keeping with the principles of the Reformed Faith. It has been argued in chapter two that Calvin's view of worship was located in his doctrine of the Church and the doctrine of God, and Dougan's liturgical practice would make no sense without these two essential doctrines. Calvin's theology which is given expression in these doctrines, moulded Dougan's liturgical views, and was expressed in three ways:

(1) In an address to the General Assembly in 1956, he said, "The Church exists only in Christ; that is the clue to the interpretation of Calvin's statement that outside the Church there is ordinarily no salvation."[21] The Church is not just an earthly organization, and membership is simply by way of self interest. Dougan was concerned that the Church as community called by God, could lose its distinctiveness by becoming a legal corporation or just merely an organization. He questioned whether or not the Church was a

reflection of the civil organisation of Australia. Although he cannot prove it he suspected that as the Church grows as an organization it loses spiritual power, just as when the State tends to become increasingly bureaucratic it tends to become less democratic.[22] It is interesting to observe the sequence of his logic as he arrives at this point of view.

> Never was our organization so developed; never were our committee so adequate; never were the loose ends of control more tightly tied together in our Church; never before have we had so many special departments; never were our works more supervised, our undertakings so carefully planned, our results so tabulated, and yet, personally, I do not think our Church is as religiously as strong as it was when I first sat a humble Exit student in the back benches of this house.[23]

He expressed concern that in the Church in which we live as Christian, and where there is a highly developed organization and efficient business management, there is the danger of losing the spiritual life which alone is the essence of the Holy Catholic Church, *"Ubi Christus, ibi ecclesia"*.[24]

Fundamental to Dougan's concept of the Church is that the Church is not of man rather the Church is of God's creation. He argues in this way, "the Church is Christ's, He created it, He redeemed it to Himself by His precious blood, it is His Holy Bride and His own gift to it is the Holy Ministry of the Word and Sacrament". For Calvin not only is the Church Christ's foundation, but membership into the Church and into the Kingdom of God is by way of forgiveness of sins, without which there is no covenant nor union with God.[25] Here are the same theological presuppositions in Dougan's thought:

- Both Calvin and Dougan accept that the Church is the creation of Christ.
- Calvin insists that membership is achieved through the atoning sacrifice of Christ –Calvin refers to it in his term "forgiveness", as forgiveness is secured by the atonement, but Dougan refers to it as "redemption by his precious blood".
- Calvin insists upon a covenant "relationship" or special "union", whereas Dougan embraces the same thought in his statement on "the Bride of Christ". In this phrase there is implied a covenantal relationship between Bride and Groom, and their union is one.

In a sermon preached at St Stephens, Bathurst, Dougan says, "the Church was right in emphasizing that the way to God must lie through the path of confession and redemption".[26] This simple public statement embraces the substance of the above theological analysis.

The spiritual life of the membership of God's church is critical for Dougan because without a definite relationship with Christ, the Church can fall into organisational decadence. The essential nature of the relationship between Church member and Christ is aptly described by Calvin in terms of "mother". "Let us learn from her single title of Mother, how useful, nay, how necessary the knowledge of her is, since there is no other means of entering into life unless she conceives us in the womb and gives us birth, unless she nourish us at her breasts, and, in short, keep us under her charge and government, until, divested of mortal flesh, we become angels."[27] This means that the Church as institution, complete with true spirituality through union with Christ is essential to the wellbeing of Christianity. With doctrine of the Church true Christianity can never be defined in terms of a general philosophy by which man can acquiesce to a set of academic propositions. Calvin's doctrine of the Church with its notion of "Mother" can only convey not just an "institution" controlled by man, but rather a family of sons and daughters who posses a real dynamic of life. From this perspective Dougan was right in describing the essential nature of the Church as Holy and Catholic. Writing to the *Western Times* newspaper, Dougan argues that the Church is one of the largest and strongest movements in the world which finds its inspiration and power "in the Divine Lord Jesus Christ". There is nevertheless a profound unity, despite differences of attitude by some Christians who are exclusive in matters of organisation. Unfortunately there are those who believe that the essence of the Church is in the organisation, but others find the essence in the ministry, and still others see that spirituality is more important than form. However says, Dougan there is the "unity of the Spirit".[28] For Calvin the Church is Holy because Christ has redeemed the Church by His atoning Sacrifice. The Church is "sanctified" when "forgiveness" is accomplished and applied. This forgiveness and regeneration to new life is applied by the action of the Holy Spirit.[29] Calvin also argues in his Institutes that the Unity of the Church is found in our ingrafting into Christ. It is this principle of ingrafting that opens up the notion of the Church being Catholic and Universal.[30] Furthermore Calvin also sees the Unity of the Church as the basis that members are "called into one inheritance and one life; and hence it follows that we cannot obtain eternal life without living in mutual harmony in this world. One divine invitation being addressed to all, they ought to be united in the same profession of faith and to render every kind of assistance to each other".[31] Dougan says the same as Calvin in a different way when he states, "Only one thing really matters in Church—that the Spirit gathers God's people with one accord into one place that people may hear the living word of God".[32] Dougan understood that his commitment to the Reformed Faith meant that an understanding of the doctrine of the Holy Spirit was critical to Calvin's theological system and the life and function of the Church. He calls for a "new thinking" about the role of the Holy Spirit. Commenting on the introductory essay to *An Experimental Liturgy* by Dr J. G. Davies who commented on the "Epiclesis" in Eastern rites, Dougan says "new thinking needs to be done about the theology of the Holy Spirit's role in the Eucharist if the Epiclesis is used as we use it now without the Prothesis and the Great Entrance".[33] The suggestion here of course is that the Epiclesis as used today has been torn out of its ancient symbolic context. It would be interesting to know how Dougan would have responded to the contemporary Scottish theologian Dr Andrew McGowan's claim that the Epiclesis in the 1940 Book of Common Order is an exercise in "sleight of hand", as it is a prayer for the Holy Spirit to come down upon the elements and produce the miracle of transubstantiation.[34] Irrespective of how Dougan would have responded, what is of interest is that Dougan's words were somewhat prophetic in that these matters are now being discussed, two decades after his death.

(2) Another glimpse of Dougan's Calvinism is his perception of the Purpose of the Church and the Church's Ministry.

Unlike the contemporary popular view that the Church exists for Mission, both Calvin and Dougan sees the Church's prime function is that of Worship. Writing in the *Western Times* newspaper on two different occasions Dougan says: "The duty to which we are called on Sunday is our supreme task—it is God's worship. By obeying this call we are asserting our faith. Faith only lives so long as it is expressed"[35] and "The Church's supreme task is worship. It is as though God says, 'on My Day it is your task to gather together to express for me the things that are of worth eternally.' And so the Church calls for Sunday October 28th 1945, as she has called every Lord's Day for twenty centuries, 'O come let us worship".[36]

In the *New South Wales Presbyterian* he expresses concern about the downgrading of Worship into forms of entertainment in which the dignified standards of the Church are being lost. With sadness he notes that popular services where there are many other popular innovations are topical sermons, and prayers that are addressed more to the people than to almighty God. He warns "this spells doom for us we must stop fooling ourselves, that this is God's worship. It is possible for that which we do in Church to be blasphemy".[37]

This view of Dougan is contrary to the current context, as modern young evangelicals, even within Reformed circles, believe that the Church exists for Mission and Evangelism. The whole notion of a marketing approach to the work of the Church is expressive of this idea. For example George Barna argues that Churches must adopt a market approach if they are to grow and survive. He writes,

> Most Churches' inability to grow is not due to a lack of desire, or even a lack of resources. The truth is, we simply have not grasped the basic principles of marketing and applied them to the Church. The opportunities for successful church marketing are plentiful. All we as a community of believers need to do is gain a proper perspective on the church and how it can be marketed effec-

tively. To successfully market your product, you have to identify its prospective market. The key to market identification is to be as specific as possible in selecting the audience to whom you will market the product. By matching the appeal of your product to the interests and needs of specific population segments, you can concentrate on getting your product to your best prospects without wasting resources on people who have no need or interest in your product.[38]

In stark contrast Dougan says the "supreme task of the Church is worship"! Worship is not and cannot Biblically be selective. Worship is an injunction for the whole people of God. To be selective as marketing techniques suggest may be successful in terms of numbers attending a worship service, but at the same time diminishing the command to go into the world and preach the gospel. The Gospel cannot be limited to just various interest groups, be they young, old, or of some ethnic dominion. Dougan's outlook on the worshipping community is comprehensive and there is no suggestion of a selection process. It is at this point that we observe Calvin's views are enunciated by Dougan. Calvin claims in his exposition on the Law, that the "first foundation of righteousness is the worship of God" and when the foundation of worship is subverted, "all the other parts of righteousness, like a building rent asunder; and in ruins, are racked and scattered".[39] From this Calvin pursued a reformation in worship which was discussed in chapter two. He argued for a redefinition of the liturgy, not its abandonment. The content of worship was to adhere to the New Testament principles which were consistent with Reformational theology. Worship for Calvin was sacred and holy. It was, where worshipers being united with Christ, encounter the worship of Christ. There is no room in worship for popular and entertaining innovations. In worship man is confronted with the Word both in preaching and in the sacrament. Here, Dougan embraces Calvin.

(3) Dougan's Calvinism also emerges in his views on "Ministerial Office". Calvin argues that believers within the Church are kept together in one body, and encouraged in the faith by ministers whom God has called into this high office. He argues "the ministers to whom he has committed this office, and given grace to discharge it, he dispenses and distributes his gifts to the Church, and thus exhibits himself as in a manner actually present by exerting the energy of his Spirit in this institution, so as to present it from being vain and fruitless".[40] It is in this way says Calvin that the body of Christ is edified and renewed, "In this way we grow up in all things unto Him who is the Head, and unite with one another; in this way we are all brought into the unity of Christ".[41] The office of ministry is so important that Calvin sternly warns those who seek to abolish or disparage it as of major importance as he, "plots the devastation, or rather the ruin and destruction of the Church".[42] The office of ministry must be held in "the highest estimation as among the most excellent of our blessings". Calvin then proceeds to enumerate the

importance of office in terms of Apostles, Prophets, Evangelists, Pastors and Teachers. Only the office of Pastor and Teacher has an ordinary office in the Church.[43]

This teaching of Calvin is in contrast to what prevails in the Presbyterian Church in New South Wales today. The high office of ministry has been downgraded on the basis of the doctrine of the Priesthood of all believers, which is made to mean that ministers render a service that is no different from what others do in the Church, except that the minister is usually employed full-time. Oz Guinness sees the pursuit of this downgrade in terms of status. He claims that the Church in the modern world has lost its status and relevance because of this hunger for relevance and authority, he writes, "we use things that are really effective in the world. The managerial revolution is behind the idea of the pastor as a chief executive officer, just as the therapeutic revolution is behind the idea of the pastor as a psychologist. The managerial ideas are well expounded in the popular American journal *Leadership*".[44] The influential scholar Walter Brueggemann sees that the whole marketing approach is the direct result of a process of "enculturation of the Church and the Christian message". He argues that the Church has been assimilated into the consumerism of a market economy. To prove his point he points to the money raising efforts of the television evangelists and the apparent success of the Willow Creek type mega Churches. He further claims that the Church has become so identified with the dominant consumerist and technological culture that it has lost its power to believe in its own tradition or to act prophetically in the community.[45] The downgrading of office must necessarily have an impact upon the Church's commitment to the practice of "ordination and induction" into pastoral charges. In the Presbyterian Church the practice of ordination to the ministry has always been very specific. It is ordination to the ministry of "Word and Sacrament". If office is not taken seriously then the ministry of Word and Sacrament become isolated to the point that they will be at the mercy of any radical idea that believers without philosophical and theological expertise, may impose on them. Certainly the Word and Sacraments would be in serious danger of being dislodged from their historical and traditional setting.

In contrast to the modern marketing era and its degrading impact, Alan Dougan embraces Calvin's notion of office. Writing in the *Bathurst National Advocate*, he raised his concern about the degradation of office. The office of Ministry cannot and should not be minimised or downgraded, because the office "is of Christ's appointment. Ministers have been called by God and ordained into the office. The glory of it is Christ's Glory and we ourselves are but the broken vessels he chooses to use...We do little honour to Christ our Lord and King by making little the way He has chosen for the perfecting of the saints, the feeding of the flock climbing the upward road to the heavenly pastures".[46] Since the Church has been created by Christ and governed by

Christ through the office of Ministry, it means that the Calvinistic view of the Church is high, as Dougan claims, and if this is so then the ministry of the Church must also be high. Dougan continues to argue that St Paul acknowledges that God gave gifts to men for the work of the ministry, for the purpose of the perfecting of the saints. In the same article he emphasises the notion "it is God who calls", convinces him that this is Presbyterian doctrine. What Dougan says is so much in keeping with Calvin, he must have had Calvin's Institutes beside him when writing the article to the newspaper.

DOUGAN AND THE LITURGICAL PRACTICE OF THE CHURCH

Calvin insisted that order and a basic uniformity were necessary in the Church so as to bring about unity. Calvin produced a catechism for the Church in Geneva with the view for uniformity among the various protestant groupings. There were serious divisions between Calvin, Luther, Bucer, Zwingli, Westphal and others. The truth of the Scriptures had to be the unifying factor. It was essential that a catechism was produced to inculcate truth. Likewise Calvin produced a Form of Prayers and Forms of Worship. These forms were generally used at services on Sunday. The exclusion of form meant liturgical chaos. The use of forms has never been mandatory or compulsory in Reformed or Presbyterian Churches, as each minister always exercised a degree of flexibility. To Alan Dougan, forms were necessary to preserve the dignity and good order in the divine service. Without form the expression of Reformed Worship would soon be lost. The lack of form in worship services which have become popular today argues Dougan is inconsistent with the general practice of the Church's government. This he says is difficult to justify. He argues that the Church's business is conducted in a most orderly fashion; the General assembly employs a special committee with legal officers to keep its business in order. But why is it, asks Dougan, that there is such a lack of order in the worship of God? He answers:

> Order is laid down for things material, but for the things eternal, it is left to the whims and fancies, of often untrained individuals. The worshippers are at the mercy of the minister. Why should the ordering of public worship be left to the parish minister? Procedure at meetings, investment of funds these are not thus left. And since there must be some order in worship, the only conclusion to be drawn is that we don't care whether the order of worship is good or bad. That is a shocking thing for a Presbyterian to have to say.
> The Presbyterian communion has always recognised a due and proper order in Divine Service. This can be clearly traced through Calvin, John Knox's Genevan Service Book .The Westminster Directory for Public Worship (which is our recognised subordinate standard), the various editions of the service book of the Scottish Church Service Society called "Euchologian", and now the magnificent "Book of Common Order" of the Church of Scotland,

which is recognised by our General Assembly's Committee as setting the norm for the services of our Church.

The order of worship thus laid down surely merits the study both of ministers and people. It follows faithfully the traditions of the Church Universal and Reformed.[47]

It is here that we see yet again Dougan's adherence to Calvin's general principles of worship and office.

In chapter one of this work reference was made to "a Pattern of Conflict". Such a pattern of conflict can be very useful and healthy for the Church as it can promote meaningful discussion on important theological issues. This is no less true with Alan Dougan's perception and adherence to Calvin's liturgical principles. Dougan was at pains to define Presbyterianism and enunciate Presbyterian liturgical practice in terms of his scholarly research into the history and development of Presbyterianism and that includes the many variations of liturgical practice. His task of conveying his understanding of Reformed practice was made difficult by the perception that Presbyterianism was determined by what was experienced "in our own parish Church, and has become for us, be it good or bad, Presbyterianism".[48] The outcome, says Dougan is often "a rich heritage that is thrown away and services become sectarian".[49] This meant that the liturgical views expressed by Dougan were deemed by many in the Church as an expression of a "high churchman" who was anxious to promote "ritualism". This unfortunate tag was soon understood in terms of innovations of non-Presbyterian practices. Any kind of ritual in the mind of some people meant either a capitulation to Rome or a failure to understand Calvin's linkage of knowledge of God and the true worship of God.

In an Article submitted to the *New South Wales Presbyterian* [50] entitled, "The Worship of the Church", Dougan argued that liturgical practice in the Presbyterian Church was determined by the pattern of the whole Reformed Church not just one branch of it, and that it was in keeping with the Reformed Doctrine. Judgements can only be made on issues of what Presbyterianism is or is not by studying a wide range of various reformed theologies and manuals of practice. He specifies for those who stand in the Scottish tradition manuals such as: John Knox's *"Book of our Common Order"*, the *Westminster Directory* (remembering this is a composite directory and many of the things the Presbyterian representatives fought for were defeated by the English Puritan representatives), the various editions of the *"Euchologian"*, the *"New Directory of the United Free Church of Scotland"*, The Church of Scotland's *"Prayers for Divine Service"* 1923 & 1929, and the *"Book of Common Order"* 1940. Dougan also cites other Reformed texts. So it is by a study of these that determines Presbyterian liturgical practice is determined.

This article evoked a strong reaction, particularly from the Rev. T.P. McEvoy. McEvoy argued that true Presbyterianism Worship is "The Church discovered that its true genius lay not in the realm of the set form of service, but along the path of that rugged yet dignified simplicity of worship ..."[51] In this response he suggests that this was the real reason why Knox's liturgy was "quietly interred", and the ritual of the English Church was to be avoided. For this reason the Church turned away from what Mr. Dougan terms as "the Catholic and Reformed tradition of worship".

In the next edition of the same journal the Rev. McEvoy continued his line of argument. On this occasion McEvoy expresses his concern about "formalism in the Church". He notes that in the tradition in which he was brought up, "form and ceremony in worship were regarded as anathema. Anything tending towards formalism was strictly taboo". McEvoy attempts to define, though poorly, what he means by formalism. Reference is made to the following, the "singing of the Doxology", the "chanting of the Lord's Prayer", the "reading of Prayers" and the use of the "Lectern, with its obtrusion of the officiating minister", the "repetition of the Creed", and "other usages which Mr Dougan styles as Catholic and Reformed".

Not only is McEvoy out of step with Calvin but he incurs the wrath of Dougan. In a scathing response to McEvoy's letters, Dougan claims that McEvoy, "cares nothing for the honoured tradition of the whole Reformed Church, the Holy Catholic Church itself, the example of our Divine Lord who attended not only the synagogue but went up to the Temple feasts and who said, 'when you pray say "Our Father ..."[52] He also ridicules McEvoy's suggestion that the Lectern "obtrudes" the officiating minister. He argues that a high central pulpit "obtrudes" the officiating minister more so. It seems strange to Dougan that McEvoy argues as he does against the use of "forms" when he claims that "confession and contrition" should come late in the order of service as they are the outcome not the beginning. Dougan then points out that McEvoy is in good company with the Romanists and Anglo-Catholics, with that claim. Besides it was the Protestant party who insisted on the penitential introduction to the morning and evening prayer in the English *Book of Common Prayer*. McEvoy failed to understand the difference between form and formalism. Dougan saves his most strident criticism until last. This criticism deals with McEvoy's reasons for the dropping of Knox's *Book of Common Order* by the Church of Scotland. McEvoy had claimed that it was because the people repudiated liturgical form. Not so, says Dougan. "It is a very poor liturgy, drawn up in the hot spirit of protest." He quotes from the Scottish Liturgical scholar D.H. Hislop, "the Church has little or nothing to learn from Knox about liturgical prayer. His public devotions appear to me to lack range of sympathy and sweep of spirit. Knox's service is singularly inadequate".[53] Comparing Knox's liturgy with the Anglican Prayer book, Bullock makes the significant observation that the prayers of Knox's liturgy are verbose and lack the grace of the Anglican collects, as Knox did not have the literary skill of Cranmer.[54] Hislop also claims that the Communion rite is lacking in many of the precious aspects of the celebration in the early Church. Knox, claims Hislop, drew up his service so as to avoid certain abuses. "Knox is so afraid of idolatry coming to man through the eye that he is ever seeking to lift the eyes of men from the visible elements lest they worship material things". Although Knox's liturgy may well have been poor and lacking in liturgical significance, it must be remembered that Knox was a product of the age in which he lived. His contribution to the life of the Church in Scotland is immeasurable. It is interesting to note that a prestigious Scottish theologian such as Professor Andrew McGowan states that of the implementation of Calvin and Knox's liturgies in Scotland today, people would say "that's Catholic"; "We don't like that." McGowan suggests that it is time to revisit the doctrine of worship with a better historical perspective.[55] Dougan also refers to Hislop's claim that another reason that Knox's liturgy was dropped, was because in Scotland the assertion of freedom was linked with political aspirations toward liberty; the historic structure of worship was sacrificed on the altar of liberty. The outcome says Hislop, was that the Lord's Prayer became suspect, the beauty of Holiness in worship was a "night of darkness" and worship as an art was demolished.[56]

In this interchange Dougan proves himself to be the liturgical scholar who draws on the historical and theological literature of the Reformed Church, to re-emphasise and to implement the rich liturgical heritage of the Church, whereas McEvoy remains captive to the doctrinal and liturgical prejudices of "the parish church" of his narrow upbringing.

The debate between Dougan and McEvoy shows how there are those within the Church who have either misunderstood or have failed to understand the Calvinist worship tradition. In the contemporary era, the failure of Reformed Liturgical practice is primarily due to the influence of "revivalism", which relies more on "evangelical efficacy" and "experiential power", rather than the building up of the Church, through Word and Sacrament. Such is the influence of revivalist culture there is the tendency to rely on individualistic or non–churchy forms of Christian devotion.[57]

This is in keeping with postmodern acculturalization of the Church with its rigid individualism that has already been noted.

NOTES

1. Robert Willson, *Life and Times of Alan Dougan,* Address at the Annual Meeting of the Friends of the Ferguson Library, 19 March 2005.
2. Robert Willson, *The Presbyterian Review*, 2005.
3. Peter Cameron, "A.A..Dougan", *The St. Andrew's College Magazine*, 1974, 18.
4. M. Horton, "Pledge and Promise", *Australian Presbyterian Life*, March 2007.

5. *Catholic* is defined in terms of, the presence of the living Christ and the "wholeness" or "totality", the wholeness of the Gospel. The unity created by Christ consisted in a whole *via vitae* which included belief, worship and morals. Only that Church, or communion, or tradition, is in the full sense catholic which possess the "wholeness" of the Gospel, and such "wholeness" can be derived only from Christ, His message of the Kingdom of God, His work of salvation and His way of life for mankind. See R. Flew and R. Davies, *The Catholicity of Protestantism* (London: Lutterworth Press, 1951), 23.

6. The Rev. Robert Willson has collected all known material, in three volumes, located in the Ferguson Memorial Library, Sydney.

7. R. Willson, *Life and Times of A.A. Dougan,* an address to the Friends of the Ferguson Memorial Library, 2005.

8. W. Kinmont, "Our Church's Worship", *New South Wales Presbyterian*, 14 July 1937.

9. G. K. Bell, *Documents on Christian Unity* (London: Oxford University Press 1958), 2.

10. Bell, *Documents,* 12.

11. Bell, *Documents,* 81.

12. Bell, *Documents,* 87.

13. Bell, *Documents,* 88.

14. Ian Henderson, *Power without Glory* (London: Hutchinson, 1967), 115.

15. Henderson, *Power without Glory*, 121.

16. A.A. Dougan, "The Origin of Presbyterian Worship", *New South Wales Presbyterian*, 29 December 1937, 9.

17. A.A. Dougan, "Some Problems of Contemporary Liturgical Reform", *Australian Church Quarterly*, September 1972, 14.

18. A.A. Dougan, letter, "Turning Back to Faith", *Western Times*, 2 June 1945.

19. W.D. Maxwell, *Genevan Service Book* (Westminster: Faith Press, 1965), 19.

20. Robert Willson, *Rev. Principal Alan Dougan M.A.* (Canberra: Private Publication 2004), Vol. 1 (2005), Vol. 2.; Robert Willson, *The Bathurst Years of Alan Dougan* (Canberra: Private Publication, 2005).

21. A.A. Dougan, "Moderator Addresses General Assembly", *New South Wales Presbyterian*, 18 May 1956, 1.

22. Dugan, *Address.*

23. Dugan, *Address.*

24. Dugan, *Address.*

25. Calvin, *Institutes*, Bk 4, Ch. 1, Sec. 20.

26. A.A. Dougan, Sermon at St. Stephen's, *Western Times*, 11 July 1944.

27. Calvin, *Institutes*, Bk 4, Ch. 1, Sec. 4.

28. A.A. Dougan, "A Movement for All", *Western Times*, 27 October 1945.

29. John Calvin, *Commentary*, Ephesians (Grand Rapids: Baker Book House, 1979), Vol. 21, 318–19.

30. Calvin, *Institutes*, Bk 4, Ch. 1, Sec. 3.

31. Calvin, *Commentaries*, Vol. 21, 268.

32. A.A. Dougan, "Moderator Address General Assembly", *New South Wales Presbyterian*, 18 May 1956.

33. A.A. Dougan, "Some Problems of Contemporary Liturgical Reform", *The Australian Church Quarterly*, September 1972, 15. Davies notes that in the Eastern Rites the Epiclesis is the last of the three closely interconnected elements; the Prothesis, when Christ is slain in a figure by the piercing of the host with a miniature lance. The second is the Great Entrance, in which the dead Christ is solemnly born to the altar. Then comes the Epiclesis when through the Spirit of Christ, the Christ is raised to be present as the living Lord in the midst of the faithful.

34. Andrew McGowan in *Conference Paper* 2006, 3. The Conference date is unknown.

35. A.A. Dougan, "Our Supreme Task", *Western Times*, 18 August 1945.

36. A.A. Dougan, "A Movement for All" *Western Times*, 27 October 1945.

37. A.A. Dougan, "*New South Wales Presbyterian*, 27 September 1944.

38. George Barna, *Marketing the Church* (Colorado: Nav Press, 1988), 40.

39. Calvin, *Institutes*, Bk 2, Ch. 8, Sec. 11.

40. Calvin, *Institutes*, Bk 4, Ch. 3, Sec. 2.

41. Calvin, *Institutes*. Sec. 2
42. Calvin, *Institutes*. Sec. 2
43. Calvin, *Institutes*, Sec. 4.
44. Interview with Oz Guinness in *The Briefing*, 9 June 1992, 8.
45. M. Budde and R. Brimlow, eds, *The Church as Counterculture* (New York: State University of NY Press, 2000), 54–56.
46. *Bathurst National Advocate*, 28 February 1952.
47. A.A. Dougan, "The Worship of the Church", *The N.S.W. Presbyterian*, 27 September 1944.
48. A.A. Dougan, "The Worship of the Church", *The N.S.W. Presbyterian*, 22 November 1944, 7.
49. Dougan, "The Worship of the Church".
50. Dougan, "The Worship of the Church".
51. T.P. McEvoy, "Exchange of Views", *The New South Wales Presbyterian*, 6 December 1944, 2.
52. A.A. Dougan, "Exchange of Views", *The New South Wales Presbyterian*, 3 January 1945, 2.
53. D.H. Hislop, *Our Heritage in Public Worship* (Edinburgh: T &T Clark, 1935), 193,195.
54. J. Bullock, *The Kirk in Scotland* (Edinburgh: St. Andrews Press, 1960), 116.
55. A. McGowan, in *Australian Presbyterian Life*, April 2006, 6.
56. Hislop, *Our Heritage*, 197.
57. D.G. Hart, *Recovering Mother Kirk* (Grand Rapids: Baker Books, 2003), 16.

Chapter Four

A Brief History of the Theological Aetiology of Liturgical Minimization

The intention of this chapter is to define "Liturgical Minimization" and to trace the development of the process from the time of Zwingli and Calvin through to the modern era. Specific reference will be given to John Knox and other important Scottish personalities. The Liturgical Minimisation process reached an apex when the Scottish Parliament approved the "Westminster Directory of Public Worship", in which set forms and ceremonies of the English Prayer Book were regarded as offensive. It is our intention to argue that the minimisation process was linked with the new popular philosophical paradigm associated with the names of Galileo, Bacon, Descartes and Newton. The ideals of the minimization process were planted in Australian soil through Scottish immigration during the early part of the nineteenth century. This historical approach concludes with the argument that Liturgical Minimization was in fact a theological question of how the principals of authority and sufficiency of Holy Scripture should be applied to the Church's ministry.

The last two chapters defined the practice of worship in the Presbyterian Church, and in particular, liturgical worship reached its zenith in New South Wales during the ministry of the Rev. Alan Dougan. The theology of worship within the Reformed tradition was Calvinistic and the practice of worship was "Trinitarian". It is at this point that the major theme of this book begins.

Liturgical minimisation in the context of Australian Presbyterianism has its origins in Scotland. The first Presbyterian Church was established by Scottish free settlers who met for worship each Sunday and who built the first Presbyterian Church by 1809 on the banks of the Hawkesbury River. They called it *Ebenezer*. It was there that the Rev. Dr John Dunmore Lang M.A., D.D. first celebrated the sacraments, according to the rites of the Church of Scotland, on Australian soil in 1823. The Scots brought with them all the variations of the conduct of public worship that had existed in Scotland.

It is therefore essential to understand what liturgical minimisation is, as it is foundational to this book.

Liturgical Minimization *is the process of removing from a liturgy anything that is theologically unacceptable or anything that is indifferent which has no direct command in Holy Scripture.* This latter aspect is of particular interest to the more radical of the religious reformers. For example, the sixteenth century protestant reformers declared that transubstantiation was an unacceptable doctrine as it was the foundation building block of the Roman Mass. This meant that in the eyes of the protestant reformers, all references to this doctrine had to be removed from the liturgy, and thus it is said that the liturgy is minimised. According to some of the radical of the reforming party, especially some of the English and Scottish Puritans, other parts of the liturgy may also be removed if there was no definitive Biblical command to worship any other way than suggested by the bare outline of the Westminster Directory of Public Worship.

It is to be understood that there were varying attitudes towards reform among the Puritans, hence the existence of a number of different groups. There were two fundamental groups; one was to seek the reform of the Church of England from within as a post reformation Church. The other group sought change which would see the structure of the Church of England change into another reformed Church model. This latter group ran foul of the Elizabethan settlement. The Acts of Uniformity saw the ejection of many Puritan clergy especially those who advocated a reformed national church system that was essentially Presbyterian. They looked towards the Calvinistic model established in Geneva. As with any broad definition it is to be understood that there were the extremists who advocated separation. The Scottish Church possesses much more flexibility for reform because the Acts of Uniformity in England had no authority. The Laudian attempt to impose the Book of Common Prayer on the Scots was met with a riot, and the attempt was a failure.

By using the blunt cleansing instrument, known as the Regulative Principle, all liturgical responses such as the Gloria, the Creed, and the Sanctus etc. may be removed. Other parts of the liturgy such as the Agnus Dei are removed as it could be interpreted as being a prayer to the Host, implying transubstantiation. Once this minimisation process is applied either to the English Book of Common Prayer or to John Calvin's Strasbourg liturgy, a worship service is reduced or minimised to the barest simplicities of Prayers, Scripture Readings, Singing of Psalms and Preaching. Worship as an art form that preserves the dignity of the "beauty of holiness", of the "Wholly Other", which speaks to the "awe struck soul", to use the key words of Evelyn Underhill, is simply minimised, in favour of worshippers being fitted for their Christian responsibilities by instruction, education and preaching. Gordon Donaldson comments that the appeal of worship services was to be to the intellect through the spoken or written word, rather than the senses.[1]

PRIVY KIRKS

It is appropriate to briefly explain, something of the historical and theological context at this point. Essential to the progress of the protestant reformation in Scotland was the establishment of the "Privy Kirks". Secret communities of Protestants transformed themselves into Privy Kirks, wherein the Holy Scriptures, and Protestant literature were studied and prayer and worship were practised. James Kirk[2] sees that by 1549 a number of earls like Glencairn and Lennox[3] promised to cause the Word of God to be taught and preached. Preachers were recruited to help organise and strengthen the secret communities into a Calvinistic Church. Although the Privy Kirks played an important part in the progress of religious reform in Scotland, especially after John Knox became minister of St Giles in Edinburgh, Y. Chung concedes to James Kirk's view that the Privy Kirks did not by themselves produce the Reformation victory of 1560:

> The Privy Kirks might breed a sense of purpose, self- reliance and esteem among the converted, the privy kirks alone could not hope to . . . bring about widespread revolution. The townspeople and country-dwellers who attended their meetings were still accustomed to looking above and beyond their own religious communities for direction and leadership . . . Political action was imperative for sustained religious change.[4]

The reformation of the theology and ecclesiology of the Church in Scotland was prosecuted with a sense of freedom; the end result was liturgical chaos. The rejection of transubstantiation and certain ceremonies was based on the progressing theological reform which arose out of the acceptance of the plenary inspiration and authority of Holy Scripture as well as the central Pauline doctrine of justification by faith. In Europe, Luther, Calvin and Zwingli made adjustments to the liturgy to ensure a degree of theological consistency. Unfortunately serious differences of opinion led to a serious lack of unity. This did not prevent Calvin from reconfiguring the liturgy whilst he ministered in Strasburg. As explained in chapter two of this dissertation, he retained much of the historic aspects of the liturgy but it was essentially a work of minimisation, in the sense of minimising the liturgy of all specific doctrine that related to transubstantiation. The Strasburg liturgy expressed a consistent and coherent view of his reformed theology. It was unfortunate that he was unable to implement this liturgy in Geneva, due to prejudice and political factors.

THE BOOK OF COMMON PRAYER

In England there were two serious attempts to produce a reformed liturgy. The second *Book of Common Prayer* authorised by Edward VI was regarded as the most Protestant. This was widely accepted and used throughout England and was in usage in Scotland, (especially in the privy kirks) as it formed part of the important liturgical mix at the time.[5] This did not mean that the Scots used the *Prayer Book* in a slavish manner. Donaldson points out that at the time there is no evidence for the idea of conducting worship without written or printed form, and there was a demand for common prayers. The Scots did not approve of everything in the Prayer Book but they had the complete freedom to pick and choose from its pages.[6] However there were many Puritans in the English and Scottish Church who did not believe that the reforms in the liturgy went far enough.

John Knox, when ministering in the dioceses of Durham had misgivings in respect to the English Prayer book and took advantage of the Bishop of Durham's failure to enforce the Act of Uniformity and Knox chose not to use it. He also ministered to a congregation of English exiles in both Frankfurt-on-Main and Geneva; it was at this time that he wrote his own liturgy despite the fact that Calvin had already rewritten the liturgy. It was in Frankfurt that he became more aware of the serious differences among the English Puritans and himself.[7] W.C. Dickinson in his introduction to Knox's History of the Reformation in Scotland, refers to this time in Knox's life. While being the unwilling minister of the English congregation in Frankfurt, he became embroiled in a serious quarrel over unprofitable ceremonies. There was a serious division within the congregation over the use of the English *Prayer Book*. Knox and others held to the view that all ceremonies and inventions were a barrier between God and man. Others including Ponet, Scorey, Bale and Cox, all of whom had been bishops or high in the hierarchy of the Church establishment, were happy with the use of the Prayer Book. Cox had quite a reputation as he was formerly a tutor of Edward VI and Chancellor of Oxford University, and had a large involvement in the preparation of the second Prayer Book. Pressure upon this group came from the Archbishop of Canterbury, Edmund Grindal, for them to take over the work of the Church in Frankfurt. When Cox and his group gained the majority within the congregation, they refused Knox the right to preach. They were somewhat ruthless in their determination to preserve and retain the *Prayer Book* for the English exiles. D.M. Lloyd-Jones comments that many of the English exiles were also influenced by Zwingli who was regarded as a radical reformer. It was Zwingli who denounced ceremonialism and clerical dress. Those who were influenced by him, including Knox, were not content with exposing erroneous Roman Catholic doctrine but they also insisted on the actual removal of all ceremony and clerical dress. It was at this time that Zwingli established many of the practices of worship that became part of the Reformed heritage. These include, for example, the idea of quarterly communion, the complete break from liturgical custom in form and phraseology, the idea of remaining seated for the distribution of the elements, and being served by the deacons. Try as he might John Calvin was unable to retrieve the divorce between the liturgy of the Word and the Eucharist. By 1525 Zwingli had dispensed with the Canon of the Mass completely and replaced it with what appears to be the medieval Prone service. He also omitted most of the ancient formulae of worship, such as the *Sursum Corda,* the *Sanctus,* the *Kyries* and *Agnus Dei.* It is in Zwingli that we see the most through going process of liturgical minimisation. By 1531 Zwingli was dead and John Calvin would take an entirely different approach to worship. So extreme was Zwingli's influence that Lloyd-Jones cites as an example one of the exiles in Frankfurt, John Hooper, who upon returning to England refused to wear the customary vestments for his installation as Bishop of Gloucester. Justification for these extreme Puritan views says Lloyd-Jones takes the form of a syllogism:

Major Premise–*all things to be required in the Christian Church are either ordained in the Bible or are things indifferent.*
Minor Premise–*Vestments are neither ordained in the Bible for use in the Christian Church nor are they things indifferent.*
Conclusion–*therefore they are not to be required in the Christian Church.*[8] The quarrel destroyed the effectiveness of his ministry. He consequently left the congregation and went to Geneva where he was elected as the minister of the English congregation. It was in Geneva that he had the opportunity to "study the government of a 'perfect city' according to the Word of God".[9]

The time Knox spent on the Continent exposed him to the ideas and convictions of the English Puritans but it also provided valuable preparation for the reformation of the Church in Scotland. On a short visit to Edinburgh in 1555, Knox saw the small beginnings of a Protestant Church. Taking advantage of what appeared to be a more tolerant spirit on the part of the Queen Regent, Mary of Guise, Knox wrote a letter suggesting that she study how that the true worshipping of God may be promoted and the tyranny of ungodly men repressed.[10] The letter was passed on to the Bishop of Glasgow who excommunicated him and his effigy was burnt in Edinburgh. His visit to Scotland was indeed brief! However in 1557 when Scottish politics changed for the better, Knox received an invitation to return to Scotland. Encouraged by John Calvin and other Godly ministers, he accepted. When Elizabeth succeeded Mary Tudor to the Crown in 1558, the English exiles returned to England and Knox arrived in Scotland in 1559. Knox began a ministry that changed the face of the nation. His influence was very wide as it extended from the ecclesiastical to social and political reform. The upheaval of the

Church both in England and Scotland brought about by the Protestation Reformation caused leaders to think through the important issues in theology and ecclesiology, as there was little cohesion between various groups who demanded reform. The outstanding feature of D.M. Lloyd-Jones's work on the Puritans is that he sees the issues clearly and objectively, and concludes that John Knox rather than John Hooper, Bishop of Gloucester, is the founder of Puritanism as suggested by Thomas Carlyle in his book *On Heroes and Hero Worship*. He puts forward the following arguments for his claim:

- Knox has independence of thought. A Puritan is not a man of the establishment.
- He enunciated the guiding principle of Puritanism, as he sees the supreme authority of the Scriptures as the Word of God.
- He believed in root and branch reformation. i.e. reformation not only in doctrine but also the practice of Christianity.
- He desired a New Testament idea of the Church. The conduct of worship and the administration of the Sacraments had to be according to New Testament principles. The Church had no right to devise religious ceremonies and impose significations upon them.

Lloyd–Jones rightly considers that Knox is a stand out in his conscientious application of what he believed to be the New Testament pattern regarding the nature of the Church, the ordinances, the ceremonies and the exercise of discipline.[11]

It was Knox's independent thought and his desire for a liturgy, which was consistent with his interpretation of the Scriptures, led him to compose his own liturgy for the English congregation at Geneva. From a more modern perspective Knox used his own *regulative principle* to govern what was to be retained in the liturgy. It comes as no surprise that he did not adopt Calvin's Strasbourg liturgy even for the sake of uniformity, considering Calvin was well known for his outstanding scholarship. It is an example of Knox's independent spirit and sense of freedom. This action could only highlight the already serious divisions and lack of unity of continental Protestantism. Luther, Zwingli, Calvin and now Knox were driving the liturgical functions of the Church in all different directions. The *Book of Common Order* also known by the common title "Knox's Liturgy" embraced a far simpler version of the liturgy and it went a long way towards satisfying some of the English exiles. This work of Knox minimised the liturgies of the English Prayer Book and the Strasbourg liturgy of Calvin, the process excluding various component parts. Knox's liturgy became the real rival to the *Book of Common Prayer* in Scotland. From this perspective it is understandable that Lloyd-Jones makes the claim that Knox was the founder of Puritanism. Although this claim could be challenged, it is nevertheless true to say that he was the outstanding leader of the Puritan cause in Scotland. And his influence went well beyond the shores of his native land.

Such was Knox's influence even in liturgical matters that it is claimed that Knox was largely responsible for the insertion of the *Black Rubric* into the 1552 *Book of Common Prayer*[12] such was his commitment towards a Puritan liturgy which overcame many of the objections to the 1552 Prayer Book.

By 1560 the year that the Scottish Parliament made the celebration of the Mass a criminal offence, the English *Book of Common Prayer* was still in use in many parish Churches. J.M. Ross claims that although the *Prayer Book* is not followed in every detail they continued to use it because Knox's Book of Common Order was not available.[13] It is worth noting that before Knox arrived back in Scotland the Earls of Argyll, Glencairn, Morton, Archibald Lord of Lorne and John Erskine of Dunn, and others, had in 1557 promised "before the Majesty of God, and his congregation, that we shall with all diligence continually apply our whole power, substance, and our very lives, to maintain, set forward, and establish the most blessed word of God and his congregation; and shall labour at our possibility to have faithful Ministers purely and truly to minister Christ's Evangel and Sacraments to his people.[14] To that end by 1558 this Band, the Lords and Barons who professed Christ met frequently in council deciding that: (1) "all parishes of this realm the Common Prayers, ie the 1552 English Prayer Book, be read weekly on Sunday, and other festival days, publickly in the parish kirks, with Lessons of the New and Old Testaments, conform to the order of the *Book of Common Prayers*". (2) "It is thought necessary, that doctrine, preaching, and interpretation of Scriptures be had and used privately in quiet houses, without great conventions of the people thereto, while afterward that God move the Prince to grant publick preaching by faithful and true ministers."[15]

In the light of these developments it is argued that the way was being prepared by important people for the ministry of Knox. They saw it necessary to have a liturgy which would encourage the people in the doctrine and worship of the Reformation. The Scottish ministers had the freedom and flexibility to use the Prayer book as they saw fit. That is, they were at liberty to minimise the content of the Prayer Book if they so desired.

By 1562 Knox's work was sufficiently known for the General Assembly to approve the *Book of Common Order* for the celebration of the Sacraments, and two years later for the use of Common Prayers. For the next eighty years successive editions were printed and it became the official service book of the Church of Scotland. The *Book of Common Order* reveals the extent to which Knox was influenced by the theology of John Calvin and the ideas of the English Exiles on the Continent who were influenced by Zwingli. Knox was thorough in his reform. It was essentially a root and branch attitude towards reform. The work is very different from that of the English *Prayer Book* and the work of Calvin in Strasbourg. Knox was now the liturgical radical. He removed everything that was in any way associated with Catholicism, or anything which did not have its justification in the New Testament. The liturgy was now reduced to the barest necessities, without the lectionary guide. In other words it was a leap forward in the process of minimisation. In this practical respect of liturgical reform Knox was more influenced by Zwingli, as both reduced or minimised the liturgy to the barest minimum.

Gordon Donaldson however notes that the Knox's liturgy was not a fixed liturgy, but it was not a mere directory either as the instruction to ministers sometime runs, "the minister prayeth in these words or like in effect". Elsewhere there seems to be no possibility of deviation.[16] Donaldson in his larger work, notes that some set forms were retained, namely, The Lord's Prayer, the Apostles Creed and the Doxology (to be sung after the Psalms). In later editions of the Book there were appended metrical versions of the Veni Creator, the Creed, the Ten Commandments, the Lord's Prayer, the Nunc Dimittis and the Magnificat each with its tune.[17] These appendages recognise that these items may have a claim to be part of historical liturgies, but are to be optional for the ministers of the Word. All congregational responses are also removed as they were in Zwingli's format. It may be concluded that this has a direct relation to his time on the Continent and the influence of the radicals in Frankfurt. The Service conducted was very much at the discretion of the minister, so long as he followed the bare basics. Future generations of Scots continued to embrace the liberty of freedom of choice but reserved the right to continue the process of minimisation. Eventually for some, the Lord's Prayer and the Creed, along with the kneeling posture for prayer, were all removed. The saying is true that you cannot satisfy all, only some.

The Early impact of the Book of Common Order on the Scots

George Sprott and Thomas Lushman in their notes and introduction to the Book of Common Order supply two descriptions which show a continuing minimisation process; one from Calderwood in 1623 and one from Alexander Henderson twenty years after, about the way Holy Communion was celebrated. It is worthwhile quoting Calderwood at length:

> Among us, the Minister, when the sermon is finished, reads the words of institution, gives a short exhortation and admonition, then blesses. The blessing or thanksgiving ended, he says, "Our Lord, on that night on which He was betrayed, took bread, and gave thanks, as we have already done, and break, as I also now break, and gave to His Disciples, saying(then he hands it to those nearest on the right and the left), This is my body," etc. He

adds nothing to the words of Christ, changes nothing, omits nothing. Then those next break a particle off the larger fragment or part, and hand what is left to those sitting nearest, so long as there is any portion of the fragment over. Then those who serve the tables, when one fragment is done, offer the paten, from which another in like manner takes a similar larger fragment or . . . . And breaking, hands to the next, and so on. In like manner the Minister delivers the cup to those nearest, repeating the words of Christ, without addition, mixture, change, or omission, and they hand it to those sitting beside them; and when the wine is done, those who serve fill it anew. As soon as he has delivered both elements to those sitting nearest to him, using only the words of Christ, whilst they distribute among themselves the bread and the cup, the Minister, as the action of eating and drinking lasts, addresses those at the table . . . Whilst they are rising from the table, and others are taking their place, the Minister is silent, and those leaving and those approaching the table, together with the whole Congregation, either sing, or the Reader reads the history of the Passion. But when the Minister is speaking, and when the communicants hand to one another the elements neither is the history of the Passion read nor Psalms sung, as it is not expedient . . . If the whole communicants could sit at the one time at the tables, it would be more agreeable and advantageous, as they could thus all together eat, drink, meditate, sing, and hear the Minister's address. . . . In this form our Church has now for sixty years celebrated the Holy Supper.[18]

Twenty years later, Alexander Henderson's description of the Holy Communion order of service is somewhat different:

After the sermon, immediately the Pastor useth an exhortation, and debarreth from the table all ignorant, profane, and scandalous persons . . . (then going to the table) he first readeth and shortly expoundeth the words of institution; . . . next he useth a prayer wherein he giveth thanks . . . and prayeth earnestly to God for His powerful presence, and effectual working to accompany His own ordinance . . . The elements thus being sanctified by the Word and prayer, the minister sacramentally breaketh the bread, taketh and eateth himself, and delivereth to the people . . . saying *Take ye eat ye; this is the Body of the Lord, which is broken for you: Do it in remembrance of Him.* After all at the table have taken and eaten, the minister taketh the cup, drinking first himself, he giveth it to the nearest, saying, *This cup, & etc* . . . The Minister, . . . after the giving of the elements, doth either by his own speech stir up the communicants to spiritual meditations, . . . or causeth be read the history of the Passion . . . After all at the table have received the cup, they rise from the table . . . (and) another company cometh, . . . during which time of removing . . . the whole congregation singeth some part of a Psalm, as Ps. 22 or 103. After the last company hath received, the Minister . . . goeth to the pulpit, where after a short speech, tending to thanksgiving, he doth again solemnly give thanks to God, . . . The prayer ended, all join in singing a Psalm of praise, suitable to the occasion, and are dismissed with the blessing, before which none are to depart unless in case of necessity.[19]

When one places Calderwood's and Henderson's versions beside Knox's Book of Common Order, the minimisation process is clearly seen in the differences. By placing the liturgies of Calvin, Knox, Calderwood and Henderson side by side the minimisation process can be seen (see Table 4.1).

From these tables it can be clearly seen how minimisation affected the liturgy from Calvin to Henderson. Knox minimised Calvin by excluding the following:

The opening Scripture Sentence from Psalm 124:8
Words of Pardon
Absolution
The Sung Decalogue with the
Kyrie Eleison
The Lection (this may be unintentional as a lection may have been included in the sermon)
The Lord's Prayer
Post Communion Collect
The Nunc Dimittis
Aaronic Blessing

Most of the congregational responses in the English *Book of Common Prayer* are also missing. The liturgies that are reported by Calderwood and Henderson show not only the further minimisation of Knox's liturgy but also a freedom to modify the practice of the liturgy. In the case of both Calderwood and Henderson in their formulations, all the liturgical items after the Sermon to the Institution in Knox's version have been removed, i.e. Prayers of Intercession for the Church, the Creed, the Singing of Psalm and Prayers. Both Calderwood and Henderson retain Knox's Institution and Exhortation and Prayers of Thanksgiving, except that in Henderson's version the Prayers of Thanksgiving include a prayer for the "powerful Presence of the Lord". This latter inclusion sounds very much like a substitute for the Epiclesis.

The Fraction and Delivery (distribution) is the same for Knox and Calderwood, but in Henderson, the Minister partakes before the people. The distribution of the Elements is accompanied by the formulae: "Take ye eat ye this is the Body of Christ", "This Cup is the New Testament in the Blood of Christ".

Henderson then takes the liberty of including a short message after the Distribution and the reading of the Passion.

Calderwood on the other hand was anxious to preserve a minimalist perspective when at the Fraction and Distribution, Sprott and Leishman note that he adds nothing to the words of Christ, changes nothing, and omits nothing, thus suggesting an extreme application of the Regulatory Principle which ensures that nothing is admitted to the liturgy without direct biblical sanction.

Table 4.1.

Calvin, Strasbourg 1540	Knox 1564
Scripture Sentence Ps.124:8	
Prayers of Confession	Prayers of Confession
Words of Pardon	Singing of Psalm
Absolution	
Metrical Decalogue sung with Kyrie Eleison	
Collect for Illumination	Prayer for Holy Spirit
Lection	
Sermon	Sermon
Collection	
Prayers of Intercession	Prayers of Intercession
Lord's Prayer	
Preparation of Elements	
Apostles Creed, sung	Apostles Creed
Consecration Prayer	Singing of Psalm
Lord's Prayer	Benediction (if service concludes)
Institution	Prayers
Exhortation	Institution
Fraction/ Delivery	Exhortation
Communion during singing of Psalm	Prayers of Thanksgiving
Post Communion Collect	Fraction / Delivery
Nunc Dimittis	Prayer of Thanksgiving
Aaronic Blessing	Singing of Psalm 103
Calderwood	*Henderson*
Sermon	Sermon
	Exhortation and debarring
Institution	Institution
Exhortation	
Blessing or Thanksgiving	Prayers of Thanksgiving
Fraction/Delivery	Fraction — minister partakes
	Delivery with formulae "Take ye, eat ye..."
Singing or Story of Passion Read	Reading of the Passion
	Short Message
	Prayers of Thanksgiving
	Singing of Psalm

The idea of minimisation and flexibility is clearly evident and should not come as any surprise as Knox's liturgy in Scotland was never a fixed liturgy.

THE WESTMINSTER DIRECTORY OF PUBLIC WORSHIP

The next step in liturgical minimisation was even more radical. In 1645 the Scottish Parliament and the General Assembly approved the "Westminster Directory of Publick Worship".[20] This was a monumental shift in the official minimised liturgical practice. The Scottish Commissioners to the Westminster Assembly were advocates of minimisation as they regarded the prescribed prayers, set forms and ceremonies of the English Prayer Book as an offence.[21] In contrast to the Book of Common Prayer,

Donaldson says that the structure of the service at best would be as follows:

Summons to Worship
Prayer of Approach
Readings and Psalm
Prayer of Confession Sermon Great Intercession (Including the Lord's Prayer)
Blessing (if the service concludes at this point)
Elements of Holy Communion brought in
Exhortation
Words of Institution
Prayer of Consecration (including a form of an Epiclesis)
Fraction and Distribution
Post-Communion Prayer

The common features of the Directory of Public Worship and Knox's liturgy were reflected in the barest simplicities but also the liturgical responses for the congregation disappeared with the exception of the Lord's Prayer in some instances. Although the Directory adheres to the barest simplicities the more radical feature was that the Directory does not contain (as did Knox's *Book of Common Order*) any recommended prayers. The Directory brought the Scots closer to the English Puritan ideal.

Donaldson comments that the Scots were under some pressure to conform to the ways of the English Puritans and that the interpretation put on the Directory, despite the Assemblies qualification (that the Directory was to be no prejudice to the order and practice of the Kirk, in such particulars as are appointed by the Books of Discipline and Acts of the General Assembly), was that what it did not expressly sanction was forbidden. Thus the use in public worship of the Doxology, the Creed, the Ten Commandments, were laid aside. The practice of kneeling in worship also disappeared as it was thought to be too ostentatious. This narrow interpretation of the Directory meant that there was a greater emphasis on preaching. Donaldson notes that the public reading of Scripture gave way to "lecturing" or "Exposition" which amounted to an additional sermon and at Holy Communion there were additional "table addresses".[22]

Due to the nature of the Directory and the sense of freedom and liberty on the part of the Scots, there was little consistency in worship practice in the land.

Sprott and Leishman in their commentary on the Directory argue that there is a close relationship between the Scots and English Puritans. That means that the Directory expresses moderate Puritan views in respect to worship. The Scottish ideal, it is argued, is made explicit, popular without being democratic, national without being a department of the State, catholic without dependence on foreign Churches for its life.

The Scots upheld the idea of a federal character of the Christian Church, wherein there is freedom and flexibility in worship practice. By contrast an Independent Church could only recognise the confines of its own worshipping community whereas a State Church religious unity can only be in terms of decrees of civil courts rather than that of Church Councils.

Setting the Book of Common Order beside the Directory, it becomes evident that the directory is a minimised version of the Book of Common Order (see Table 4.2).

Sprott and Leishman conclude that the Directory was less comprehensive in its range than many other works of the same kind. In the Directory there is at least one Psalm excluded but the real minimisation occurs with the exclusion of the Creed. However, the political and ecclesiastical gains achieved by the Scots came to an abrupt end in 1661 when the Scottish Parliament passed

Table 4.2.

Book of Common Order	Directory
Prayer	Prayer
Scripture from both Testaments	Scripture from both Testaments
Psalm	Psalm
Prayer	Prayer
Psalm (morning only)	
Prayer(morning only)	
Sermon	Sermon
Prayer	Prayer
Lord's Prayer	Lord's Prayer
Creed	
Psalm	Psalm
Benediction	Benediction

the Rescissory Act which repealed all legislation enacted since 1633. The effect was to overthrow Presbyterianism and restore Episcopacy. That meant that the Directory which encapsulated the liturgical minimisation process was officially removed from the Scottish Church. However, in another dramatic turn of events at the Restoration, the Scottish Parliament offered the throne to William and Mary accompanied by the offer of a "Claim of Right" which went further than the 1689 Bill of Rights in England. The feature of this was the Crown would give up controlling the Church of Scotland through Bishops and would recognise Scotland as fully Presbyterian. This William accepted.

Since the Restoration the Directory has never been acknowledged by the civil authority. However there have been a number of statutes passed by the General Assembly which in effect restored the basics of the Directory. In practice there was simply a revival of Knox's liturgy in so far as the Book of Common Order was used as a Directory rather than a liturgy.[23] This was more preferable than trying to impose a fixed liturgy. The relevant statutes are as follows:

- 1694 Sess.9. Act. anent Lecturing , — the Assembly of the National Church commends to the several Presbyteries that, they endeavour that the ministers . . . in the exercise of lecturing, read and open up to the people some large and considerable portion of the Word of god: and this to the effect the old custom introduced and established by the Directory may by degrees be recovered.
- 1705. Sess. 12. The General Assembly of the National Church recommends, that all ministers and others within this National Church the due observation of the Directory for the Public Worship of God, approved by the General Assembly held in the year 1645, sess. 10.
- 1736. Sess. 8. The General Assembly recommends to all ministers and preachers to "seriously consider and observe the Directory of this Church, concerning the preaching of the Word".
- 1856 Sess. Ult. The General Assembly approved the overture which says, "Whereas it has always been the desire of the Church of Scotland, that in every part of its bounds the people should, as far as practicable, enjoy in an equal degree the benefits of public instruction and the administration of Divine ordinances, . . . that a Recommendation or Declaratory Act shall be issued for the purpose of reminding all who labour in word and doctrine that every congregation, at each diet of public worship, should have access to the advantage of hearing a portion of the Old and New Testament read, — that there should always be included in the service of every Lord's Day, not only a sermon, but a lecture on a passage of the Holy Scriptures."[24]

These *Acts* of the General Assembly not only impose but they legitimised the liturgical minimisation process. In each of the quoted Statutes there is specific recommendation to observe the Directory and the importance of preaching and lecturing. The Statute of 1856 is of special importance as it recommends that on a Sunday worship service there is, not only a sermon, but a lecture on a passage of Scripture. Through the lapse of time, from 1562 when the General Assembly first approved the *Book of Common Order*, composed by Knox, to 1856 with the introduction of the Declaratory Act, a period of two hundred and ninety-four years, the minimisation of the liturgy had become the tradition, and deeply ingrained into the Scottish psyche. Despite the fact that the National Church adhered to a Calvinist theology this doctrinal orientation was not followed through with Calvin's liturgy. Moreover in the same two hundred and ninety four years, the primacy of preaching/lecturing was legislated for by the General Assembly, but to the exclusion of the frequency of the Sacrament. By contrast, Calvin considered the sacrament of Holy Communion was a necessary part of a service of worship as the sacrament was reckoned to be the word in action.

By the 1803 the Principal of St Andrew's University, the Rev. Dr George Hill, was able to say to his students:

> The Church of Scotland, in adopting a Directory instead of a Liturgy, considers its men of understanding, of taste, and of sentiment, capable of thinking for themselves, who without being confined to the repetition of a lesson that has been composed for them may be permitted to exercise their talents, with a becoming independence upon Divine aid, in the sacred and important office of leading the devotions of Christian worshippers.[25]

These sentiments, however, fail to recognise that all ministers are not as theologically capable as those who are especially gifted with a sharp intellect and literary skills. Not all have the theological consistency to compose prayers and sermons every week consistent with the Westminster standards. Besides, the Directory is unable to provide a meaningful liturgy for a long pastoral vacancy. The laity may well lead a minimised service of worship but there can be no guarantee that the prayers or sermon /lecturing would have any theological consistency. The advantage of the English Book of Common Prayer is that it is able to provide prayers and readings for the laity, in a rubric that is meaningful and consistent.

The Puritan Scots did not have it all their own way. Although the Church of Scotland became the National Church and Presbyterian, the Scottish Parliament was forced to recognise the English liturgical tradition as the English Parliament passed the 1712 Toleration Act, which basically recognised two Churches in Scotland.

The importance of the Scottish minimisation process to Australian Presbyterianism lay in the fact that all the early ministers that came to Australia in the nineteenth century were mainly Scots who came from the various Presbyterian groups in Scotland. That is to say all the minimised liturgical practices of Scottish Presbyterianism were planted in Australia.

THE LITURGICAL TRANSPLANT ON AUSTRALIAN SOIL

Up to 1865, fifty three ministers arrived in Australia from Scotland, many of them recruited by the Rev. John Dunmore Lang. Of these: 30 came from the Church of Scotland; 20 came from the Free Church of Scotland; 2 came from the United Presbyterian Church and 1 came from an independent Church.[26]

In other words in the formative years of Presbyterianism in Australia every minister bar one, up to 1865 came from Scottish Presbyterian denomination that had minimised the liturgy and had been influenced by the various statutes of the Church of Scotland in accepting the Directory of public Worship.

It can be shown that the early Scottish ministers in Australia not only implemented the practice of minimised worship but the practice became entrenched. By 1891 the Federal Assembly of the Presbyterian Church in Australia[27] met in Brisbane and it received a report from a committee under the convenor-ship of the Rev. Dr. Robert Steel M.A., Ph.D. on the revised "Directory for public Worship". The Assembly approved the following deliverance unanimously: "The Federal Assembly approve generally of the draft of the Revised Directory for the Public Worship of God, as submitted by the convenor: thank the committee for their labours and resolve that it be recommended for the adoption by ministers of the Church as far as possible".

The Assembly also formed a committee made up by Rev. Dr Robert Steel, Rev. Dr. James Nish and the Rev. James S. Lang, to be authorised to produce and publish the Directory in book form. The passing of this resolution unanimously implied that the substance of the Directory was already being practised, and was readily accepted. The minimised practice of worship in Scotland had been successfully transplanted into Australia and had become entrenched in Australian Presbyterian life.

The detail of the Directory is as follows: It is recommended that the order of Divine Service in the Public Worship of God should be uniformly observed by all the congregations of the Church according to the following arrangement:

1. Introductory, Praise of God
2. Brief prayer of Invocation
3. Reading a Lesson or portion of Scripture from the Old Testament
4. Prayer of Confession, Petition and Thanksgiving
5. Praise

6. Reading a lesson from the New Testament
7. Prayer of Intercession for all conditions of men, and the Church of Christ, with the Lord's Prayer before or after.
8. Praise
9. Sermon or Lecture.
10. Praise
11. Prayer
12. Praise
13. Benediction

Public intimations may most conveniently be made before the Sermon, or at such other time as may be arranged by the minister. Collections may also be taken at the doors of the Church.

This arrangement may, at the discretion of the minister, be abridged in special circumstances, or slightly changed in the parts of Prayer and Praise.[28]

Comparing this Directory with those already mentioned, a number of things can be noted: The freedom of the minister is preserved, the Directory is "recommended" and the minister has the discretion to change the order if necessary. This Directory as with the ones in use in Scotland in the nineteenth century is at pains to preserve the simplicity and bare essentials of worship without a set liturgy. It is also worth noting that the Lord's Prayer is included. The Sermon is associated with lecturing which indicates the high priority of preaching as a medium of instruction and encouragement.

The Service of Holy Communion is not part of the regular Sunday service. The Scottish practice of infrequent celebration of the Sacrament has also found its way into the Australian Church. The Directory for Holy Communion is found separately in chapter nine.

The format for Holy Communion is as follows after the Sermon:

Sermon

Exhortation: The minister warns the profane, the ignorant and scandalous and those that secretly indulge in any known sin, not to approach the Holy Table.

Hymn during which the communicants take their places

Reading of the Institution 1Corth. 11: 23–27

Fraction of Bread with a prayer of the Holy Spirit to sanctify and bless the elements of Bread and Wine (a form of Epiclesis)

Creed (the minister recites)

Distribution of Bread with the words, "Take eat, this is my Body broken for you. Do this in remembrance of me".

Cup, with the words, "This cup is the New Testament in my blood, shed for many for the remission of sins".

The Elders distribute the elements to the communicants in an orderly manner.
Brief Address
Hymn
Benediction (This is not specifically stated but is assumed as there is a Benediction at the conclusion of the weekly service format.)[29]

This Directory appears to be modelled after Alexander Henderson's format which has already been mentioned. It is fundamentally the same except for the inclusion of a hymn and the minister reciting the Creed. After the Sermon, the Directory follows the same format. The specific items are: The Exhortation to the profane, ignorant and the scandalous; Immediately before or during the Fraction, there is the prayer for the Holy Spirit. This is another way of expressing Henderson's Prayer for the "powerful presence of the Lord". The brief address after the distribution, also follows the Henderson format.

It can only be concluded that this Australian version of the Directory has its foundation in the extreme Puritan model of the sixteenth century. That is to say that the process of liturgical minimisation found its way, with acceptance, into the Australian Church. It also reinforces the powerful Scottish connection and influence.

THE PHILOSOPHICAL BASIS OF MINIMISATION

The life of the Church in the medieval period was dominated by the ecclesial hierarchy, and the authority of the Church was exercised on the whole of society, as the accumulated dogma gave expression, that the Church was the receptor of all truth. The rise and influence of Francis Bacon came at a time when the Protestant reformers were challenging the Aristotelian premises of Roman dogma. The Puritans were demanding liturgical and ecclesiastical change at a time when there was a serious challenge to the accepted philosophical paradigms upon which theology and science functioned. Throughout the medieval period the underlying philosophy was that of Aristotle and Plato and it was thought that nature was impregnated with ultimate causes, so that an eternal pattern could be read off the face of nature, (in effect substituting nature for God which gave rise to natural theology). Apart from that understanding of the eternal pattern, real knowledge of nature was not possible.[30]

T.F. Torrance quotes John Baillie who says, "to interpret nature in the light of final and primary causes left little room for the element of real contingency in nature, to the recognition of which modern experimental science owes its existence".[31] This philosophy permeated medieval science and theology. It was held that there was an intrinsic relation of Grace between the being and existence of the Church and the nature of the truth of revelation once and for all deposited in the apostolic foundations of the Church. Since the Church is full of Grace it is held to represent in its forms and dogmas the objectification of the truth, in its institutional and rational structures, that is in the ordinances, decrees and dogmatic definitions promulgated in the Church.[32] Theology was therefore at a standstill, unable to move, because of the impregnation of ultimate and primary causes arising from Plato and Aristotle.

It has been noted by Laura in a study of educational ideology that indoctrination (which in this instance also applies to medieval theology) is "tantamount to a paralysis of intellectual imagination. The mind becomes closed on those issues which are fundamentally open and the inability to imagine things as they are not imprisons the human being in the world of things as they are".[33]

Laura's view is also reinforced in Torrance who declares that, "the questions which medieval thinkers asked were so philosophically controlled from behind that they were not properly free and open, nor were they put in the mode and idiom of a rationality that was congruent with real contingency".[34]

This philosophical paradigm gave way to a new paradigm which had far-reaching effects for the sciences as well as theology. At the most critical time in Reformational history there arose four outstanding thinkers who were to change the philosophical landscape for ever. They were Galileo Galilei, Francis Bacon, Rene Descartes and Isaac Newton. The eventual impact of these philosophical landscapers was such that a full-blown reductio mechanical paradigm became the accepted model for epistemology. It was thought that only that which could be weighed or measured belonged to the realm of genuine knowledge.

Francis Bacon 1561–1626 argued in his Novum Organum (1620) that "power over nature" would never be realised through the definitions of knowledge held by Aristotle and Plato. The wisdom of the Greeks, "abound in words but are barren of works .For fruits and works are as it were sponsors and sureties for the truth of philosophers".[35] Laura interprets Bacon in terms of a new paradigm that fosters the view that nature exists as an object of investigation and exploitation as something to be subdued, subjugated and conquered.[36] For Bacon the objectivity of science is secured by the distinction between the observer and the observed. J. Rivkin explains this more fully:

The new method Bacon alludes to is the scientific method, an approach that could separate the observer from the observed and provide a neutral forum for the development of "objective knowledge". According to Bacon, objective knowledge would allow people to take "command over things natural . . . "Every school child is weaned on Bacon's method. From the time we are able to form conception, we are informed that there is in fact an objective world out there whose secrets can be discovered and exploited to advance human ends. We are encouraged to create distance between ourselves and the world, to detach ourselves so that we can sever our natural relationships with things and turn them into objects for manipulation. The scientific method reflects our consuming passion for predictability and order. We have transformed all of physical reality into a giant testing site and then attempted to discover predictable patterns of behaviour that can be exploited over and over in such a way as to advance our control over the forces of nature. The more successful we are at imperializing our environment, the more secure we feel. The long history of Western consciousness, which reached its zenith with the flowering of the Baconian revolution, can be summarized as follows: Knowledge is power, power is control, control is security".[37]

This scientific methodology freed up theology to progress without the philosophical baggage of Aristotle and Plato. The ensuing inductionist methodology instead of being applied to nature was applied to the Holy Scriptures. Biblical and theological scholarship immediately had a new lease of life as the Scriptures were dismantled, examined and analysed to produce works that were to be influential in the Reformed theological world for the next several hundred years. John Owen, the Dean of Christ Church Oxford and Vice Chancellor of Oxford University is a case in point, as he produced a sixteen volume work covering the important aspects of Reformed theology, and a seven volume commentary on the Epistle to the Hebrews. The success of the new Baconian methodology in theological disciplines was such that some one hundred and fifty years later the famous Edinburgh scholar Dr Thomas Chalmers was able to declare his dependence on the Baconian approach to Biblical and Theological scholarship: "Butler is the Bacon of Theology; and certain it is, that as the one, in the construction of his Novum Organum, which points out the right way of philosophizing".[38] Referring to Owen's commentary on the Epistle to the Hebrews, Chalmers said to his students, "Let me again recommend your studious and sustained attention to the Epistle to the Hebrews and I should rejoice if any of you felt beholden on my advice to grapple with a work so ponderous as Owen's commentary I promise you a hundred fold more advantage from the perusal of this greatest work of John Owen, than from the perusal of all that has been written on the subject of the heathen sacrifices. It is a work of gigantic strength as well as gigantic size."[39]

The revolutionary ideas of Bacon eventually filtered through to the educational institutions in which many of the Puritans and their sympathisers had an influence.

P. R. May notes that the seventeenth century Puritan pastors had an important part to play in educational theory, as Cranmer, Latimer and Bacon and other Reformers were actually involved in the teaching of children and students. The most prolific Puritan writer on education was the well-known moderate Puritan, Richard Baxter 1615–1691. Baxter was a prominent member of the Puritan movement, excluding the extremist minority, which formed the backbone of English life for most of the seventeenth century. Their main task says May was twofold: "to teach a full knowledge of the Bible, their supreme authority in all matters of faith and conduct and to apply Scriptural teaching to life".[40] Instruction in most schools and Universities, says May, remained rigidly traditional as did the curriculum in which Latin and Greek grammar, speech and composition predominated in the Grammar Schools while scholasticism, disputation and classical study continued at Oxford and Cambridge. Baconians like Hartlib and John Hall, collaborators of Comenius, attacked the curriculum of the Universities by making a plea for less abstract teaching, and a greater use of models, maps and experiments.

R. Hooykaas, quotes John Hall's address to Parliament in 1649 entitled "The Advancement of Learning", which itself shows the influence of Francis Bacon, and he makes a plea to parliament to reform university education. His main complaint is the Universities' humanistic one-sidedness:

> I have ever expected from a University, that though all men cannot learn all things, yet they should be able to teach all things to all men, and be able either to attract knowing men from abroad out of their own wealth, or at least be able to make exchange. But how far short come we of this, though I acknowledge some differences between our Universities? . . . Where have we anything to do with chemistry, which hath snatched the keys of nature from the other sects of Philosophy, by her multiplied experiences. Where have we constant reading upon either quick or dead *Anatomies*, or ocular demonstration of herbs? Where any manual demonstrations of Mathematical Theorems or Instruments?[41]

Baxter provides a book list which provides the makeup of a personal library. The list discloses his sympathy to the new philosophy of Bacon. Some of the recommended works are: Books by Comenius, Lord Bacon, Mr Boyle, Samuel Gott, Dr Wallis and Isaac Barrow. In his approach to educational practices of the day, he preferred to be positive, to examine, in the Baconian spirit of the day, educational principles and methods in question.[42]

Adopting the revolutionary methodology of Bacon, the Puritan movement empowered the Reformational process in the English Church. The authority and inspiration of the Holy Scriptures was of critical importance as it replaced the authority and dominion of the prelates of the medieval Church. The Scriptures in the hands of the Puritans were to be all authoritative in matters of faith and practice. The ideal of Richard Baxter in this regard was representative of the puritan movement.

It was the application of the authority and sufficiency of the Scriptures that lay at the heart of the prolonged and passionate debate over worship. On one side were the traditionalists within the Church of England and on the other side were the Puritans who advocated the minimisation of the liturgy.

James Packer, a specialist in Puritan theology, is helpful in this debate as he sees little point in resurrecting all the details of the prolonged emotional debate, as it is better to acknowledge that both sides upheld the authority of the Bible, as most of the reformers accepted the theology of John Calvin. For Packer the central issue in the debate lay in the question, "In what sense are the Scriptures authoritative for Christian worship?"[43] Initially Luther and Calvin differed in their judgements on this question. For Luther the ordering of public worship was to allow traditional things that could be helpful but were not contrary to Scripture. Calvin judgement was that nothing should be admitted into the worship that was not specifically prescribed by Scripture. The Church of England followed Luther's judgement whereas the Puritans followed Calvin. It was therefore a matter of logic that the Puritans accused the Church of England of having no regard for Holy Scripture as the constitutive and authoritative rule for worship. Packer argues that much of the debate was in fact misleading, as both parties upheld the authority and sufficiency of the Scripture in all matters of personal and Church life. Packer shows that they were all agreed on so many of the important issues that he argues that the real issue was "the interpretation and content of Holy Scripture, rather than the formal principle of the nature and extent of its authority". It is difficult to better the argument as it is explained by Packer:

> German, Swiss and English Reformers held common basic principles about worship. They agreed that Christian worship must express man's reception of, and response to, evangelical truth, and they were substantially in agreement as to what that truth was. They agreed in analysing worship as an exercise of mind and heart in praise, thanksgiving, prayer, confession of sin, trust in God's promises and the hearing of God's word, read and preached. They were in agreement also to the nature and number of the Gospel sacraments, and their place in the Church's worship. They took the same view of the office of the Christian minister in the leading the worship of the congregation. They agreed too that each Church . . . is responsible for settling the details of its own worship in accordance with the apostolic principle that all must be done "unto edifying" (1Corth.14:26) and that as a means to that end everything must be done decently and in order. Finally, they were all agreed that each Church has liberty to arrange its worship in the way best adapted to edify its own worshippers . . . The only real differences regarding worship between any of the first generation of Reformers were differences of personal judgement as to what would edify and what would not—differences of the kind reflected in Calvin's judgement that the second Edwardian *Prayer Book* of 1552 contained *multas tolerabiles ineptias* (many bearable pieces of foolishness), or in the troubles at Frankfurt in 1554, when the "Coxian" group of exiles adhered to the 1552 *Prayer Book* as being sufficiently sound and edifying, while the "Knoxians" felt obliged to abandon it in favour of an alternative order drawn up on the Geneva pattern".[44]

Packer therefore concludes that "Biblical warrant, in the form of precept or precedent, required to sanction every substantive item included in public worship of God was in fact a Puritan innovation, which crystallised out in the course of the prolonged debates that followed the Elizabethan settlement".

The liturgical minimisation process was therefore a question of agreement as to how the principle of the authority and sufficiency of Holy Scripture should be applied. Once the personal judgement of Calvin was accepted as truth, and the implication that the judgement was biblical truth rather than the formal principle of the nature and extent of Biblical authority, the Puritans were able to proceed with the idea of minimisation. The underlying philosophy of minimisation can be seen within the context of the Baconian revolution, but the actual process depended on a personal judgement and the application of the principle of deduction. That is akin to the theological method of the medieval period wherein the expression of a Thomist theological view, based on Aristotelian precepts, was accepted as divinely appointed truth. In the context of the protestant reformation, particularly in England, a medieval deductive ghost pervaded the thought of Puritan notions of worship.

The Puritan minimisation process was an innovation which saw the removal of set prayers, kneeling, the Christian Year, weekly Communion, the practice of confirmation as well as the liturgical responses. The central issue was still nevertheless a question of how should the sufficiency of Scripture be understood in connection with worship. There can therefore be only three possible ways of conducting ordinary public worship, says Packer, there can only be a set Prayer Book or a Directory such as the Westminster Directory for the general guidance, or the worship is left in the hands of the individual minister.

In Scotland a similar set of circumstances existed when the General Assembly was debating matters of Subscription or Adherence to the Confession of Faith, raised by the Duchess of Sutherland and Countess of Cromartie and the Duke of Sutherland who set up a Petition to the General Assembly which asked the Assembly to "inviolably maintain the Westminster Confession of Faith as the doctrinal standard, and secondly to secure adherence to the simple forms of the Church, and preventing any change from being made in the same without competent authority".[45] This petition arose at a time when some issues within the Confession of Faith were being questioned by some high profile ministers, such as Principal Tulloch one of the Clerks of the Assembly. Principal Tulloch had said of the Confession of Faith, it was impossible to understand it without studying it in the light of its age –that it was not a broad catholic statement, calm, and large, and impersonal for all time, but a marked and characteristic product of a most marked, individual, and warlike age".

The real problem as the Rev. Dr Robert Lee saw it was that the Westminster Confession was being exalted to the same position as the Word of God.

Lee argued that this view was very common throughout Scotland. He points out that the Confession contains many issues that are not matters of faith. He mentions that the United Presbyterians, who were proposing to unite with the Free Church, had already renounced the chapter on the Civil Magistrate. The unique relationship between Church and State in Scotland insisted on adherence to the Confession, which was binding in government statute. But says Lee, the law, "only sanctions the general doctrine and does not give its sanction to every particular doctrine or position in that Confession". The petitioners' actions in the General Assembly were in effect trying to enforce the minimised liturgical practice of the Directory of Public Worship. They wanted the simple forms of the Church to have the same authority as the general doctrinal stance of the Confession. Had the Petition been successful, liturgical minimisation would have had the force of divine authority. Lee cogently argued that this Petition is not necessary as the State has written the Confession into law and ministers are bound by it. Lee asks the question "what do you require men to do now?" To elevate non-doctrinal matters to doctrinal status is to have serious consequences. In answer, Lee, says, "you require them to declare that Presbyterianism is not only true, but according to the Word of God".[46] The import of Lee's argument for the purposes of this book is that minimization cannot be regarded in the same way as the essential doctrinal content of the Confession. It may be related to, but it is not the same; it is a device of man not a theological presupposition. In the next chapter, the relevancy of Dr Robert Lee's argument in the contemporary Presbyterian Church will be shown. At this point we would suggest that a subscriptionary attitude has once again overwhelmed the Church's liturgical practice.

LITURGICAL DEVELOPMENT SINCE 1901

In a somewhat strange twist of history, within just ten years, The Presbyterian Church of Australia was constituted on the 24th day of July 1901. In the constitution of this new Federated Church, the Directory drawn up by Dr Robert Steel is not included as a primary document, neither is it specifically mentioned. The basis of Union of the various state Presbyterian Churches, simply stated the Supreme Standard of the United Church shall be the "Word of God contained in the Scriptures of the Old and New Testaments". The Subordinate Standard shall be the "Westminster Confession of Faith" read in the light of the Declaratory Statement:

> That in regard to the doctrine of redemption as taught in the subordinate standard, and in consistency therewith, the love of God to all mankind, His gift of His Son to be the propitiation for the sins of the whole world, and the free offer of salvation to men without distinction on the ground of Christ's all-

sufficient sacrifice, are regarded by this Church as vital to the Christian Faith . . . .That liberty of opinion is allowed on matters in the subordinate standard not essential to the doctrine therein taught, the Church guarding against the abuse of this liberty to the injury of its unity and peace . . .[47]

To explain this extraordinary turn of events it is necessary to move on to the General Assembly of 1918. It was at this meeting that *A Book of Common Order*, as a guide to the orderly administration of the sacraments and other officers of the Church was approved.[48] The only reference to a Directory of Public Worship is the statement, "The Westminster Directory for the Public Worship of God may likewise be consulted".[49] This would seem to suggest that the Assembly was still desirous to preserve the liberty of opinion and freedom for ministers to conduct public worship as they please, by the use of the words, "a guide", and "consult". We would claim that in the intervening ten years there was the awareness that the liturgical minimisation inherited from the Scottish Church was indeed an extreme approach to worship. The approval in principle of the 1918 Book of Common Order offers a greater scope of historic worship in that there is the reappearance of the Lord's Prayer and the Apostles Creed in the service for Holy Communion and there are printed Prayers. The structure is still simple. The structure is as follows:

First part of service as in any other Sunday
Prayers, Praise, Readings in keeping with the occasion
Sermon
Hymn Para 35
Apostles Creed or the Beatitudes
Lord's Prayer
The Institution
Brief Address
Prayers of Thanksgiving
Distribution with the Formulae Bread: The Lord Jesus in the night in which He was betrayed took bread and when he had given thanks, he break it and said "This is my body which is broken for you, do this in remembrance of me".
Wine: In like manner also the cup after supper, saying, "This cup is the new covenant in my blood: this do, as oft as you drink it, in remembrance of me".
Prayers of Supplication
Offering
Hymn Ps 103: 1–5
Benediction

In 1920 the General Assembly resolved to call the publication "*The Book of Common Order*", and authorised its publication. The book contained much more than the Communion Service. The Assembly also approved other services complete with printed prayers for the following services:

Administration of the Sacrament of Baptism
Administration of the Sacrament of Baptism for Adults
The Admission of Catechumens
The Solemnization of Marriage
Visitation of the Sick
Burial of the Dead
Burial of a Child
Ordination and Induction of Elders
The Licensing of Candidates for the Ministry
The Dedication of Deaconesses
The laying of the Foundation Stone of a Church
Dedication of a Church
Dedication of Memorial Gifts

In 1930 the General Assembly received a report from the committee which oversaw the publication of the *Book of Common Order*. It expressed satisfaction with the results of the first edition. The Committee was directed to proceed with a second edition which was to incorporate an Order of Service for the dedication of Sunday School Teachers as suggested in the Report.[50] The Assembly also resolved to publish a book of Responsive Readings.[51]

The new approach to worship, although in simple format found its way into the Church's broadsheet journal, *The Messenger* which printed complete services including prayers and a sermon, to be used by laymen in vacant Churches. The Format was akin to the Directory Format:

Hymn
Lord's Prayer
Hymn
Bible Reading
Prayers of Thanksgiving and Intercession
Sermon
Hymn
Benediction

The publication of the new *Book of Common Order* marked the end of the minimisation process and the beginning of a revival of liturgical practice. This was to reach a zenith in 1954 when the General Assembly approved the publication of a new Book of Common Order which embraced the greater part of the liturgies developed and approved by the Church of Scotland. The Order for Holy Communion is complete with congregational responses, including *Sursum Corda*, and *Sanctus*, there was the inclusion of an *Epiclesis*, which denies the doctrine of transubstantiation but elevates the elements to express the wonder and unique presence of Christ within the sacrament that comes through personal faith: "send down Thy Holy Spirit to sanctify both us and these Thine Own gifts of bread and wine which we set before Thee, that the bread which we break may be the Communion of the body of Christ, and the cup of blessing which we bless the Communion of the Blood of Christ; that we receiving them, may by faith be made partakers of His Body and Blood, with all His benefits, to our nourishment and growth in grace".

Giving consideration to the liturgical minimisation process to the revival of liturgical practice in the Presbyterian Church, the words of Dr. James Moffatt are appropriate at this point:

> The reaction against liturgies (in Scotland) was partly due to an honourable but exaggerated devotion to freedom and spirit in worship, as though this was incompatible with the use of any forms of prayer, and partly to the fact that, as in the case of Scotland, the King sought to impose a new liturgy upon it, and thereby created a distaste for liturgies in general. It is a pity when minds work by reaction: in the Church, as individuals, it may sound strong, mainly because it goes readily into strong words, but it is a sign of weakness. Progress is not attained by recoiling as far as possible from what some other people hold, nor by discarding a practice incontinently either because it is being abused by contemporaries or because it has acquired some compromising associations. Unluckily, Presbyterians for a time parted with some precious elements in their heritage of worship, for reasons into which it is needless to enter here; and one of these was orderly liturgical prayer, which like good music acquired odium from its connexion with episcopacy. It was for a long time believed that spontaneous, unpremeditated prayer was more inspired than any carefully drawn up collect. Even the Lord's Prayer has been tabooed! These sad days are over . . . It is at least becoming more and more recognised that we are as free to use forms of prayer as to do without them in worship. As a result of this slow and difficult revival, there is now, at any rate in Scotland, a welcome variety and wealth of worship, from the simple, most impressive service of a small congregation, to the more elaborate worship in our cathedrals, abbeys and larger Churches.[52]

This liturgical change of direction which occurred in Scotland also occurred in New South Wales and was championed by the Rev Alan Dougan who became the denomination's liturgical leader. His influence has been dealt with in another chapter of this book.

This, however, was not the end of liturgical minimization. The Church Union movement which culminated in the formation of the Uniting Church in Australia in 1977 took place at the same time as a resurgence of Puritanism within the Presbyterian Church. It will be argued that it was the result of this movement that liturgical minimization once again was pursued and gained the ascendancy.

NOTES

1. Gordon Donaldson, *The Making of the Scottish Prayer Book of 1637* (Edinburgh: University Press 1954), 37.
2. Referred to by Y. Chung, *Consolidation and Revolution. Journal of Oxford University History Society*, 2005, 5.
3. See the text of the promises in W. Dickinson, *John Knox's History of the Reformation in Scotland* (London: Thomas Nelson, 1949), Vol. 1, 136–37.
4. Chung, *Consolidation and Revolution*.
5. Andrew Laing, *John Knox and the Reformation* (London: Longmans Green, 1905), 275–76.
6. Gordon Donaldson, in *Studies in the History of Worship in Scotland* (Edinburgh T&T Clark, 1996), 38–39.
7. An excellent summary is found in W. Stanford Reid, *The Trumpeter of God* (New York: Charles Scribner and Sons, 1974), 123–29.
8. D.M. Lloyd-Jones, *The Puritans* (Edinburgh: Banner of Truth, 1987), 242–43.
9. Dickinson, *Knox's History*, Vol. 1, xxxvi.
10. Dickinson, *Knox's History*.
11. Lloyd Jones, *The Puritans*, 267–69.
12. The Black Rubric is the name given to the declaration of kneeling printed at the end of the Holy Communion Service in the 1552 BCP. At the Elizabethan Settlement it was removed but was replaced in 1662 together with the words "real and essential" presence were altered to "corporal" presence, thereby indicating that its purpose was rather to guard against popular and debased medieval ideas of Eucharistic doctrine than to deny altogether Christ's presence in the sacrament.
13. J.M. Ross, *Four Centuries of Scottish Worship* (Edinburgh: St. Andrew Press, 1972), 1–4; Ross describes the details of what a worship service at the time was like.
14. Dickinson, *Knox's History*, Vol. 1, 136.
15. Dickinson, *Knox's History*, Vol. 1, 137–38.
16. D. Forrester and D. Murray, *Studies in the History of Worship in Scotland* (Edinburgh: T&T Clark, 1996), 40.
17. Donaldson, *Making of the Scottish*, 14–15.
18. G. Sprott and T. Lushman, *The Book of Common Order* (Edinburgh: William Blackwood & Sons, 1868), xxxlx–xl.
19. Sprott & Lushman, *Book of Common Order*, xl–xli.
20. The Westminster Assembly was called by the English Long Parliament to reform the English Church. The Assembly was made up of 151 nominated members. Among the diverse clergy were four distinct groups: Episcopalians, Presbyterians, Independents and Eurasians. Despite the Assemblies importance to Presbyterian history, the Assembly was in no sense a creation of Presbyterianism. It met from 1643 and was never formally dissolved.
21. Donaldson, in *Studies in the History of Worship in Scotland*, D. Forrester and D. Murray, eds (Edinburgh: T&T Clark, 1996), 59.
22. Donaldson, "Covenant to Revelation", in *Studies in the History of Worship*, Forrester and Murray, eds, 257.
23. Sprott and Leishman, *Book of Common Order*, 271–72.
24. Sprott and Leishman, *Book of Common Order*, 269.
25. George Hill, *Theological Institutes* (Edinburgh: Bell and Bradfute, 1803), 294.
26. The United Presbyterian Church was formed in 1847 by the union of two groups: The United Secession Church with the Relief Synod. In 1900 apart from a small minority the U.P. united with the Free Church of Scotland to form the United Free Church of Scotland.
27. The Federal Assembly existed from 1886–1901. It drew up a basis of Union upon which the State Churches could enter into a Federal Union and at the same time preserve their separate entities.
28. *Directory of Public Worship of God* (Sydney: Angus and Robertson, 1892)
29. Op.cit. 30–34.
30. T.F. Torrance, *Theological Science* (London: Oxford University Press, 1969), 60.

31. J. Baillie, *Natural Science and Spiritual Life* (London: Oxford University Press, 1951), 22.
32. Torrance, *Theological Science*, 78.
33. R. Laura, *Empathetic Education* (London: Falmer Press, 1999), 74.
34. Torrance, *Theological Science*, 61.
35. Francis Bacon, *The New Organon and Related Writings* (New York: Bobbs Merril, 1960), Aphorisms LXXI–LXXIII.
36. Laura, *Empathetic Education*, 105.
37. Laura, *Empathetic Education*, 105–106.
38. Thomas Chalmers, *Prelections on Butlers Analogy, Paley &Hill* (Edinburgh: Thomas Constable, 1849), Posthumous Works, Vol. IX, 489.
39. Chalmers, *Prelections on Butlers*, 282.
40. P.R. May, "Richard Baxter in Education", *British Journal of Education* 104, 1 (1967), 60–73.
41. R. Hooykaas, *Scientific Progress and Religious Dissent* (Milton Keynes: Open University Press, 1975), 21.
42. May, "Baxter in Education", 72.
43. J.I. Packer, *A Quest for Godliness* (Illinois: Crossways Books, 1990), 246.
44. Packer, *Quest for Holiness*, 246–47.
45. R.H. Story, *Life and Remains of Robert Lee D.D.* (London: Hurst and Blackett, 1870), Vol. II, 269.
46. Story, *Life and Remains*, 276.
47. For the full text of the Declaratory Statement see *Basic Documents on Presbyterian Polity* (Blackburn: Board of Christian Education and S.R. Laing and Co., 1961), 92.
48. *Minutes of the General Assembly of Australia*, Report, 83. Approval to submit the final draft, 54.
49. *Constitution Procedure and Practice* (Melbourne: Board of Religious Education, 1950), VIII.
50. Minutes of the General Assembly 1930 (*Blue Book*), 116.
51. *Blue Book*, 17.
52. J. Moffatt, *The Presbyterian Churches* (London: Methuen, 1928), 140.

Chapter Five

Minimization since 1977 in the Presbyterian Church of Australia

The objective of this chapter is to show that a radical form of liturgical minimisation in Australia took place after the formation of the Uniting Church in 1977.

To achieve this we shall examine in detail the extent of the changes that took place in the revision of the *Worship Book* that was authorised by the General Assembly of Australia in 1998. The revision was the work of a new "Public Worship and Aids Committee" elected by the Assembly in 1991. We shall argue that the minimisation process was so radical that it turned the Presbyterian Church of Australia into a non-symbolic and non-liturgical denomination. It is here that Dr. Lee's argument in the previous chapter is so relevant. The question that needs to be asked is whether the *Worship Book of 1998* is a subscriptionist's view of the Westminster Confession. The ramifications of this revision have been extensive, penetrating the political and theological outlook of the denomination. A brief introduction to the main task is required at this point.

In chapter three it was shown that the Rev. Principal Alan Dougan laboured for many years to inculcate a theology of worship that was true to the Church's historical and theological heritage. A large section of the ministry of the Church, however, did not take Dougan seriously, as his liturgical views were contrary to the freedoms offered in the "Directories of Public Worship". In the late nineteenth century the General Assembly of Australia had approved and published a *Directory of Public Worship* that was formulated by the Rev. Dr Robert Steel.

To break free from the herd mentality in liturgical matters is always a risky business. Dougan soon found that he was the object of ridicule, whereby his views were cast aside as being "ritualistic" and "high Church". For a young theological student during the 1960s, there was an awareness of the tension within the Church over liturgy. Popular opinion among some fellow students at the time was that Dougan's liturgical views were not to be taken seriously, as they were not at all part of the evangelical stance. It was during the year of 2007 that a fellow student of the 1960s made the comment, "you don't still believe all that rubbish Dougan taught us do you?"

Never the less the influence that Dougan had within the Church led many ministers to embrace his views willingly, believing that they were consistent with the Church's theological position. On the other hand there were those who, like the Rev. Tom McEvoy rejected Dougan's views completely. Although the General Assembly had published a *Book of Common Order* in 1954, which was a reprint, with minor changes, of the 1940 Scottish *Book of Common Order*, most ministers had little interest in a theology of worship. Most accepted the forms in the *Book of Common Order* as being broadly Presbyterian. When one of the authors of this book, Dr John Webster became a theological student in 1965, he was appointed as an assistant to a minister in several parishes. During those years as an assistant, most ministers that he came to know used the various forms of worship within the *Book of Common Order*, with a great deal of discretion. *The Book of Common Order* was regarded as an essential tool in a minister's ecclesial tool-box.

All the liturgical advances made during the Dougan years were soon to come to an end. Dougan retired and by 1982 he was dead, and there was no other liturgical scholar in the Church to replace him. However, there were other key ministers who were greatly influenced by Dougan's liturgical views, but their expertise lay in pastoral ministry, not in academic disciplines. The Rev. Douglas Murray, the Rev. James Bruce, Rev. Peter Boase, the Rev. Robert Willison and the Rev. Dr. John Webster were all greatly influenced by Dougan. By 1992 Murray had retired and a short time later, Peter Boase retired from active ministry and Bruce died in 1999.[1] Unfortunately, due to the passage of time and death, those who were influenced by Dougan have been overtaken by a newer generation with very different liturgical ideas. The Dougan era is now definitely over.

The greatest challenge to a sound liturgical practice within the Church was to occur after "Church Union" in 1977.[2] Indeed, we wish to argue that since 1977 a liturgical minimisation process has been in operation. This is a process as defined in chapter four, and though its exposition shall not be restated here, it is important to clarify some of the history surrounding it.

The General Assembly of Australia which met in 1965 proclaimed that the 1965 edition of the *Book of Common Order* was the basis for Presbyterian worship in Australia. In 1979, only two years after the Union the Public Worship Committee of the General Assembly was instructed to begin a revision of the *Book of Common Order* as the current book had been published in 1920, revised in 1929, and reprinted several times with only minor changes.

The Committee was instructed to make a revision and to make service formats available in draft form from time to time. The convenor of the committee was the Rev. Douglas Murray, a Dougan sympathiser. Mr. Murray was the minister at St Stephens, Bathurst for many years, the last pastoral charge in which Alan Dougan served. In 1985 the General Assembly required the Committee to continue its work on the preparation of the *Book of Common Order*, and to provide from time to time provisional services for the use and study within the Church, and to endeavour to finalise the production of the Book for presentation to the next General Assembly.[3] The book was published in 1990 with a blue cover and titled *Worship*.

REVISION OF THE 1990 PROVISIONAL WORSHIP BOOK

However, the 1991 General Assembly referred the provisional book back to the Public Worship and Aids Committee for complete revision. At this Assembly a new committee was appointed and there was only one member of the old committee re-elected, the Rev. R. Humphreys. The previous convenor the Rev. Douglas Murray stated in the course of debate that he was prepared to be part of the new committee but not prepared to be its convenor. Unfortunately Douglas Murray was not elected onto the new committee. This came as an awful shock and Douglas Murray was deeply hurt.[4] In hindsight this was an *ecclesial coup d'etat*. The new committee held to a very different theological persuasion. The new committee's convenor was the Rev. Paul Cooper.

It is from this point in time that a more radical form of liturgical minimisation began to be expressed in the work of the committee. The General Assembly also approved the following motion:

> Request ministers, sessions, and presbyteries NOT to use or recommend the provisional Book of Common Order, known as *"Worship"* and refer the book back to the Committee for complete revision.[5]

The passing of this motion suggests that an opportunity was now at hand to radically change the content of the *Worship Book*. The rapidity of the minimisation process was astounding. The revision was completed and approved by the General Assembly of 1998.

This change of personnel and the conviction that there should be another comprehensive revision came as a complete shock. The previous convenor, the Rev. Douglas Murray, though not re-elected to the new committee has made the comment that the previous committees from 1977 to 1991 were:

> almost 100% of the view that the new Book of Common Order should reflect the Church of Scotland 1940 Book. The members had received training for the

ministry at a time when there was a 'high view' of the sacraments, i.e. an adherence to the Westminster Confession of Faith, the Shorter Catechism both of which in their turn reflected the emphasis which John Calvin had made at the time of the Reformation.[6]

The decision of the previous committee to publish the 1991 *"Worship"* book was based on the fact that there were no indications from Sessions and Presbyteries that the book would not be accepted. This was a reasonable assumption especially since the content of the book had gone down to all Presbyteries and Sessions for consideration and report.[7]

The new committee comprised the following ministers: Professor Principal A. Harman, C. Balzer, P. Hastie, M. Ramage, J. Davies, K. Gardner, C. Able, P. Cooper, R. Humphreys, D. Tsai, D. Geddes and M. Grieve. Two things can be said of the elected personnel: first, there is not one liturgical scholar in the list, and second, all but two are well-known for their commitment to the Reformed faith as expressed by many of the more extreme ideas of the English and Scottish Puritan Divines. The new committee lacked theological breadth. Those who were elected all held to similar theological convictions which did not reflect the differing theological viewpoints held by the wider Church. In other words there was a lack of theological balance. Comparing the provisional book of 1990 to the 1998 revision, there are a number ofissues, both in content and structure that reveal a minimisation process.

1. The first noticeable change is the omission of orders of service for the:

Dedication of a Church
Dedication of Church Furnishings
Dedication of Church Memorials.
In their place six new services have been added:
Commissioning of a Deaconess
Commissioning of a Home Missionary
Dedication of Christian Teachers
Commissioning of a Youth Worker
Commissioning of a Missionary Family
The Decommissioning of a Missionary Family.[8]

The implication of this change is that people can be commissioned for all types of ministries, but inanimate objects, such as Church Buildings and furnishings are of little value, as ministry is all about people, not things.

In hindsight this resolution of the Assembly to approve the above changes,unwittingly pointed the Church in a liturgical direction that was to prove unwise, as no one envisaged the extent of liturgical denial that would plague the Church in the years ahead.

THE REMOVAL OF SYMBOL

The removal of this section raises serious questions in respect to the role of symbol in Christian worship. Church buildings and furnishings are powerful symbols of gospel ministry. Although the Assembly's resolution was not specifically formulated to reject the notion of symbols, it nevertheless signalled the secondary importance of symbols, as the new thinking within the committee and the new spirit within the Assembly was that the proclamation of the Word is of such paramount importance, everything else becomes secondary. It was by implication that the whole notion of symbol was left to wither on the vine. This was all part of a minimisation process.

What was being overlooked was that symbols are an essential part of human life. Metaphors and allegories have a connectedness with reality, and in the context of the Christian Church, a spiritual reality. To neglect the importance of symbols from Christian worship is as unwise, as it is inconsistent with the rest of life. A wedding ring, for example is simply a circle of precious metal, but it is readily accepted as a symbol of the reality of marriage. The ring itself is not love, commitment, fidelity or family, but it does represent in a powerful way, all those things for which it stands. Its potency is far greater than its commercial value. The realist not only believes in symbols but accepts them as contributing to an important and essential part of life from advertising to quantum physics and the various grades of mathematics. Language itself is made up of words that are symbols of reality. To deny the use of symbols in Christian worship is to deny an important aspect of life and knowledge. The poet Ralph Waldo Emerson is reputed to have said, "a good symbol is the best argument, and a missionary to persuade thousands". John Dewey, in *The Quest for Certainty* writes, "The invention or discovery of symbols is doubtless by far the greatest single event in the history of man. Without them no advance is possible; with them, there is no limit set to intellectual development except inherent stupidity".[9]

The concept of symbol and its relevance, albeit subjective, to all compartments of life was ignored by the Assembly when it voted the way it did. Symbols help to create a resonant mythos that expresses the moral and spiritual values of the Church community, and helps to create a sense of solidarity between religious adherents. Thomas Stafford argues that many elements of Christian supernaturalism can only be suggested to the human mind through symbolic words and signs. He further sees that representation of spiritual truths and abstract notions by analogous phenomena in the physical world has been common to all people and religions.[10] The early Christian Church used symbols freely for the many illiterate Christians and during periods of persecution. Gordon Calthrop states that the Fish was the earliest Christian symbol, partly as the symbol of water and the rite of Baptism, and also because the five Greek letters which express the word "Fish" form the anagram of the name of Jesus Christ. Calthrop also points out that the Fish had largely disappeared by the tenth century and the Cross replaced it as the principal symbol. The Lamb in Christian art became the symbol of the Redeemer, as the sacrifice without blemish. Similarly the Dragon became the symbol of sin.[11] The physical centre for worship should not be regarded as an unimportant symbol or be relegated as an obsolete symbol of secondary importance. The Old Testament is rich in symbolism and it has the ring of divine authority. In 1 Kings 6–7, the Lord gives clear instruction as to how the Temple was to be constructed including its beautification and furnishings. The Ark of the Covenant was brought into the Temple with a solemn procession and placed in the "Holy of Holies". The Temple complex was symbolic of the greatness and majesty of Israel's belief in the sovereign creator God, who had entered into a covenantal relationship with his people. It was the symbol of God's presence within the nation it was the public centre for worship and a centre for instruction so that the faith could be passed from one generation to another. The Temple, in all its grandeur, was never to be a substitute for personal faith and commitment. At the dedication of the Temple, Solomon, when pronouncing a blessing on the people, said: "may he (God) be with us, may he turn our hearts to him, to walk in all his ways and to keep his commandments, decrees and regulations he gave to our fathers. But your hearts must be fully committed to the Lord our God, to live by his decrees and to obey his commands, as at this time".[12] The early Church met for worship in various buildings. After Christianity became a state religion, buildings became more important as places of public worship as distinct from private worship. The building, varying in size and beautification, was regarded as only symbolic. The early Church taught that Christians were living stones of the new Temple, indwelt by the Holy Spirit.[13]

CHURCH ARCHITECTURE

In the years since 1977 when new Churches have been built or old Churches renovated, there is a marked tendency to reduce or omit all symbols and beautification. In some Churches Pulpits, Communion Tables and Baptismal Fonts have been removed. The sanctuary area becomes as simple as it is bare except for a centrally located Lectern and band equipment. It seems as though art and beauty of a worship area is in some way a hindrance to genuine worship. Electronic mixing desks have become common place from which sound, overhead projection and lighting are controlled. We have observed that in some Church buildings the worship area could easily be a drama theatre or just a meeting area for Bible Study, Prayer or any other activity. People become aware that the building is a worship centre, because of the information on the public notice board at the entry of the property.

At this point in the argument, it is of immense value to define more precisely what symbolism really is, and to elaborate its function within the life of the worshipping community.

DEFINING SYMBOL

Professor John McIntyre the noted Edinburgh theologian suggests that:

> A religious symbol is a phenomenon existent in space and time, and identifiable materially or conceptually by both believers and unbelievers alike, but its differentia as a religious symbol is that for believers it carries a reference to a supernatural reality, this reference being specifiable in a complex variety of ways . . . A sign is unifunctional; it is an indicator to the presence of another reality, and its role is exhausted when we have reached or discovered or identified that reality. The symbol may be a marker to a reality beyond itself.[14]

McIntyre argues that in religious life there is a definite cognitive role for symbols, especially in the practice of prayer. He argues, "in knowing the symbol in some way we are also given to know the reality. The symbol is not simply an occasion of knowing; it is a means of knowing".[15] It is here that we get the first glimpse of McIntyre's differentiation between the epistemological and ontological aspects of symbol. He specifies three points to clarify the relation between symbol and the reality it symbolizes, which enables the latter to be known through the former:

(a) It is not our creation. God gives the symbol and in doing so constitutes the unique relation which it holds to himself. He cites four scriptural passages: Genesis 9:12, the rainbow, "This is the sign of the covenant that I make between me and you and every living creature that is with you, for all future generations: I have set my bow in the cloud and it shall be a sign of the covenant between me and the earth". In the Book of Exodus, McIntyre cites the pillar of cloud by day and the pillar of fire by night as a symbol by which God's people would be aware of his encompassing care for them. In the New Testament the lilies in the field are a symbol, a means of knowing the continuing providence of God. Likewise the bread and wine through which, in partaking, we know the body and blood, the renewing forgiveness of Christ and of God.

(b) There is the popular view that symbol is simply an "associative mechanism which we adopt, to recall the sacred object to mind, a stimulus which we employ to activate the religious reality". Although this view is very different in character to that of the former, it nevertheless shows man's dependence on symbolic usage.

(c) Symbolism, says McIntyre, should never be taken as "a basis or premise of inference to the religious reality as a proof of divine existence" The religious symbol "is in a more direct relation to the symbolized than the inferential process permits; the relation is more akin to that which obtains between the overt observable activities of a person and his or her inner intentions and purposes, where we know the inner reality in terms of outward expression".

McIntyre then concludes that the cognitive role of religious symbols (especially in the matter of prayer) "rests on knowledge, or the acknowledgement of God".[16]

In contrast to this epistemological approach to symbols, McIntyre expounds another approach which explains why liturgical minimalists find the need to abolish the symbolism in the dedication section of the *1990 Worship Book*. This is what McIntyre calls the "ontological" role of symbols. This theory suggests that knowing the symbol, we are given the reality which it symbolises. This theory says McIntyre, is seen in the work of Paul Tillich,[17] where he sees that there is an ontological relationship between symbol and the symbolised. The clearest expression of this view is found in Roman Catholicism. Specific mention is made to the Mass, where the participation of bread and wine is the reality of the body and blood of Christ which warrants the claim of transubstantiation. As McIntyre points out, however, it is no less clear in the Protestant Orthodox doctrine of Scripture, according to which the written word of God becomes the Word of God *simpliciter* or even in a non-sacramental service of dedication where the liturgy followed, shares in the holiness of the God to whom the child is dedicated. This ontological relation "is the basis of the veneration of relics no less than of the honour for God which requires us to take off our hats in Church or cross ourselves before the altar".[18]

It is this ontological notion of symbol that adherents of the Reformed Faith find so objectionable. It was this understanding which gave rise to the destructive iconoclastic movement of the sixteenth century. In the contemporary situation, in an endeavour to abolish the objectionable ontological aspect of symbol, the formulators of the *1998 Worship Book* have also excluded the epistemological explanation of symbol. It is a case of the proverbial throwing the baby out with the bathwater.

So the new committee established by the General Assembly began its work of minimisation by omitting all services that are not people-related and, by implication, removing the rich heritage of Christian symbolism. This action of the Committee is not always supported by more recent liturgical scholarship in the Reformed tradition. R.G. Gore argues that "God has made use of natural symbols in the Church and the Church would be foolish to deny the power and influence such symbols contain". What is important says Gore is that there should be "balance between Word and Symbol and between Word and Sacrament".[19]

2. Revising the Liturgy of Holy Communion

The aim at this point in this thesis is not to examine all aspects of the 1998 *Book of Common Order*, but rather to limit the analysis in a way that is in keeping with the foregoing chapters and analyse specifically the liturgy of Holy Communion. In Chapter 4 different liturgies are set side by side in order to show the impact of the minimisation process. For consistency the same is done with the liturgy of the provisional 1990 and the authorised 1998 *Worship Book*.

By setting the liturgical details of both the 1990 and 1998 versions of *Worship* side by side, it can be seen that the structure and form of both are identical, except for the omission of the dedication section, and except for some minor issues, such as language expression. It is not until an examination is made of the content of the forms however that there is an immediate awareness of a change in theological direction. This is achieved through a minimisation process that deletes significant paragraphs in the liturgy. The theological change is, towards being more Zwinglian in flavour, in place of the rich sacramental heritage of Calvin, which has been already discussed in a previous chapter. Zwingli was rationalistic in his theological outlook and less mystical than Calvin and Luther. In Zurich, where he ministered, ceremonies and rituals were reduced to their barest form. The liturgy was reduced to the point that the Eucharist was a service of remembrance of Christ's death in a spiritual way.[20] Zwingli's approach to the Eucharist was minimisation in its form and structure. Maxwell points out that

Zwingli, in the early years of the Reformation, did not regard the Eucharist as a means of Grace or as the norm of Christian worship.[21]

In a letter to Matthew Alber in 1524, Zwingli explained how he interprets St Luke 22:19 where Jesus said at the Last Supper "Take this and eat, this is my body which is given for you". Zwingli argues; "Take and eat. This signifies my body which is given for you see the purpose for which he ordered them to eat, "Do this as a memorial for me". It is simply a "commemoration of himself . . . This meal is a symbol by which you recall the body of the very son of God.[22] Zwingli was also at pains to show that the Eucharist is not a sacrament of sacrifice and claimed that holding to such a view is to dishonour and deprecate the body and blood of Christ.[23] By repudiating the doctrine of transubstantiation with its Aristotelian metaphysic there was no other philosophical means of explaining the real Presence of Christ in the sacrament. Refusing to accept Calvin's view of the sacrament, Zwingli was only left with a memorialist interpretation which was a better option, than to re-crucify Jesus Christ every time the sacrament was celebrated, which transubstantiation strongly suggests. Thus Zwingli adopts a consistent rationalist methodology in his view of the sacrament.

If the Eucharist is only a means to remember Christ's death in a spiritual way then there is no need for symbol, it is merely a sign. Certainly there was no place for an ontological perspective of symbolism. We would claim that Zwingli completely failed to understand the "epistemological" perspective of symbol. This is completely understandable as Zwingli's early years of ministry were immersed in Roman Catholicism.

The Zwinglian influence is obvious in the omission of key sections of the *Great Prayer of Thanksgiving and Consecration*, in the 1990 version of *Worship*. The prayer of 1990 is evidence of the change that had been effected in the 1998 version:

Almighty and everlasting God, it is indeed our duty and delight always and everywhere to give You thanks and praise. In the beginning You created the heavens and the earth and all that is therein:

> You made man in your own image and Your tender mercies are over all Your works.
>
> (Here may be added the Preface according to the season of the Christian Year.)
>
> Mighty God, heavenly King, we magnify and praise You. With all the company of heaven we worship and adore You, evermore saying: Holy, holy, holy, Lord God of hosts, Heaven and earth are full of your glory. Glory to You, O Lord most high. Blessed is he who comes in the name of the Lord. Hosanna in the highest.
>
> Almighty and merciful God, You loved the world so much that You gave Your only Son that whoever believes in Him should not perish but have eternal life.
>
> Not as we ought but as we are able, we bless You for His holy incarnation, for His perfect life on earth, for His precious sufferings and death upon the cross, for His glorious resurrection from the dead, for His ascension to Your right hand where He ever lives to plead our cause, for the promise of His coming again, and for His gift of the Holy Spirit. Remembering, therefore, the life and work of our Saviour Christ, and pleading His eternal sacrifice, we do this in obedience to His command. By the presence and power of the Holy Spirit bless and consecrate these gifts of bread and wine which we set before You, so that the bread which we break may be a sharing in the body of Christ, and the cup which we bless a sharing in the blood of Christ, that as we receive them we may receive by faith the body and blood of our Lord Jesus Christ, to our spiritual nourishment and growth in grace, and to Your glory.
>
> Most gracious God and Father, accept this our sacrifice of praise and thanksgiving; and for the sake of the offering made once for all upon the Cross, grant unto us and all Your people the fullness of Your redeeming love: and receive the offering of our selves which we now make to Your service; through Jesus Christ our Lord. Amen.[24]

The 1998 version of Worship edits this prayer in a serious way. While retaining the form, there is the deletion of:

- The recommended Preface according to the Christian Year. This deletion signals the view that the Christian Year is not necessary and that the Church will not conform to the collective wisdom of historic Christianity.
- The words "eternal sacrifice" are replaced by, "His perfect sacrifice". It is difficult to understand why this change was made as "eternal sacrifice" understood in the light of the *Westminster Confession of Faith*, assumes that Christ's death was perfect. While this reference to the sacrifice of Christ is a reference to the historical event of Christ's actual death on the Cross, it should not be interpreted as suggesting a re-sacrifice at the point of the celebration of the Eucharist. The new committee was determined to reassert the Church's commitment to a Puritan liturgical position.
- The complete paragraph relating to consecration, "By the presence and power to your glory." The removal of this prayer of consecration is an admission that there is no relation between the symbol and that which is symbolised. The elements become only a sign, which McIntyre says is "unifunctional and is only an indicator to the presence of another reality and its role is exhausted when we have reached or discovered that reality". Since the Holy Table has been fenced earlier in the liturgy and only the faithful engage in the Communion, then there is no need for a prayer of consecration. This in itself conveys the strong Zwinglian overtones.
- Upon reflection, from a Zwinglian perspective, it could be argued that the last paragraph beginning and ending "Most gracious God . . . Amen", especially the words "the fullness of your redeeming love", may be linked to the elements ontologically, as the grace of redeeming love is conveyed through the reception of the elements and not through faith. In the context of the paragraph, the "grace of redeeming love" is linked with the sacrifice of Christ on the Cross, which may be suggestive that grace is conveyed *ex opera operato*. If this was the thinking of the committee then there is no need for the prayer. On the other hand, the blessing of God in the sacrament comes when we recall the events of Christ on the Cross, and nothing that we do changes the blessings that come through our union with the Christ. If this be so, why have the prayer?

3. In the new 1998 version of *Worship* the prayers of Intercession are deleted.

The following is the prayer in the 1990 version of *Worship*:

> We believe it to be your will, our God, to bless in answer to prayer.
> Hear us as we pray:

> For the whole world, for all nations and their governments, that there may be freedom, peace, and plenty in all parts of the earth;
> For the Church in all its branches, that its zeal may be rekindled, its faith renewed, and its unity restored;
> For one another, that we may all truly receive the benefits of Christ offered in the sacrament of His body and blood;
> For those of our fellowship not with us today through illness, work, absence from home, or carelessness, that the presence of Christ may be known to them also;
> For our homes and families, for our neighbours, and for the places where we work and those we meet there, that in the encounters of each day people may learn through us of Your Son's love for them;
> For the schools and colleges of our parish that in them our children and young people may be prepared in mind and spirit to meet the opportunities and face the confusion of our times;
> For the sick and suffering, the careworn and the sad, remembering in silence any whose need lies heavily upon our hearts . . . and for the dying, that they may depart unafraid and in peace;
> For . . . *(here any other intercessions)*
> This we ask in the name and for the sake of Him who lives to make intercession for us: Jesus Christ our Lord. Amen.

This prayer in the 1990 version of Worship enjoins the concept of fellowship where Christians express their common relationship to Christ, their needs and concerns for each other. Such a prayer is a requisite according to Christ's injunction to Love one another, as I have loved you.

The 1998 version of *Worship* omits this prayer. The question arises, "why is this so?"

In answer to this, it is necessary to understand that the new committee appointed by the General Assembly in 1991 to "completely revise" *Worship* was predominately made up of personnel who were well known for their commitment to the Reformed Faith. The understanding of the Reformed Faith was more in keeping with the English and Scottish Puritan theological tradition, with its strong links with rationalism and Zwinglianism and its abhorrence of Catholicism. From this perspective it is obvious that there are sections of this above prayer that were found to be theologically awkward. The paragraph beginning and ending "For the Church in all its branches restored;" would be viewed as unworthy. It was held by many at the time that not all Churches were true Churches. Calvin's notion of the marks of the true Church was taken very seriously, viz, Berkhof in his *Systematic Theology* notes that Reformed theologians differed as to the number of the marks of the Church. There were those who considered there was but one mark that is preaching of the pure doctrine of the Gospel (Beza, Alsted Amesius, Heidanus, Maresius). Others thought there were two marks, the pure preaching of the word and the right administration of the sacraments (Calvin, Bullinger

Zanchius, Junius, Gomarus, Mastricht, a Marck)Others insisted on three marks by including with the above the faithful exercise of discipline (Hyperius, Martyr, Ursinus, Trelcatius, Heidegger, Wendelinus). The acceptance of any of the three marks, and especially those who accepted all three, provided a mechanism whereby serious judgements could be made in respect to the Churches that were or were not faithful to the cause of Christ. Given this mechanism it is easy to deduce that the Roman Catholic Church was not a true Church as the Pope was referred to as the Antichrist. This naturally led to an ecclesial exclusivism.

4. The next noticeable difference in the 1998 version is the Prayer for the Communion of Saints is removed.

The Prayer in the 1990 version is as follows:

> O God our Father, You have greatly loved us, and mercifully redeemed us, and now You have fed us and strengthened us at Your table: give us grace that in everything we may give ourselves, our wills and our works, a continual thank offering to You;
> And rejoicing in the communion of saints, we thank You for all your servants who have departed in the faith; and especially those dear to us who are at rest in You...
> Keep us in unbroken fellowship with Your whole Church in heaven and on earth, and grant that we may rejoice together in Your eternal kingdom; through Jesus Christ our Lord. Amen

This Prayer has been replaced by:

> O God our Father, you have greatly loved us and mercifully redeemed us, and now you have fed us and strengthened us at your table: give us grace that in everything we may give ourselves, our wills and our works, as a continual thank offering to you. May we live in peace and fellowship with our brothers and sisters in Christ and rejoice together in your eternal kingdom; through Jesus Christ our Lord. Amen.

This substituted prayer is restricted to the self. It is in keeping with the rugged individualism of the modern age and has no corporate sense and appeal. In receiving the sacrament we not only share the worship with Christ by virtue of our union with him, we also share with each other. We are present because of the faithful witness of countless servants who have served faithfully over many centuries, but also those who still labour in the cause of Christ. There is no meaningful acknowledgment of those who have gone before us. On the broader theological perspective there is an inherent denial of the Church's catholicity as there is no reference to the whole Church on earth and heaven. The words, *"...your servants who have departed in the faith; and especially those dear to us who are at rest in You ... "* in the 1990 version may suggest to some that the Church may be giving approval for prayers for the dead, so the inclusion of such a prayer was too risky for a Church that was intent on a liturgical cleansing mission. This strongly suggests that public membership of the Church is seen through the periscope of private worship where the self alone is seen in terms of a personal relationship with Jesus Christ. The subtle implication being that membership can only be defined in terms of a Reformed soteriological perspective, and anything outside of that perspective is viewed with suspicion. This would explain why the statement "The Table of the Lord Jesus Christ is open to all who are in communion with the Church universal", is excluded. The omission of all reference to the membership of the historic Church of the past only devalues the ministries of those who have contributed so much to the Church's mission in the world.

R.J. Gore, on the other hand argues that Reformed believers need to be catholic in outlook and be prepared to learn from other traditions and not to allow their confidence to lead them to suppose that they have cornered all truth. Gore sees this catholicity as being grounded in the Great Commission in St Matthew 28.[25] He also cites the well known reformed scholar Richard B Gaffin, "What reformed believers have in common with everyone who calls on the name of the Lord (Romans 10:13) is more basic than the differences, because above all they share in Christ, and Christ is not divided 1Corth. 1:13.[26]

With the omission of the four sections within the prayers as discussed above there is the minimisation of the liturgy in a way which changes the theological direction from that of Calvinism to that of Zwinglianism. The means of achieving this liturgical cleansing is through the removal of all notion of symbol. The removal of symbol and the reduction of the liturgy to its barest and most simplistic form and the exclusion of any notion of an epistemological explanation of symbol is perfectly consistent with Zwinglianism. The Eucharist was only a means of remembering Christ's death in a spiritual way; such a remembrance does not need a symbol. In Zwingli's early years he did not regard the Eucharist as being a norm for Christian worship. This of course explains the infrequency of the sacrament in many Reformed denominations. Calvin saw the role of the sacrament very differently, insisting that the Eucharist be the norm for worship. The preaching of the Word ought not to be separated from the Eucharist as it was the Word in action. The Eucharist was more than remembrance as it implies the reality of the Real Presence of Christ which defies rational or empirical explanation. It should also be noted that in the Zwinglian rite there is the deletion of the prayer of consecration and prayers of intercession.[27] With the deletion of the prayers of intercession there is also no reference to prayers for the communion of saints. The 1998 version of Worship follows closely the Zwinglian format.

However there is a further minimising of the 1990 version of Worship. It takes the form of minimising the structure of the liturgy. The structure of the 1990 version will be set out and the items in italics are those items that were deleted in the 1998 version. Presenting the form outline in this way clearly shows how minimisation of the structure has taken place. Italics will not be used for any item that has only a change in language or a minor adjustment in the place of occurrence. It is more important to see the impact of the removal of theologically sensitive items.

The Preparation of Approach to God
Call to worship
Psalm or Hymn
Scripture Sentences
Prayers of Approach and Confession
Assurance of Pardon
Prayer of Supplication
Gloria in Excelsis or other suitable Canticle or Hymn
The Word of God
Old Testament Lesson
Psalm or Hymn
New Testament Lesson
Prayer for Illumination
Sermon
Ascription of Praise
Apostles' or Nicene Creed
Announcements
Prayers of Intercession
Offering and Prayer of Dedication
The Sacrament of the Lord's Supper
Invitation to the Lord's Table
Communion Psalm or Hymn
Unveiling of the Elements
Prayer
The Grace
Warrant and Setting Apart
"He took the bread and wine"
Prayer of Thanksgiving *and Consecration*
The Lord's Supper
"He gave thanks"
The Action, "He broke the bread"
The Delivery and Reception of Holy Communion

"He gave it to them"
The Peace
Prayers of Thanksgiving *and Communion of Saints*
Psalm or Hymn
The Blessing

With the deletion of the items in italics, the structure of the liturgy had been minimised. The setting apart of the elements and the prayer of consecration and the removal of all the congregational responses leave the liturgy seriously truncated and reduced to the barest and most simplistic form. As it now stands, it is very akin to the structure of Zwingli's Communion service. The similarities of Zwingli's service and that of the 1998 version of *Worship* is evident when set side by side for comparison. The comparison is only for the Holy Communion Service after the sermon (see Table 5.1).

Note the uncanny similarity. Although the similarities are strong, the 1998 Version of *Worship* even minimises the Zwinglian model, in that there is no fraction and the minister's communion is at the same time as the congregation.

The 1998 version of *Worship* has become truncated due to the many omissions and it gives the impression to the naive that the liturgies' structure is consistent with historic Christianity but is in fact void of the symbolic

Table 5.1.

Zwingli	1998 Version
Exhortation	Invitation to the Lord's Table + hymn
Fencing of the Table	
The Lord's Prayer	Prayer and the Grace
Prayer of Humble Access	
Words of Institution, with:	Words of Institution + Prayer of Thanksgiving
Fraction	
Ministers Communion	
Delivery	The sharing of the bread and wine (delivery)
Post-communion Psalm	
Post-communion Collect	The Peace & Prayers of Thanksgiving
Dismissal[1]	Post-communion Psalm or Hymn
	The Blessing (Dismissal)[2]

1. Maxwell, *Outline of Christian Worship*, 84–85. 2. Presbyterian Church of Australia, *Worship*, Sydney, 1998, 35.

beauty and mystique of the 1990 version. Sadly the bare outline of the 1998 version has become nothing more than a "directory" of public worship.

EXPLANATION FOR THE DIFFERENCES

The liturgies in the two *Worship Books* are so radically different that it begs the question whether or not the author or authors of the 1998 version had given sufficient consideration to what Michael Horton calls issues in transcendence and immanence, the priority of Word and the sacraments. The fact is says Horton, style (which accompanies such a change) is never neutral as liturgies embody our belief about God, ourselves, redemption and the chief end of human existence.[28] The final composition of the Holy Communion liturgy in the 1998 version of *Worship* is due, in the greater part, to the Rev. Christopher Balzer who headed the subcommittee dealing with the Holy Communion liturgy, and the Rev. Paul Cooper the convenor of the whole Committee.[29] Both men at the time were lecturers and colleagues at the Presbyterian Theological Centre. It should also be noted that the Rev. Dr John Davies, who was also on the Committee, was Principal of the College. In a penetrating article which appeared in the *Reformed Theological Review*, Christopher Balzer provides a valuable insight into his theological thinking, which in turn explains the radical change in the *Worship Book*. Balzer comments on the growing view of John Woodhouse and George May who claim that the evidence of the New Testament does not lead to the conclusion that Jesus instituted a sacramental meal which the Church had kept from the beginning of the Church's establishment.[30] Balzer began his response by referring to three key verses: St Luke 22:17 "Take this", St Matthew 26:26 "Take eat" and St Mark 14:22 "Take". He observes that this was an instruction by Jesus to those gathered for that particular Passover Feast. He claims that the longer passage in St Luke 22 is more foundational and reliable due to the MS evidence. It is also the passage that Zwingli used to justify his particular view of the sacrament. Particular attention is given to verse 19b, τουτο ποιέιτέ ἐις τήν ἐμην ἀνάμνης. He argues that ποιεῖτε can be either indicative or imperative, but he cannot find an English translation which takes it as an indicative. He says, "The imperative seems to make more sense as the present imperative, (in the case of this verb) is a command to continue the practice". As Balzer sees it, it is legitimate to use 1 Corth.11 to interpret Luke 22.[31] Using this methodology Balzer understands the instruction of Jesus, specifically referring to things which the disciples were to remember:

- They would have understood what was meant by this command only after the cruxification and resurrection. With this Balzer is in agreement.

- By 55 AD the Church's practice of the Lord's Supper was closely linked with the words of Jesus at the last Supper. To disagree with this says Balzer is to fly in the face of the evidence.
- Balzer tends to agree with John Woodhouse[32] that 1Corth.10 refers to the practice of Christians meeting together for meals in a non sacramental sense. He sees that the logical conclusion that 1Corth. 10 and 11 is making explicit reference to the Last Supper. This conclusion is supported by the correspondence of the reference in 1Corth10:16 with the bread which we break being and sharing in the body of Christ to that of St. Luke 22:19 where Jesus says of the bread that he had just broken, "This is my body which is given for you". It is a very short step (and a necessary one) from here to the conclusion that the early Church practice referred to in 1Corth 10:16 is the Christians doing what they were commanded at the Last Supper by Jesus, "Do this in remembrance of me".
- Balzer is in partial agreement with George May, that the Last Supper narrative is used "illustratively and catechetical to remind the Corinthians of the basis of their unity" and not as a directive for liturgical practice.[33]
- Pointing to 1Corth. 11:24–26, Balzer sees the meal referred to be "remembrance and proclamation of Christ's sacrificial death."

Drawing upon the above Balzer comes to the conclusion that, "1 Corth 10 and 11 and Acts 2 all refer to common meals which the early Christians shared. These meals included some sort of ritual words and actions which served to help Christians attending to think again about the death of Jesus on the Cross for them and to bring home the reality of their redemption in a tactile way." Arriving at this conclusion, Balzer cannot have any regard for the formal liturgy of the 1990 version of *Worship,* as it is contrary to his stated theological position. Balzer saw little value for the symbol and the mystique that are found in the *Worship* book of 1990 which is dependent on the evolution of historical liturgical process of the Christian Church, particularly that of the Church of Scotland.

The revision of the liturgy of the Lord's Supper in the 1998 *Worship* is perfectly consistent with Balzer's memorialist/ Zwinglian views of this sacrament. Balzer's argument together with the radical changes to the Book of Common Order on the whole is suggestive of an imperative need to recast the liturgical tradition in terms of an adherence to the simplicities of worship found only in the Holy Scriptures. The Holy Scriptures being viewed as the infallible Word of God becomes the central force of recasting the liturgy. Although a detailed study of apostolic worship in the New Testament and that of the Church Fathers would be useful at this point the intention of this work is to show how the contemporary Presbyterian Church in New South Wales has compromised its liturgical heritage from the time of John Calvin, whose Strasbourg liturgy embraced New Testament principles. There are many works that outline in detail the parameters of worship in the New Testament and the Church Fathers.[34]

WIDER CHURCH CONSULTATION

The revision proceeded only after in depth consultation within the wider Church. The Rev. Dr John Davies prepared a statement of the Committee's mandate for the revision of *Worship*. It was sent down to all Presbyteries for consultation and response. The response was very disappointing, as there were only ten replies. Principal Davies suggested that the Church at large does not consider the issue as being of vital concern.[35] This was another way of saying that the Church at large has a serious problem with an adequate understanding of a theology of worship. By implication, a similar situation existed during the life of the previous Committee. As mentioned already in this chapter the Rev. Douglas Murray sent his Committee's Revision down to all Presbyteries and Sessions for comment and report. At that time there were no suggestions that the wider Church was in any way dissatisfied with the revision. Thus from 1990 to 1998 the wider Church's limited interest in *Worship* was due in part to the closure of the Dougan years of influence and to the failure of the Presbyterian Theological College to inculcate an effective Calvinistic Theology of Worship. In order for a College to inculcate an effective theology of worship it needs to provide the opportunities of critical analysis of the history, philosophy and theology of worship.

In the 1994 Davies' report there were a number of responses from Presbyteries that suggest that the denomination should be a non-liturgical Church. This suggested that there were people in the Church's system of government who were happy with a Zwinglian interpretation of the sacrament. For example,

> Worship does not consist of a set of events which one performs. Rather it is a total response to the character and work of God in Christ, a reciprocating of the friendship initiated by the sovereign Lord.
>
> To worship God is to acknowledge him as our creating and redeeming Lord, to love and serve him with our whole being and to join with others in giving expression to this in all we say and do.[36]

In these two statements worship is defined more or less in terms of a Christian's lifestyle: "total response", "a reciprocating friendship", "love and serve him with our whole being". The traditional and formal concept of worship seemed to be misplaced, so long as Christians meet for fellowship for mutual concerns and personal Christian development. Formalised ritual in worship, although rich in history and symbol, seemed not at all necessary. This view of worship is currently shared by many ministers of the Presbyterian Church of Australia, particularly in New South Wales, especially those who studied for their theological degree at Moore Theological College in the years after Church Union in 1977.[37] Students at Moore College were exposed to the peculiar doctrine of the Church and its liturgy advocated by the Principal, Dr Broughton Knox and Donald Robinson (later Archbishop of Sydney). Knox's vision for Moore College was a large institution more concerned for the teaching of theology than with the training of men for ordination.[38] John Reid stresses that by 1961 Knox was preoccupied with faith as a key to understanding the New Testament. But by 1967, faith had developed into the idea of "fellowship". It was this issue that led to a theological revolution at the College. Reid points out that, the doctrine of the Church was now re-examined in the light of "fellowship". In Knox's view, the Church was to be seen only as the gathered people of God when they physically met together for "fellowship" in the local congregation, or as the gathering of all the redeemed in heaven.[39] Reid claimed that this view of the Church means that all denominational structures and agencies must be regarded as nothing more that the corporate activities of individual Christians with gifts or interests in that area. According to Knox, Reid claimed that Christians did not meet primarily for praise of God so much as for the strengthening of the fellowship of believers.[40] For the purposes of this book, the issue is the commitment to a rationalist propositional view of revelation. Muriel Porter argues that for Broughton Knox, God "cannot be truly worshipped with the senses, the emotions, the feelings or any other bodily or sensory aspect. Religious art and symbols, colour, music and fragrance (such as incense) and bodily posture and movement—let alone the beauty of nature or any form of Christian meditation or mysticism, are at best irrelevant and at worst dangerous to true Christian worship".[41] This needs to be seen in the context of Knox's philosophical and theological outlook. Robert Banks describes Knox's philosophical outlook as empirical realism. Strange as it may seem the structure of Knox's system runs parallel with the structure of the atheist philosopher John Anderson who held the chair of Philosophy at Sydney University. Quoting E. F. Osborn, empirical realism takes the following form:

- "Meaningful" means "propositional". The Bible is only revelational because it is from beginning to end a series of propositions.
- "Revelational" means "verbal". This is part of the meaning of "propositional", for biblical statements are ultimately utterances of God.
- The "concepts" inherent in events and visions are "relational" not the events and visions themselves. It is only when the latter are put into propositional form that they become "revelatory".

- "Interpretation" of events and visions is by God Himself and takes "propositional" form.
- "Faith is towards propositions". Fellowship with God is more than intellectual, but revealed knowledge of Him is entirely a cognitive affair.

Robert Banks then sets out Osborn's comparison of Dr Knox and Professor John Anderson, side by side (see Table 5.2).

This philosophical theory, says Osborn, fails on two counts. Firstly the account of reality itself as the abstract experience such as love and beauty etc. need to be reduced to truth statements. Such an approach results in a monochrome view of the Bible. Secondly, the role of the imagination and emotion in understanding of the Bible retreat as the intellect takes complete charge. The Bible's capacity to stimulate our vision evokes our associations, and move us at the most profound level of our feelings and intuitions, tends to diminish in the cerebral search for systematic information about God.[42] In one sense man's communicative skills are in many ways reliant on propositions for meaningful cognition but, in the case of Broughton Knox, the mind of man takes centre stage as it uses logical reductionism to arrive at truth. This is the methodology of the Enlightenment. In God's creative purpose mankind has been gifted with the aesthetic and as emotional beings. To deny these gifts of creation in worship is to limit God's power to speak.

From a theological perspective Peter Carnley acknowledges that Knox established a "firm theological mindset which influenced generations of theological students",[43] by intellectualising faith and doctrine, by forming propositions. In doing so the experience of the holy or a deepening engagement with the communion of God disappears. "The role of the Holy Spirit is intellectualised so that its role is confined to illumination of the individual's understanding." Carnley therefore argues that the Sydney Diocese's approach to the Eucharist is not so much a deeper entry together into sacramen-

Table 5.2.

Dr Knox	Professor Anderson
Meaningful means "Propositional"	Meaningful means "Propositional"
Revelational means "Propositional"	Truth is "Propositional"
Revelational means "verbal"	Truth is "verbal"
Events must be interpreted	Knowledge is a relation
God interprets	There is only one kind of truth
Faith is in propositions	Knowledge is of propositions
Revelation is inerrant	What is true is completely true

tal presence, as upon a bringing to mind of the more abstract belief that Christ died for our sins upon the Cross.[44] Elsewhere, Carnley refers to the approach to the Eucharist in terms of, a rationalistic mental act, a remembering with gratitude of the saving death of Christ upon the Cross in the past. Instead of doing something in liturgy of an experiential kind in commemoration of the death of Christ, it is a matter of mentally remembering in the course of doing something, an entry into liturgical experience thus become incidental to the having of right thoughts. This essentially is the outcome of a purely propositional approach to faith.[45]

Furthermore there is another consequence. Porter says at the heart of worship in the Sydney Anglican Dioceses is an "expository style of preaching aimed at locking intellectual commitment into a set of rationalist propositions".[46]

From a Presbyterian point of view the appeal of Broughton Knox and Donald Robertson is that their theological perspective is Calvinist/Reformed, but it is unfortunate that Knox's particular view of the Sacrament was Zwinglian in nature. This led to an extreme Puritan liturgical practice. But it is precisely here that Christopher Balzer fits into the equation. Balzer was a faithful product of Knoxian thought.

The influence that Moore Theological College has had on the Presbyterian Church cannot be underestimated, as so many of the students who received their degrees through that institution between 1977 and 1990 are now in leadership positions in the Presbyterian Church, including lecturing positions in the Presbyterian Theological College. It is no accident that the description of Sydney Anglican worship put forward by Muriel Porter is precisely that which is found in most Presbyterian Churches in New South Wales today. In other words the Presbyterian Church of Australia, through its 1998 *Worship Book,* now struggles to contain the dictating ghost of Anglican Knoxianism. The peculiarities of the of the theological world view which governs much of the ecclesiology, epistemology and eschatology of Knox, Robinson and of latter times Woodhouse could well be a worthwhile topic for a major dissertation of the distinctive and unique role of the Reformed tradition in the Anglican Diocese of Sydney.

This means that Liturgical minimisation in the Presbyterian Church, in New South Wales in particular, is linked with "propositional revelation". The real challenge in the future will be the ability of the Church to change its liturgy again, when the tide of theological opinion changes as propositional revelation is challenged. The Scottish theologian Professor Andrew McGowan has unwittingly created a challenge, by arguing that, "we must not make the mistake of imagining that revelation is simply the communication of information, as if God used prophets and apostles to communicate facts that human beings need to know. Rather, we must view revelation as part of the overall plan and purpose of God whereby he acts to save his people. Revelation is a way of indicating the communicative force of God's saving, fellowship-creating presence. God is present as saviour, and so communicatively present. The idiom of revelation is as much moral and relational as it is cognitional.[47] McGowan argues for a reconstruction of the doctrine of Scripture by suggesting that it would be more helpful if the Doctrine of Scripture was not placed as the first head in a theological system. Most Reformed theologians assume that the Doctrine of Scripture is placed at the head of all other Doctrine. Considering the history of the development of the Doctrine of Scripture, it is better to relocate it into the Doctrine of God, because the doctrine of Scripture was not an independent *locus* or *quaestio* in the theological system until the second half of the sixteenth century, and even then it remained closely linked to its systematic place of origin, the prolegomena.[48] It is essential "that we explain the way in which our epistemology relates to our doctrine of Scripture. He quotes the story of Karl Barth who was a visiting lecturer at Princeton Theological Seminary and Chicago Divinity School in 1962. Karl Barth was asked by a reporter to sum up the teaching of his Church Dogmatics. Barth responded with the children's hymn "Jesus loves me this I know for the Bible tells me so". This response says McGowan is a profound epistemological statement of the relationship between Scripture and our knowledge of God. Barth was arguing that our knowledge of the love of God in Christ comes to us through the voice of God speaking in the Scriptures. God's truth is not arrived at by way of logical reductionism rather it is by reason, logic and evidence which have their place in our thinking only because we live in a world God has created, which is therefore inherently rational.[49] There will be challenging days ahead for the Presbyterian Church as McGowan becomes more widely accepted and influential on the world stage of Reformed Theology. The influence of Moore Theological College, particularly the views of Dr. Broughton Knox on Propositional Revelation have been cited, but what will the consequences be, if the ministerial community of the church takes up the suggestion of McGowan, that the doctrine of scripture needs to be reconstructed? This could have serious impact upon the way in which ministers understand doctrines such as the Penal Substitutionary theory of the atonement, and it could even challenge the current Zwinglian understanding of the sacrament. If that were to occur would the General Assembly, be challenged to revise the *Worship Book*?

Another statement from the Davies report is also of particular interest in this matter of worship:

> Though there are some indications of the practice of the Church in the apostolic period (prayer, singing of praise, reading of Scripture, instruction, exhortation, the sharing of a fellowship meal), the New Testament does not contain a

description of an order of service. We must avoid confusing worship with particular forms and styles (including set orders of service) which may serve as appropriate vehicles for expressing genuine faith. Within biblical guidelines, it is for each culture and each successive generation to demonstrate its heartfelt response to God's greatness and love in appropriate ways.

If worship is not to be confused with forms and styles, and if the worship is to be linked to the culture and each successive generation, of the day, then worship will always be in flux and there will be the danger of its being divorced from the Church's history and theology, and worship will always be at the mercy of popular public opinion. It must be realized that in any social context the prevailing culture has a powerful pull. It is always a delicate balancing act to prevent the worship activities of the Church from being submerged by popular opinion. In many ways current social context is similar to that of a Corinthian culture that was suffocating and challenging to the Church in the first century, but St Paul was not intimidated by it as he said in 1 Corth.2:5 "Your faith should not stand in the wisdom of man, but in the power of God". From a historical perspective, Michael Horton argues that the major contribution of the Protestant Reformers was that they never tried to transform culture into Christian culture; rather they sought to liberate culture – not in a godless way – but so that it could exist in its own right.[50] The Church in the future therefore needs to be very cautious in the way it seeks to borrow from popular culture as it may be inconsistent with the denominational theological perspective.

The 1998 version of *Worship* has been so minimalized that the authors have gone a long way towards the fulfilment of the ideas of non-liturgical worship contained in the above quotations. Therefore the 1998 version of *Worship* seeks to deny the rights and privileges of those ministers who want to uphold the Calvinistic liturgical traditions of the Church.

Fortunately one of the principles of Presbyterianism is that Books of Common Order is still only a guide for worship. The various forms of worship need not be adhered to; they can be changed to suit the occasion. If it is the minister's wish to use a liturgical form which previous Assemblies have authorised, he may do so. The 1998 version of *Worship* may well express the mind of the contemporary Church, but it is divorced from the Church's past and the evolution of worship practice in the Reformed Church on the Continent and in Scotland, since the seventeenth century is conveniently ignored.

The revised *Worship Book* was presented to the General Assembly in 1997. In its report the committee acknowledged that not everyone would be happy with its content, but it believed that the book was in conformity with the standards of the Church. It was hoped, said the report that it would provide some measure of uniformity within the Church's practice of worship and act as a guide to all responsible for the conduct of worship.[51]

The General Assembly approved the revision and consented to its publication in orderto set a standard of the kind of service the Assembly commends.

The Rev. J.J.T. Campbell recorded his dissent on the grounds that the Lord's Supper "is defective by the measure of the Westminster Confession of Faith chapter 29 section 3".[52]

The Rev. J.J.T. Campbell was indeed perceptive in his theology of the sacraments and history may yet justify this action of this humble parish minister.

RECENT CONSEQUENCES OF MINIMISATION

In recent years there has been a distinct move away from the use of Books of Common Order. It is now commonplace for ministers of the Church to celebrate the sacrament without any formal structure. This practice extends from the General Assembly down to the parish level. For example, The General Assembly of Australia met for Holy Communion on Tuesday, 11 September 2007 within Scots Church Sydney. The Moderator General, the Rt Rev. Robert Benn, had printed an order of service. The structure was as follows:

Call to Worship
Hymn
Lesson
Hymn
Apostles Creed
Lesson
Hymn
Sermon
Hymn
Invitation to the Lord's Table
Hymn
Lord's Supper
Prayers of Intercession
Hymn
Benediction

This structure does not outline what happens in the Lord's Supper. The actual sequence of events within the liturgy was pencilled on the back of the Order of Service by the Rev. Dr John Webster, as they occurred:

Invitation
Reading of the Institution
Short Address
Hymn
Presentation of the Bread and Wine with the formula "Take Eat", "This Cup is the New Testament in My Blood"
General Prayer of Thanksgiving
Distribution
Prayer of General Intercessions
Hymn
Benediction.

This format excluded all the historic items of the liturgy of the past. It excluded, for example all congregational responses such as the Sanctus, Gloria, Agnes Dei, Kyrie Eleison etc. It excluded the historic Great Prayer of Thanksgiving, Prayer of Consecration, and the Prayer for the Communion of Saints. In short it was a very crude attempt to minimise the liturgy without the aid of a Book of Common Order. Although the service was conducted with the utmost sincerity, the Holy Awe and Majesty of a Calvinist liturgy was missing, as was any sense of historical development of the liturgy over the centuries since the Reformation.

Another consequence of liturgical minimisation includes minimisation of any service that has to do with office. At the New South Wales General Assembly in 2000, the Hunter Presbytery Overtured the Assembly to implement a Liturgy for the Induction of a State Moderator. Up to this point in time there was no induction service as such. The moderator nominate was greeted by words of good will and a prayer by the moderator. With a shake of the hand the change over of Moderator took place. The proposed liturgy for the installation of a State Moderator was the work of the Rev. Dr. John Webster. It is as follows:

> The Moderator shall say: The Grace of the Lord Jesus Christ be with you:
> Hear what the Apostle Paul has written:
> Our gifts differ according to the grace given. If your gift is prophecy, use it as your faith suggests. If administration, use it for administration. If teaching, then use it for teaching. Let the preachers deliver sermons, the almsgivers give freely, the officials be diligent, and those who do works of mercy do them cheerfully. Do not let your love be pretence, but sincerely prefer good to evil. Work for the Lord with untiring effort and with great earnestness of spirit. There are different gifts, but it is the same Spirit who gives them. Each one is given a gift by the Spirit, to use it for the common good. Amen.

The Moderator shall say the following:

The Presbyterian Church of Australia, as part of the Holy Catholic or universal Church, worshipping one God, Father, Son and Holy Spirit, affirms its belief in the Gospel of the Sovereign Grace and love of God, wherein through Jesus Christ, His only Son, incarnate, crucified and risen, He freely offers to all men, upon repentance and faith, the forgiveness of sins, renewal by the Holy Spirit and eternal life, and calls them to labour in the fellowship of faith for the advancement of the kingdom of God throughout the world.

The Presbyterian Church of Australia holds as its subordinate standard the Westminster Confession of Faith, recognising liberty of opinion on such points of doctrine as do not enter the substance of the Faith and claiming the right, in dependence on the promised guidance of the Holy Spirit, to formulate, interpret, or modify its subordinate standards, always in agreement with the Word of God and the fundamental doctrines of the Christian Faith contained in the said Confession, of which the Church itself shall be sole judge.

The Moderator shall say to the newly elected Moderator:

Do you promise to seek the unity and peace of this Church, to uphold the doctrine, worship, government and discipline thereof, and to cherish a spirit of brotherhood, understanding, tolerance and fellowship toward all followers of the Lord?
Answer: I do.
And do you engage in the strength of the Lord Jesus Christ to live a Godly and circumspect life and faithfully and diligently and cheerfully to discharge the duties of your ministry, seeing in all things the advancement of the kingdom of God?
Answer: I do.
(Name) . . . you have been called by God to this special work of State Moderator, you have prepared yourself for this office through prayer and your diligent searching of the Holy Scripture. Knowing that the Holy Spirit has prepared you for this high office, I ask you:
Are you willing to be installed as State Moderator in New South Wales?
Answer: I am.
Will you serve the General Assembly and the Churches in the State of New South Wales with energy, diligence, imagination and love, relying on God's mercy and rejoicing in His promises through Jesus Christ, our Lord?
Answer: I will.

The Past Moderator and the newly elected Moderator will face the congregation. The past Moderator will then ask:

Do you members of this General Assembly accept the Rev./ Mr/ Dr (Name) as the State Moderator for the year . . .
Answer: We do.

The newly elected Moderator will kneel, as the past Moderator leads the Assembly in prayer saying:

> Almighty God, who for the work of Your Son's kingdom, have sanctified in all ages those who have been called to be your servants, and through His Apostles, did order the governance thereof; mercifully behold Your servant.
>
> (Name) . . . whom we have elected to be Moderator of this court of your Church, bestow on him, we ask you, the spirit of wisdom and understanding, of council and strength, that he may fulfil his office to the glory of Your name and the welfare of Your Church, for the sake of the Good Shepherd who gave His life for the sheep, even Jesus Christ, Your Son, our Lord. Amen.

The past Moderator shall declare the commissioned Moderator installed into office, saying:

> (Name) . . . You are now installed as Moderator of this General Assembly. Whatever you do, in word or deed, do everything in the name of the Lord Jesus Christ, giving thanks to God the Father, through Him.

The past Moderator will leave the centre of the sanctuary with his chaplains to suitable seating in the sanctuary.

The newly inducted Moderator will call forward his two chaplains and introduce them to the Assembly, and offer the following prayer:

> God of Grace, You have called us to a common ministry as ambassadors of Christ, entrusting us with the message of reconciliation, give to our Moderator courage and grace to be alert and courteous to the needs of this court and to its officers, so that where your servants rightly lead, we may declare your wonderful deeds and show love to the world, through Jesus Christ the Lord. Amen.

Then shall be sung the hymn *Veni Creator Spiritus*, "Come Holy Ghost, our Souls Inspire". The Moderator shall lead the worship with the following collect:

> O God, You who have prepared for those who love you such good things as pass men's understanding, pour into our hearts such love toward you, that we loving you above all things, may obtain your promises, which exceed all we can desire, through Jesus Christ our Lord. Amen
>
> Lessons Old and New Testament
> Hymn
> Sermon/Moderator's Address
> Liturgy of Holy Communion
> Hymn
> Benediction
> All stand as the Moderator and his chaplains leave the sanctuary, followed by the past Moderators.[53]

This liturgy of induction recognises the importance of the office of Moderator, it acknowledges the solemnity of the occasion and it presents publicly that the Presbyterian Church is a Church that does its business with decorum and good order. Besides it is a public recognition that God calls those who have the gifts to fulfil the responsibilities of office.

The overture was lost, as it was thought that such a liturgy was unnecessary.

Another consequence of liturgical minimisation is the ongoing process that inculcates the notion that the Presbyterian Church is a non-liturgical Church. During the past few years the Presbyterian Church in New South Wales has implemented the Metro Scheme,[54] which provides a pathway for people considering training at theological college. *The Ministry Paper* entitled "*Leading Church*" encourages a non liturgical format for a service of worship. However, the paper does recognise the value of a liturgical approach. In a liturgy model says the Metro Papers, the words are amazingly passionate and honest, well thought out and inspirational. This comment is in stark contrast to the preferred worship practice:

> For many of us, liturgy (a set form of words, e.g. a prayer book) is an unfamiliar way of running our Church meetings. More and more it's becoming a thing of the past.
>
> The whole concept of the "Church meeting" is the conveyance of the Word. At church we try to cater for the listener by preparing messages that convey one big biblical concept or one Big Idea that will be clear and challenging to all who listen. To take it further still, not just the sermon but the entire church service should be shaped around expressing that biblical concept, to try and ensure the seed of God's word is firmly implanted in the heart of the listener.[55]

The order of morning service that is suggested in the *Paper* is as follows:

Songs & prayer
Welcome & announcements Prayer
Key verse
Kids' talk, Kids' song & collection
Break
Prayer focus
Song
Bible reading
Bible talk
Prayer
Song
Food and home.

This order of service is still a liturgy, or at least a para-liturgy. The whole focus is upon an intellectual understanding of the Christian faith. The elements of beauty, art and symbol are minimised. It is a cerebral search for systematic information about God. The accumulated wisdom of the development of liturgy over the centuries gives way to a non-liturgical and overly simplistic notion of worship practice that is conducted in a spirit of informality. Another feature of the *Ministry Paper* is that the suggested order of service is not definitive worship. While our worship of God should be modelled in our church meetings, true worship involves submitting all of our life to the Lord Jesus. So, referring to our church meeting as "worship" can be unhelpful. It fuels the wrong idea that worship stops at the end of the last song. This statement is over simplistic and does not convey the Biblical evidence that God draws near to his people in a special way when they meet in His name. The bare fundamentals of a good, minimised liturgy means that worshippers meeting in His name in fellowship, prayer, instruction in the Word and in praise are drawn face to face before the Holy Majestic Creator and Saviour, and special homage is given before the divine presence.

Harold Best expresses concern that contemporary worship, such as that being described, brings about disconnection between contemporary and the traditional. He ably argues that the contemporary advocates have not produced literature or repertoire that goes into the artistic depth of things. "There is no deep and probing equivalent in the contemporary, say, to the Brahms *Requiem* or Handel's *Messiah*. Usually in the Contemporary service, says Best, music is of the popular variety, which is popular because "it is legitimately shallow".[56]

Sally Morgenthaler rightly sees this contemporary form of service is one that is organised to culminate in what she calls a sermonic punch line. Each step in the service order is designed to achieve that end.[57] That is specifically true of the arguments presented in the *Ministry Papers*.

From a theological perspective this notion of worship is at odds with the protestant reformers, particularly John Calvin. Here, specific reference to the theology of worship in chapter two of this book. Evelyn Underhill rightly interpreted Calvinistic worship in terms of God's unspeakable Majesty and Otherness and the nothingness and simplicity of man.[58] It is in worship that man experiences the Divine Transcendence on the awestruck soul. Worship for Calvin was a serious matter. It was unthinkable to approach worship in a *laissez-faire* fashion. The Biblical notion of the sovereignty of God and the emphasis on the creator/creature distinction demanded a spirit of humility in worship in which man experiences the transcendence of the Almighty God. Worship was to be governed by God's requirements. Any notion of worship which focused on self-satisfaction rather than an obedience and submission to His authority in worship was unacceptable and by definition regarded as idolatrous. T. F. Torrance rightly comments that Calvin never divorced the doctrine of Christ from the doctrine of the Church. This was the fundamental error of Rome and it impacted on the worship of the Church.[59] Calvin argues that the unity of the Church is both physical and spiritual. He likens the external form of the Church to the body and the worship and doctrine of the Church to the soul.

Calvin's Christology cannot be ignored as a prerequisite for worship, as doctrine regulated the due worship of God. Calvin uses the term Chief foundation of worship which is to acknowledge Him to be, as He is, the only source of all virtue, justice, holiness, wisdom, truth, power, goodness, mercy, life and salvation.[60] It is from this biblical view of God that Calvin arrives at the how of worship. It is from this definition of God that gives rise to "prayer, praise and thanksgiving" as these bring Glory to Him. To this he links Adoration which acknowledges our reverence to His greatness, and self abasement which renews the mind as the worshipper renounces the world and the flesh. This is an indication of obedience and devotion to His will. If Prayer, Praise and Thanksgiving, together with Adoration and Self-Abasement, constitute the building blocks of the how of worship then the worship needs structure. It is here that Calvin insists upon Ceremonies. This term is not used in the sense of the worship practices of the medieval era where there were rituals for a multitude of religious ideas. Rather it is a means of providing opportunity of the body and soul being exercised. It is necessary, as Calvin sees it, to worship in this way for two important reasons. The first reason is that it is in this way that we establish God's authority, the second reason is not to follow our own pleasure, as to do so is to be left at liberty to go astray.[61] The how of worship is principally grounded in the acknowledgement of who God is and that He is the source of our salvation.[62] It is the doctrine of God that gives rise to the concept of "Prayer, Praise and Thanksgiving. In order not to be misunderstood Calvin insists that prayer is more than just making requests. It is in prayer that due glory is given to God where the participant feels " that God is the only being to whom he ought to flee".[63] If Prayer, Praise and Thanksgiving are the essential prerequisites of worship, then, as Calvin insists, adoration, ceremonies and self abasement must accompany them. By adoration he means our reverence due to his Greatness and Excellency. Ceremonies are not defined in terms of Church practice during the Medieval era, rather they are helps or instruments subservient to the doctrine of God. Ceremonies are not an invention of man rather they are to be justified according to Biblical principle.

From the historical perspective James Torrance is more in keeping with Calvin's notion of worship, as he defines worship more in terms of Trinitarian worship which is a view of worship that is a gift of participating through the Spirit in the incarnate Son's communion with the Father.[64] If Torrance's view is correct then serious questions need to be asked in respect to the theology that lay behind the METRO *Ministry Papers* view of worship.[65]

These radical changes in the worship practice of many Presbyterian Churches have caused considerable disquiet as the historic liturgical traditions of the Church recede into the background.

The revision of the *Worship Book* of 1998 not only radically changed the content of the liturgy but the spirit that sought the change has had far-reaching consequences in the life and practice of the Church's ministry.

NOTES

1. Of these ministers, Murray, Boase and Webster were elected as N.S.W. State Moderators. The Rev. Robert Willson became the Presbyterian Minister of Blayney in N.S.W. After four years of ministry he was ordained into the Anglican Church in the Diocese of Canberra/Goulburn. He later collected a vast amount of primary material on Dougan's life and ministry. This material is now located in the Ferguson Memorial Library Sydney. Peter Boase writes a good deal about the influence of Dougan in a letter in Willsons first volume of Dougan's material.
2. Church Union was a union of three Churches, the Presbyterian Church the Methodist Church and the Congregational Church. The Union led to the formation of the Uniting Church of Australia. The Union was not as complete as many would have liked as there was a sizable section of the Presbyterian Church remained out of the union due to an inadequate theological basis of the union. To a lesser extent this was also true for the Congregational Church.
3. See the Preface of The Book of Common Order, *Worship* (Sydney: Presbyterian Church of Australia, 1990).
4. D.F. Murray, Private Papers, 7.
5. Blue Book, 1991, Minute 49.
6. Murray, Private Papers, 11.
7. Murray, Private Papers, 7.
8. General Assembly of Australia, *Blue Book* 1997, 198–200.
9. John Dewey, *The Quest for Certainty* (London: Allen & Unwin, 1930), 146.
10. T. A. Stafford, *Christian Symbolism* (New York: Abington-Cokesbury, 1942), 17.
11. Gordon Calthrop, in *Treasury of Quotations* (Michigan: Kregel Publishing, 1977), 692.
12. *The Holy Bible*, 1 Kings 8: 57, 58, 61.
13. For greater detail see C. Jones, *The Study of Liturgy* (Lincon.: SPCK, 1983), 473–80.
14. J. McIntyre, *Theology after the Storm* (Michigan: W. Eerdmans, 1977), 237.
15. McIntyre, *Theology after the Storm*, 239.
16. McIntyre, *Theology after the Storm*, 240.
17. Paul Tillich, *Systematic Theology* (Chicago: University of Chicago Press, 1951), Vol. 1, 177.
18. Tillich, *Systematic Theology*, 241.
19. R.J. Gore, *Covenantal Worship* (Phillipsburg: P&R Publishing, 2002), 154–55.
20. W.D. Maxwell, *Outline of Christian Worship* (London: Oxford University Press 1963), 83.
21. Maxwell, *Outline of Christian Worship*, 81; see also the flowing works: A. Dickens, ed., *Documents of Modern History* (New York: St. Martins Press, 1977), 32, 89; H. Zwingli, *Commentary on True and False Religion* (Carolina: Labyrith Press, 1981), 201; G. Potter, *Zwingli* (London: Historical Association, 1977), 36.
22. A. Dickens, ed., *Documents of Modern History* (New York: St. Martins Press, 1977), 98.
23. H. Zwingli, Commentary on the Sixty Seven Theses 1523, *Documents of Modern History*, 32; also a full account of Zwingli's views on this matter is to found in his *Commentary on True and False Religion*, S. Jackson and C Hiller, Sec. 18, 199.
24. Presbyterian Church of Australia, *Worship*, 1998, 46.
25. Gore, *Covenantal Worship*, 150–51.
26. Richard B. Gaffin, "On Being Reformed", *Bulletin of Westminster Theological Seminary*, 24 April 1985.
27. Maxwell, *Outline of Christian Worship*, 87.
28. Michael Horton, *A Better Way* (Michigan: Baker Books, 2002), 143.
29. See Report to the 1994 General Assembly, *White Book*, 50.

30. C. Balzer, in *Reformed Theological Review*, Vol. 61, No 3, December 2002, 117.
31. Balzer, *Reformed Theological Review*, 120–21.
32. John Woodhouse, *The Briefing*, No 124, November 1993, 2.
33. George May, "The Lord's Supper: Ritual or Relationship? Part 2", *The Reformed Theological Review*, 61, 1 (2002): 123.
34. See Robert G. Rayburn, *O Come Let Us Worship* (Michigan: Baker Book House, 1982), Chapter 3.
35. General Assembly of Australia Reports, *White Book*, 1994, 51.
36. *White Book*, 51.
37. An arrangement was made between the Presbyterian Church in New South Wales and Moore College for Presbyterian students who wished to study towards a degree. This arrangement was made due to the fact that the Presbyterian College was unable to offer degree courses after Church Union in 1977. The Church has since developed a flourishing Theological College offering Diplomas, Degrees from Bachelors to Doctorates. This arrangement with Moore College was in place for over twenty years.
38. Broughton Knox deliberately kept the influence of the archdioceses at a distance and kept the influence of Archbishop Marcus Loane to a minimum. The Archbishop was concerned at the way in which the College was encouraging a view of the Church that was not consistent with the Elizabethan settlement. The views of Knox was seen by the Archbishop as excessive Calvinism and Independency.
39. J.R. Reid, *Marcus L. Loane* (Brunswick East: Acorn Press, 2004), 108.
40. Reid, *Marcus Loane*, 108; see also how these views have been further refined into a praxis for the contemporary Church within the Archdiocese of Sydney in *A Report from the Sydney Diocesan Doctrine Commission, 2008*. "A Theology of Christian Assembly". This paper was a supplementary Report of a Standing Committee. The paper shows a refined alignment that exists between N.S.W. Presbyterianism and the Anglican Archdioceses of Sydney.
41. Muriel Porter, *The New Puritans* (Melbourne: Melbourne University Press, 2006), 52.
42. Robert J. Banks, "The Theology of D. B. Knox", in *God who is Rich in Mercy,* eds P. O'Brien and D. Peterson, (Homebush West: Lancer Books, 1986), 395–97.
43. P. Carnley, *Reflections in Glass* (Sydney: Harper Collins, 2004), 69–70.
44. Carnley, *Reflections*, 71.
45. Carnley, *Reflections*, 6.
46. Porter, *The New Puritans*, 22.
47. A.T.B. McGowan, *The Divine Spiration of Scripture* (Nottingham: Apollos Press, 2007), 20–21.
48. . McGowan here relies on the work of Richard A. Muller, *Post-Reformation Reformed Dogmatics* Vol. 2, *Holy Scripture: The Cognitive Foundations of Theology* (Grand Rapids: Baker Books, 1993), 3.
49. McGowan, *Divine Spiration*, 32.
50. Michael Horton "Critical Connection," in *Australian Presbyterian*, December (2007), 6.
51. White Book, 1997, 29–31.
52. *Blue Book*, 1997, 241.
53. General Assembly of New South Wales, *White Book*, 2000, 74–77.
54. The METRO Scheme stands for "Ministry Equipping, Training and Recruiting Organisation". Metro is about ministry training that is geared to the local church context, and provides an evangelistic model as standard for local church ministry. It is pre- theological college training. The scheme offers one- to -one training in an apprentice style training scheme. The scheme makes extensive use of the *Ministry Papers*.
55. Presbyterian Youth N.S.W. *Ministry Papers* (Sydney: Presbyterian Youth N.S.W., 2006.)
56. Harold Best, "Contemporary Music – Driven Worship", in P. Engle and P. Basden, *Exploring the Worship Spectrum,* (Michigan: Zondervan, 2004), 123.
57. See, Sally Morgenthaler, "Emerging Worship," in *Exploring the Worship*, edited by P. Engle & P, Basden, *Exploring the Worship Spectrum*, (Grand Rapids:Zondervan,2004), 223.
58. Underhill, *Worship*, 16.

59. T.F. Torrance, ed., *John Calvin's Tracts and Treatises* (Michigan: Eerdmans, 1958), Vol.1, vii; see also, H.R. Mackintosh, *The Person of Jesus Christ* (Edinburgh: T.&T Clark, 1956), Chapter 7. It is here that Mackintosh traces the history of Christology of the Reformation Church.

60. Torrance, *Calvin's Tracts and Treatises* xxvii–xxviii.

61. Torrance, *Tracts and Treatises* Vol. 2, 128. Calvin defines in a more detailed way what he means by terms such as prayer, adoration ceremonies, self abasement, etc., 130–32.

62. Torrance, *Tracts and Treatises*, Vol. 1, 127.

63. Torrance, *Tracts and Treatises*, Vol. 1, 130.

64. James Torrance, *Worship, Community and the Triune God of Grace* (London: IVP, 1996), 20.

65. It would be an interesting piece of research to examine whether or not the author of the *Metro Papers* is divorcing the Doctrine of God from the Doctrine of the Church.

Chapter Six

Towards an Epistemology of Worship

In chapter five it was shown that the view that the rich liturgical Calvinist tradition expressed in the *Book of Common Order* of 1929 and 1954 as well as the provisional *Worship Book* of 1991, were displaced in favour of a through going Zwinglian version. The revised *Worship Book* of 1998 saw revolutionary changes in the liturgy of the Church, in which symbols were removed together with large sections of the liturgical content. The change in the liturgical perspective was generated largely due to the theological perspective of those who were in sympathy with the mien of Moore Theological College. It was further argued that the influence of Dr Broughton Knox, in particular, was very evident among those who sought liturgical change. Critical to Knox's theological perspective was the notion of Propositional Revelation.

The aim of this chapter is to introduce and apply the novel theory of Transformative Subjugation to the Church's liturgical practice. This theory is the work of Professor Ronald S. Laura (the co-author of this book) the foundational precept being Bacon's notion that "knowledge is power". The application of this theory to the Church's theological outlook and practice gives a coherent explanation to current theological and liturgical practice within the contemporary Presbyterian Church in Australia.

In order to achieve this we shall, in the first instance, define more precisely the content of "transformative subjugation", which has its foundations in the epistemology which arose out of the Enlightenment. It will be argued that this theory has become the operative epistemology of modern education of which theological education is an integral part of the same process. It will be shown that there is a long history within the Reformed Church and the Presbyterian Church in particular of the application of the scientific method in the science of theology and so opening the epistemological door that provides the soil for "transformative subjugation" to take root. There will also be an attempt to provide an alternative epistemology, put forward by Cornelius Van Til, to act as a counter balance to the dominance and control of the current theological perspective.

THE THEORY OF TRANSFORMATIVE SUBJUGATION

Since knowledge is a form of power, knowledge becomes a form of control, and the more control we have, the more secure we become. If nature can be predicted, the more readily it can be controlled. The technologies born out of this form of knowledge will themselves replicate through their own inventions in nature the obsession of our culture with domination and subjugation. It is argued that the technological process of control through *transformative subjugation* involves taking the vital things of nature and converting them into the utilitarian things of mankind. Technology thus gives us the power over nature by systematically synthesizing and reconstructing it. Technology is the tool we have created to reconstruct nature.[1] Although this theory is applied in the first instance to nature and the environment, it also can be applied to the theological perspective of the Presbyterian Church. In a Christian denomination such as the Presbyterian Church, theological knowledge is power. If theology is predictable, as the Reformed/Puritan version is, through its "Confessions of Faith", the theology that is explicit or implied is highly reductionist. The outcome of this is many Church members feel secure in their faith. Because the theology is so predictable it is also more controllable, and unfortunately also open to abuse. Control is mediated through a technological process, but the question remains, "what is the technological process for the Church? Power and control, we would claim, operates through *liturgical technology*. It is through the liturgical functions of the Church that the claims of the Gospel are conveyed and taught. Biblical theology is reconstructed into a form which satisfies the desires of those who operate the liturgical technology. The technology is itself a replicate of a value laden theological knowledge which those in control desire. Liturgical Technology is enhanced through the use of physical apparatus such as light and sound controls, the use of data projectors and musical synthesisers. As in nature the theological perspective of the Church becomes open to expropriation, exploitation and manipulation. It is important to realise at this point that the technology that has arisen out of the scientific method is not value free nor is it neutral. On the view we advance here every piece of information which is accepted as knowledge is structurally encoded to ensure a covert measure of control over every aspect our lives.[2] This presumption of knowledge encoded as power, argues Chapman, will have serious implications in the way in which education actually informs and shapes the very foundations of sociocultural values. From this it follows that the liturgical apparatus is also not neutral. It becomes a powerful tool to assert a particular theological perspective to the exclusion of all other perspectives. Control and manipulation become the essential characteristics in the liturgical process. The process of liturgical minimisation in previous chapters of this work is evidence of a process that has encoded theological presumptions which exclude traditional vitals of historic liturgical practice and by implication deem them Biblically unnecessary or not consistent with the Reformed tradition. Evelyn Underhill has succinctly described the type of Christianity that structurally encodes the liturgical technology that presently operates within the Presbyterian Church:

> The small company of keen believers ready to press the teaching of the Gospel to its logical conclusions: ruthlessly rejecting all that conflicts with evangelical ardour and simplicity, demanding personal consecration, downright costly conversion of the whole life to God's purpose, repudiating all substitutes for the offering of the self. It restores to their original position of importance the charismatic and prophetic characteristics of primitive Christianity: and hence is suspicious of set forms, and demands a spontaneous worship which shall be the devotional expression of a personal and subjective relation to God. The responsibility and capacity of each soul, the priesthood of all believers, the universal call to sanctity, are the central truths governing real Free Church worship.[3]

Current liturgical practice within the Australian Presbyterian Church suggests that the liturgical technology is saturated with power with the intent to force a narrow extreme Puritan theological perspective thereby restricting debate within the confines of accepted Reformed parameters. This specific epistemology of power is locked into a Newtonian type paradigm that excludes the possibility of new theological paradigms from emerging. On the practical level this means that there are those who see the Church emerging as the true Church of the protestant Reformation. Those who think outside of the accepted paradigm are seen as not being faithful to the Reformed tradition. This means that the integrity of genuine theological debate is compromised. We would see this circumstance as a "paralysis of the intellectual imagination", whereby the mind becomes closed on those issues which are fundamentally open, and the inability to imagine things as they are not, imprisons the human being in the world of things as they are. We would argue that the intellectual components of our individual autonomy are eroded by a narrowing of the mind's eye such that we see only those things which others want to us to see.[4]

Relevancy is seen to be one of the most important aspects of "liturgical technology" through which covert control and manipulation is exerted. In the present context the term "relevancy" is itself value laden. Relevancy is relevant in terms of a specific theological perspective and the whims of socio/

cultural acceptance. In order to evangelise, the Church structures its worship services with an aim to making its content non-threatening to outsiders while making its contemporary believers comfortable in their expression of spirituality. The idea of presenting notions of the Holy, the Mysterious or even religious, are avoided as these notions may put off those who are possible converts. This can be demonstrated when a minister was asked, "Do you still sing hymns in your worship services?" When he replied "Yes', the response was to the point and swift, "Well that is the kiss of death". This response was in the context of a discussion on the type of worship services that were required if the younger generation were to be attracted to the Church. Implied in this response is the idea that structure and tradition in worship services are a thing of the past and that Churches that continue to use such formal structures are doomed.

Since science and technology play a salient role in defining the dominant belief systems of most within the community, there exists a presumption that if Christian worship is to be relevant, then it must adopt a theological posture that capitulates to the dominant frame of epistemological reference. This being so, Rationalism and Empiricism have come to play an important role in shaping the foundational epistemology of the Christian Church and its message. Most modern theologians, argues Andrew McGowan, have accepted the Enlightenment consensus, arguing that real knowledge must be obtained from rational reflection upon the information received through sense perception.[5] Just as the Newtonian mechanistic paradigm yielded so much for the development of modern science, it is also true that the same paradigm when applied to theology also yielded a high degree of certainty of belief and practice, in a rapidly changing world. The two basic principles that undergird the Enlightenment paradigms are the autonomy of man and the final authority of reason. To appreciate fully this assumption an explanation of the epistemological foundations of the Enlightenment is required.

THE BACKGROUND[6]

It has always been strange that theologians adopted a scientific methodology that arose out of the philosophical principles of the Enlightenment, as they drove a philosophical wedge between the physical and spiritual realities.

Plato was driven to a rational understanding of the eternal world of ideas to give a teleological understanding to physical reality. Without it, a thoroughgoing scepticism would emerge. In his *Timaeus* Plato's unchanging and eternal world is apprehended by intelligence and reason, while change in the physical world is apprehended by sense. The physical world being apprehended by sense cannot be eternal and must have been created by God. Since God is good, He made the world after the pattern of the eternal. He desired that everything should be good and nothing bad. Finding the whole visible sphere not at rest, but moving in an irregular and disorderly fashion, God brought order out of confusion. Without God there can only be disorder and chaos. The created order therefore can only have its explanation in terms of God's creative intervention. Similarly the intelligence of man has its explanation in God. God, claims Plato, put intelligence in the soul and the soul in the body. God made the world as a whole and man as a living creature having soul and intelligence. Unless there is order and stability in the created order, there can be no basis for knowledge, for knowledge implies fixity and an abiding nature somewhere.

Put in another way, a world of change provides no basis for an epistemology. In the world of sense, everything is ephemeral and in constant process of change. Knowledge requires therefore the world of the Idea and Form. A. K. Rogers expresses the notion of Idea and Form as, "absolute, abiding without variableness or shadow of turning, which sensation never can attain to, but thought alone. Over against that world of flux, where nothing is, but all things seem, it is the vocation of Plato to set up a standard of unchangeable reality, which in its highest theoretic development becomes the world of eternal and immutable ideas, indefectible outlines of thought, yet also the veritable things of experience".[7]

In this there is an obvious dualism between soul and body. The soul's essence is found only in the contemplation of ideas as the world of sense is not the real world. The particulars of physical reality are known only through the senses, but the real world of Ideas can only be known through the contemplation of the mind. In his *Phaedo*, Plato argues that true knowledge is located in universals and it is the soul in its intellectual capacity that is designed to access that world.

The Christian Church has always claimed that God created all things out of nothing (*creatio ex nihilo*) and the created order was perfect. Mankind was created in God's image in terms of righteousness and holiness. Genesis chapters one to three clearly shows that God is an essential prerequisite in understanding the created order. Fiat creation implies meaning and purpose. Without God's command there can be no explanation of the existence of the physical world. Nor can there be an explanation of the differentiation between man and the animal kingdom. The Christian distinctiveness of man is well summed up in the *Westminster Shorter Catechism* Question One: "The chief purpose of man is to glorify God and to enjoy him for ever."

The Genesis account of creation is critical to the understanding of a Christian Epistemology. In a similar way the Christian Church needs to locate a biblical epistemology in Genesis. Plato established his epistemology upon universals, but the Church in a like manner must establish its epistemology, not in the "Eternal World of Ideas' but rather in the Creator God who created *ex nihilo*.

C. Van Til argues that the early Church Fathers had no well-defined and developed epistemology.[8] At best it was an implied epistemology in the general philosophy of life. Augustine, for example, differed from Plato in a major way. According to Plato man is not created in the image of God because there is no God sufficiently absolute to create man in his own image. In the Platonic story of creation God looks up to the Ideas that are next to him and is conditioned by material that is independent of him. The God of Plato does not carry within him the ultimate principle of unity and diversity, but is looking for it.[9]

This means that the epistemological foundations of Plato's work, although similar on the surface, are very different from the biblical and Augustinian thought which locates the foundations of epistemology in the doctrine of the Trinity.

THE ENLIGHTENMENT PERIOD

The Epistemological foundations of Descartes, Lock, Berkley, Kant and others not only drove a wedge deeper into Plato's dualism, between body and soul, they eventually excluded God altogether by excluding *a priori* propositions. The acceptance of *a posteriori* propositions among the "empiricists' was not always clear and consistent. As D.W. Hamlyn points out, there is a prima facie exception to the empirical thesis that the senses provide knowledge. Even in its weakest form as the propositions of mathematics, they have usually been thought to be *a priori*, not *a posteriori* – that is we can know their truth independently of experience.[10] Put another way, the full flowering of Enlightenment philosophy located epistemology in the autonomy of man and the final authority of reason. An important figure in the modern era also depended on a dualism and the authority of autonomous man. He was: Rene Descartes (1596–1650). His starting point was expressed in the phrase *cogito ergo sum*, "I think therefore I am". His system was dependent upon a marked dualism between matter and spirit. He located the foundation of knowledge in the universal *a priori* principles that are known intuitively. From these principles other truths can be deduced, by the unerring method of mathematics. Rationalists such as Descartes were greatly impressed by the cogency and exactitude of mathematics, so they had no hesitation in using a mathematical model to determine truth. He established a new code of rules which were based on mathematical reasoning.[11] There is no better example of Descartes rationalism than in his rules two and three: Rule 2 says, "We should attend only to those objects of which our minds seem capable of having certain and indubitable cognition".[12]

Commenting on this, Descartes argues: "So in accordance with this rule, we reject all such merely probable cognition and resolve to believe only what is perfectly known and incapable of being doubted, truths which suffice for the sure demonstration of countless propositions which so far they (the educated who doubt that there is very little indubitable knowledge) have managed as no more than probable". The Third Rule describes the two basic processes of attaining certain knowledge: "Concerning objects proposed for study, we ought to investigate what we can clearly and evidently intuit or deduce with certainty, and not what other people have thought or what we ourselves conjecture". Commenting on this Descartes defines what he means by intuition and deduction: "By 'intuition' I do not mean the fluctuating testimony of the senses or the deceptive judgement of the imagination as it botches things together, but the conception of a clear and attentive mind, which is so easy and distinct that there can be no room for doubt about what we are understanding". When defining deduction, he says: "we mean the inference of something as following necessarily from some other propositions which are known with certainty".[13]

At this point in his argument Descartes distinguishes between the knowledge attained by intuition and deduction, and that which is revealed by God. Since faith in these matters, as in anything obscure, is an act of the will rather than an act of the understanding. And if Faith has a basis in our intellect, revealed truths above all can and should be discovered by one or other of the two ways we have just described.[14] By locating matters of faith to an act of the will, he demotes belief in God as of secondary importance as real knowledge is an act of the intellect. Bishop George Berkeley on the other hand refuses to locate faith in God as of secondary importance. Berkley reveals his rationalism when the senses were not perceiving the required sensations when there was no vision. Belief became a necessity. His position is well summed up by Ronald Knox in this verse:

> There was once a young man who said, "God
> Must think it exceedingly odd
> If he finds that this tree
> Continues to be
> When there's no one about in the Quad".
> REPLY
> Dear Sir:
> Your astonishment's odd:
> I am always about in the Quad.
> And that's why the tree
> Will continue to be,
> Since observed by
> Yours faithfully,
> GOD.[15]

THE EMPIRICISTS

The Empiricists, while they may differ in their interpretation of the deductive process, do not reject it. What they do reject is the concept of knowledge as a closed deductive system, based on fixed *a priori* principles. The universe is to be thought of in terms of mathematical connections, as in a vast machine. The power of reductionism was later exhibited mathematically in the discovery of calculus, by Isaac Newton. This was important as, that by subdividing nature into component systems, the machinery of nature could be understood in mathematical terms. Thus reductionism becomes an essential characteristic of modern scientific thought.[16] By this means man becomes the master and possessor of nature. It can be argued that faith in the mechanical paradigm can enhance the idea that nature had no intrinsic value or purpose. This enabled man to transform the resources of nature into something of economic value, to be exchanged and consumed in society.[17]

The development of empiricism continued the growing awareness of the autonomy of man and the affirmation of the authority of reason.

In contrast to rationalism, Empiricism argued that all knowledge comes through sense perception. This says McGowan is the crucial element in modern scientific Methodology, whereby truth is obtained through experiment, followed by logical Deduction from the evidence produced by the experiment. The more notable exponents of this method were John Locke, Bishop George Berkeley and David Hume.

John Locke refused to accept innate ideas. "To imprint anything on the mind without the mind's perceiving it seems to me hardly intelligible".[18] The content of the mind is supplied through experience and observation: "the mind has its first objects, and by what steps it makes progress to the laying in and storing up those ideas out of which is to be framed all the knowledge it is capable of; I must appeal to experience and observation".[19]

The content of the mind is supplied through experience and observation. All knowledge is the result of experience in that external objects come to us by sensation and the reflection that takes place within the mind. It is through the external and internal sensations that are the windows by which light is let into (the dark room) of the mind:

> For me thinks the understanding is not much unlike a closet wholly shut from light, with only some little opening left to let in external visible resemblances or ideas of things without: would the pictures coming into such a dark room but stay there, and lie so orderly as to be found upon occasion, it would very much resemble the understanding of a man, in reference to all objects of sight, and the ideas of them...[20]

It was by this empirical understanding that John Locke's observation and experimentation came to be exalted.

The impact of empiricism was to support the ideas of man's autonomy and the final authority of reason as a basis of an effective epistemology which gave man power and control over the machine of nature. We therefore argue for this outcome in this way:

> In assuming an epistemic posture by way of which we detach ourselves from the world we investigate, for the purpose of maintaining objectivity of the mechanical paradigm, we unwittingly and almost imperceptibly sever our relationships with the natural order. In so doing we achieve the kind of epistemic view which encourages the temptation to reduce those "things" of which nature is made to nothing more than objects for commercial manipulation and exploitation.[21]

Jeremy Rifkin argues for the autonomy of man, by asserting that the mechanical paradigm was irresistible as it was simple and predictable. However there was a problem, the erratic behaviour of people and the imperfect workings of government and the economy didn't seem to square with the well ordered mechanical explanation of the world that Bacon, Descartes and Newton had put forth. As Rifken sees it the problem was resolved by human beings following natural law rather than a religious world view. By excluding God, humanity would have a new purpose in life instead of the medieval goal of seeking salvation in the next world humanity would seek the perfection in this world. History then is seen by Rifkin as a progressive journey towards a well-ordered and predictable state represented by the Newtonian world machine. Rikkin's argument is firmly located in the philosophy of John Locke: "Locke provided an argument that has continued to dominate the modern world view down to the present. Once we cut through useless custom and superstition, argued Locke, we see society, being made solely of individuals creating their own meaning, has one purpose only: to protect and allow for the increase of the property of its members".[22]

This conclusion is identical with that of the Laura and Ashton work. Science and technology grew at a rapid rate with beneficial results. The new epistemological outlook was revolutionary. Thomas Kuhn has shown clearly that the new philosophical paradigm, initiated by Descartes and the development of Newtonian dynamics, has served both science and philosophy well: "Its exploitation, like that of dynamics itself, has been fruitful of a fundamental understanding that perhaps could not have been achieved in another way".[23]

The important issue to understand for the purposes of this thesis is that in the development of both rationalism and empiricism God was being pushed further to the periphery of man's life and understanding. It was only a matter of time before David Hume (1711–1776) the Scottish sceptic pushed empiricism to its logical conclusion by removing God altogether. Hume is both a rationalist and an empiricist.

After an exhaustive attack on the evidence for miracles, he concludes that the Christian religion: "is founded upon faith, not on reason; and it is a sure method of exposing it to put it to such a trial as it is, by no means, fitted to endure ... So that, upon a whole, we may conclude, that the Christian Religion not only was at first attended with miracles, but even at this day cannot be believed by any reasonable person without one.[24]

In like manner in his Dialogues, after sceptical arguments against extra-empirical knowledge, he concludes:

> A person, seasoned with a just sense of the imperfections of natural reason, will fly to revealed truth with the greatest avidity: While haughty Dogmatist, persuaded that he can erect a complete system of Theology by the mere help of philosophy, disdains any further aid, and rejects this adventitious instructor. To be a philosophical Sceptic is, in man of letters, the first and most essential step towards being a sound, believing Christian.[25]

Without discussing the implications of Hume's thought, especially whether or not the distinction between faith and knowledge is valid, the important thing to note is that Hume's understanding of empiricism and his epistemology exclude God.

In the next century Emmanuel Kant did something similar in drawing a distinction between the phenomenal realm and the noumenal. The phenomenal realm is the real world, of sense experience, whereas the noumenal world is a world in which the normal rules of sense experience and rational deduction do not apply. Kant was committed to the idea of the autonomy of man and the final authority of reason. Although he accepted that all knowledge was derived from experience he refused to accept the Lockian idea that the mind was a blank page (*tabula rasa*). Kant argued that the mind played a part in the reception of knowledge because it processed the facts of experience. The mind, he concluded, provides the missing link between the rationalist and the empiricist. The mind provides the "objectivity".[26] Christianity was explained in terms of the "phenomenal realm" and the "noumenal realm". This meant that Christianity was stripped of its supernatural elements including the idea of faith and that of a personal God. This reduced Christianity to a non–supernatural religion that bore little relation to Biblical Christianity. This Kantian synthesis became the underlying philosophy of Theological Liberalism.

The outcome of the Enlightenment has been well expressed, although somewhat overstated by David Wells who describes the outcome in theological categories:

> The prerogatives that had belonged to God did not simply disappear; now they appeared in human beings. The revelation he had given now reappeared in the form of natural reason, which would do what revelation had done but without

the discomfort of requiring humanity to submit to the God from whom the revelation had come; the idea of salvation was retained but transformed into the drive for human perfectibility, at first achieved by moral striving and then, as we know it today, by psychological technique; grace became effort; the life of faith became the hope of personal growth; and eschatology became progress (what Lord Acton called the religion of those who have none). Thus was the Christian Trinity replaced by a substitute trinity of reason, nature, and progress. The place God had occupied was now occupied by the human being. Meaning and morality, which only God could give, were taken to be purely human accomplishments.[27]

Science, says McGowan, became the model for "all academic work and "scientific" accuracy became the standard against which all other truths claimed were judged".[28]

The Application of this scientific methodology to an Evangelical sense of Theology led to the idea that the Bible can be reduced to a set of propositions that can be demonstrated as being true. The key to understanding the transmission of a liturgical minimisation process during the 1970s and beyond, in the Presbyterian Church is via Broughton Knox who upheld propositional revelation, which necessitates acceptance of a scientific paradigm. In response to this view many prestigious scholars at Oxford and Cambridge, such as Leonard Hodgson, John Burnaby and later Archbishop Temple, all denied propositional revelation. Hodgson, for example, argued: "The Word of God is not a proposition or a series of propositions prescribing what we are to believe or think. It is a series of divine acts, when they are reflected on the mind as it seeks their significance. The revelation is given in deeds: the doctrines of the faith are formulated by reflection on the significance of those deeds".[29] Responding to these viewpoints Knox responded with this statement: "The denial of 'propositional revelation' is the denial that God reveals himself to men through the medium of words, that is to say, through meaningful statements and concepts expressed in words, for such is the only sense that can be given to the word "propositional". He argues that such a view runs counter to the biblical view of revelation. The view of the Bible is that revelation is essentially propositional.[30] There seems to be a contrast of opinion between the Cambridge and Oxford scholars and Knox. This is the result of a problematic epistemology. In a narrow sense both the Cambridge and Oxford scholars and Broughton Knox were right, as both are holding to an epistemological framework that has arisen out of the Enlightenment. The comment of Hodgson above is in one sense right in that God the Spirit is able to effect change in man's spirituality, but on the other hand Hodgson seems to be declaring that the Word of God is reflected only in the mind and not reflected upon the written page. This suggests that language is in no sense propositional. Unless language is propositional how can anything written become cognitive? The cognitive aspect of language becomes essential if a mathematical proposition is to be understood and declared axiomatic. Unless language in one sense is rational and propositional the authority of Scripture becomes meaningless. From a Christian perspective the locus of authority becomes embedded in the Christian community and not in God. Knox, one the other hand, accepting a scientific methodology, wants to preserve the authority and inspiration of the Scriptures, for to deny it is to submit to the relativism of postmodern views of truth. Both Hodgson and Knox want to say that God still speaks through the Scripture. Insisting upon the assumptions of a scientific method it is better to regard the systematic formulations of doctrine not as truth per se, but rather as a Directory of Biblical Doctrine, for the guidance of the Christian community to use in a way in which the Word of God can speak in the Scriptures. This only serves to illustrate the imperative need to develop a Christian epistemology.

If David Hume brought empiricism to its logical conclusion then, in the twentieth century, the Logical Positivists popularised the conclusions and inculcated the idea that science was the vehicle to real knowledge and that religious belief systems were unnecessary and redundant.

Another important development in the autonomy and authority of man came in the twentieth century and it was used to drive a wedge between the Church and scientific truth. This movement had a lasting impact upon the work of the Church.

LOGICAL POSITIVISTS

This school of thought popular among students in the 1960s is distinguished by the concern to separate positive science from all metaphysical and religious influence. It was necessary to find a means of freeing science from religion and metaphysics so as to provide a firm and credible epistemology. This was a real problem in that the empirical experience of the positive sciences was just as open to the possibility of bias as the religious experience, from which the positivists sought emancipation. Ludwig Wittgenstein provided the logical basis for the positivist's quest.[31]

Wittgenstein's picture theory of meaning supported the view that truth conditions must be verifiable. It can be shown how A.J. Ayer used the "picture theory" to forge a conceptual tool for eliminating metaphysical and religious statements from the realm of meaning discourse. The damaging implication of Ayer's philosophy is the implication that the propositions of religion and metaphysics limit the range of possible truth-achieving propositions to those which were meaningful by his criterion.

By the mid-twentieth century science had effectively displaced God, but the scientific method used to establish truth claims had been adopted by theologians of the Church to determine theological truth. Put another way, a secular scientific methodology which was controlled by the autonomy and self-sufficiency of man, had now become the final point of epistemic reference.

The point of this somewhat long discussion on the autonomy and final authority of man's reason is to show that the long history of this epistemological thinking has had enduring implications in theoretical knowledge as well as in theological knowledge over a long period of time. Theologians have used the same epistemological methods as their scientific counterparts. This explains the philosophical background to liturgical technology, the tool that is used to dominate and control the Church within narrow theological parameters.

INFLUENTIAL THEOLOGIANS IN AUSTRALIAN PRESBYTERIANISM

There are a number of theologians who have been influential in Australian Presbyterianism who applied the same reductionist principles of a scientific methodology to theology. This has paved the way for the process of "transformative subjugation". Specifically, these influential theologians were: Thomas Chalmers of Edinburgh and the Princetonians Charles Hodge and B.B. Warfield.

Andrew McGowan argues that although well-intentioned, the theologians who reduced the Scriptures to a set of facts must then arrange and exhibit them, usually in the form of a Systematic Theology. This, he argues, is to "change the Scriptures from their true nature as the Word of God into something cold and clinical, which we possess and which we manipulate".[32] David Wells gives expression to the same idea when he argues that Enlightenment ideology (ideology is a worldview with attitude) has the intent to control. Through the passage of time and the desire to be triumphant, "ideologies tend to become simplistic ... and they find acceptance because they tap into our need".[33] This is precisely the argument of Laura and Ashton in their book on environmental education, albeit an application in another discipline. McGowan extends his argument to the central thesis of his book, on the doctrine of Scripture. He argues that the outcome of the scientific methodology results in "a belief in the inerrancy of the autographa ... and it reduces Scripture to a set of propositions under the theologian's control".[34] One doctrine that came into prominence as a result of this view of Scripture was the penal substitutionary theory of the Atonement.

Kevin J. Vanhoozer argues that the Penal Substitutionary theory, like other theories of the Atonement in the history of the doctrine, says more about the history and culture of the people who devised it than it does about the Cross.[35] The mere fact that the Penal Substitutionary theory lends itself to "deconstruction" is in itself characteristic of a theory which is dependent on a scientific paradigm. Certainly the rise to popularity of the Penal Substitionary theory was coincidental with the wide acceptance of the Newtonian mechanistic worldview. Vanhoozer points to the work of Joel Green and Mark Baker who suggest that the model of the theory "betrays the hallmarks of modernity: an anthropocentric tendency to see the significance of Jesus' death as limited to human beings; an individualistic tendency to see Jesus' death as benefiting isolated persons; a moralist tendency to see Jesus' death as a punishment for the acts of sinful individuals. To understand the Atonement in post-modernity, then, one has to come to grips with the deconstruction (that is, the exposure of its constructedness) of the Penal Substitution theory.

After considerable struggle and argument and trust in human reason to explain the Theology of the Cross, Vanhoozer concludes that we nevertheless are fed the answer every Sunday when we take Holy Communion. At the celebration of Holy Communion we begin to realise that the sacrament transcends all the theories of the Atonement. He puts it this way:

> Post-moderns or not, we gather around the Lord's Table as we have been instructed, ("Do this in remembrance of me"), awaiting the elements that signify more than our saving theories. Then, like the five thousand, we discover that after our centuries-long banquet of atonement theology, there are still more fragments of the Cross left over. As we seek to understand the atonement in post-modernity or at any other time, let us fill our baskets and keep the feast.[36]

Even if one agrees with this conclusion of Vanhoozer, what if, while we were participating in the sacrament, we realized that the liturgy had already been minimised to the point that the worship liturgy is sterile and dead? This circumstance is indeed challenging to say the least. From a Calvinist perspective the only response is a continuing belief in the sovereign work of the Holy Spirit that transcends the actions of men's liturgical manipulations. Despite the minimisation of the liturgy God is still able to reveal His majestic and holy Presence.

The attention is now to focus on Chalmers, Hodge and Warfield who applied the scientific methodology to their theological pursuits.

Thomas Chalmers 1780–1847 was professor of Divinity at Edinburgh University. He resigned his position at the time of the Disruption in the Church of Scotland in 1843. He became Principal of the New College, a theological institution created by the newly formed Free Church of Scotland. Chalmers became a household name throughout the western theological world. His influence as a Church statesman and theologian was international. Stuart Piggin described him as Scotland's greatest modern Churchman.[37] Many of his students achieved lasting fame. Among them were John Urquhart, Alexander Duff, Robert Nesbit, John Adam, David Ewart and William Mackay all of whom devoted them-selves to missionary work in India. Chalmers' influence reached Australian shores, as many of the clergy arriving from Scotland were trained by him at the University of Edinburgh or at the New College. Some of those who were not specifically studying directly under him were nevertheless influenced by him. John Dunmore Lang was one such person. Lang's name was synonymous with the establishment of the Presbyterian Church in Australia. Lang fell under the spell of Chalmers while he was a student at Glasgow University. Chalmers at the time was an innovative minister in Glasgow where he preached his famous "Astronomical Sermons", and established a successful new Church of St John's. Lang attended St John's where the influence of Chalmers became deeply imbedded in his soul. It was from Glasgow that Chalmers' academic career began. He became the Professor of Moral Philosophy at St. Andrew's University where he had previously lectured in mathematics and chemistry. Within a few short years he accepted the chair of Divinity at Edinburgh. Throughout Australia there were many Presbyterian Churches called "Chalmers Church", so called as a testimony to the esteem in which he was regarded both by laity and clergy. Mark Hutchinson comments that Thomas Chalmers was Lang's great mentor. He argues that Lang had imbibed a great deal of the pre-1823 Chalmers programme in Glasgow, which suited the moral decadent society of Sydney. This suited Lang's character and the Glasgow experiment born out of the slums appealed to him as being suitable for a transplant in Australia. Hutchinson writes:

Hutchinson sees the Chalmers experiment at St. John's, Glasgow as an integration of activism, Biblical social concern and a renewal of Knox's vision of a Godly Commonwealth. The ministry of Chalmers in Glasgow had an emphasis on poor relief, education and a ministry to the whole of life. This approach to ministry was ideal for decant Sydney. Under the leadership the of Lang this type of ministry was prosecuted with enthusiasm.

Chalmers was exposed to the scientific methodology whist he was a postgraduate student at Edinburgh University studying chemistry and mathematics. He was indebted to Professor Robison from whom he received a profound admiration and understanding of the Baconian method of investigation.[38]

In his Institutes of Theology, Chalmers makes a firm argument to apply the analytic method to understand the science of theology:

> By the analytic, you begin with the objects or the phenomena which first solicit your regards, and these by comparison and abstraction you are enabled to resolve into their principles. It is evident that the synthetic treatment demand a full and thorough and confident acquaintance with the subject matter to which it is applied, and withal a clear and correct notion of the primitive

elements that enter into the investigation, lest in the stream of ratiocination downward some original flaw in the premises shall be found to vitiate every deduction that may have issued from an infected fountainhead. The analytic, again, is more applicable to a subject where, instead of having the principles to set out with, you have the principles to seek, and so beginning with the phenomena that are most palpable or nearest at hand, you, by a reverse process, end where the other begins. This latter mode is surely the fitter for a science beset on either side with mysteries unfathomable – a science all whose light breaks in upon us by partial and imperfect disclosures, and where we vainly try to find a ligament or connecting principle between one ascertained truth and another. With such a science we should feel inclined to proceed *modo indagandi* rather than *modo demonstrandi*. And theology we hold to be pre-eminently such a science – a science whose initial elements we cannot pluck from the dark recesses of the eternity that is past, and whose ultimate conclusions we cannot follow to the dark and distant recesses of the eternity before us, and which we can therefore only explore to the confines of the light that has been made to shine around us. There it our duty to stop, intruding not into the things which we have not seen, and to wait in humble expectancy for the day of a larger and brighter manifestation.[39]

It was clear that Chalmers was adopting an empirical approach to the study of theology. This methodological understanding turned theology at Edinburgh on its head. Chalmers refused to treat the Godhead first, as was the custom in theological circles. To do so was a breach or violation of the "analytical" principle.

In his 1843 Principal's address at the opening of the Free Church College, he teased out the connection between the sciences and theological discipline. To present day students it may seem strange that Chalmers advocated the study of mathematics as a preliminary subject to the study of theology. He argued this way: "I have a strong persuasion that both the power to apprehend and the power to convince, may be mightily strengthened—that the habit of clear and consecutive reasoning may be firmly established by the successive journeys which the mind is called on to perform along the pathway of geometrical demonstration".[40]

In the same address, he acknowledges acquisition of knowledge as of prime importance, and to that end Chalmers believed that the study of Greek, mathematics and logic are courses for the gymnastics of the mind. He also announced the desire to establish a chair in the Physical Sciences, so as to show the "signatures and set forth the glories of Him who sits enthroned on the riches of the universe".[41]

This interaction of the sciences and the study of theology assumed the dependence of the two disciplines upon a scientific methodology. In his *Institutes of Theology* Chalmers applied the inductive methodology to the Scriptures, not for the purpose of adding to proof texts but to the general truth of revelation. He argued in this way: "there remains a sufficient and most instructive analogy between the work of the observer in science and that of the Scripture critic in theology, on the one hand; and on the other, between the philosopher in science and the systematiser in theology; such an analogy in fact as might guide to the explanation and vindication of the uses of both".[42]

Chalmers drew out the analogy this way: Just as the observer of nature accumulates facts from his observation, so does the Scripture critic, who uses the Scriptural text and lexicon, instead of a microscope or similar instrument. Without basic facts, there can be only speculations, unsupported theories which have no experimental basic to rest on. The vast collection of facts are examined to discover any resemblances. It is the recognition of likeness that is important. It is the discovery of a universal likeness among all the instances of bodies approaching each other in free space that led to, or rather constituted the discovery of the universal law of gravitation. It is at this point that Chalmers leans upon the work of Robison, who claimed that a law of nature is the expression of a general fact grounded on the observations of particulars and affirming within the limits of a brief and compendious utterance of something that was common to them all. Chalmers continued to argue that there may have been thousands of similar observations in different parts of the world at different periods of time, but until the similarity was discovered, they formed a loose aggregate of individuals. The announcement of a law of nature was for Chalmers, "the revelation of nature's most magnificent harmony". The Scripture critic, using the same method groups his Biblical facts. Chalmers then argued: "when a hundred facts exhibit one and the same phenomenon, the expression of this phenomenon in its generality is the expression of a principle in philosophy – when a hundred verses speak one and the same truth, this truth, sustained on the basis of a multiple testimony, may by means of one brief and comprehensive affirmation become the article of a creed".[43]

Chalmers differentiated between the experimenter/observer and the philosopher of science: "The Scripture critic is in Christianity what the experimentalist or the observer is in science; and the systematic theologian is in Christianity what the philosopher is in science". There is a mutual agreement between the two, one cannot exist without the other. This method has its dangers and temptations. Chalmers warned that to systematise is not to theorise. "To frame a speculation from the gratuitous fancies of one's own spirit is a wholly different exercise from that of classifying according to their observed resemblances, the observed individuals which have a place and a substantive being in some outer field of contemplation".[44] This distinction, argued Chalmers, was of critical importance if Baconian principles are to be implemented. The distinction between Scripture Criticism and Systematic Theology has its counterpart in Newton's law of gravitation. This, according to Chalmers was a splendid example whereby the general doctrine and the observation of special phenomena acted and reacted so powerfully on each other. This, claimed Chalmers, is the very essence of Bacon's philosophy. It is little wonder that Chalmers has more than a scientific affinity with Bacon; it is a common affinity which has its roots in the fertile soil of Reformational theology which drew a heavy distinction between Grace and nature. Reacting against the Scholasticism of the Middle Ages, there emerged the doctrine of Grace which had dominion, primary precedence in all things, for man's salvation is due to God alone and even his knowledge of God derives its possibility solely from God's Grace and condescension; but in the realm of nature, man is given by grace dominion, primacy and precedence, for all things are given under his command. Both in the realm of Grace and nature, man is created and called to be a partner in covenant with God. This had the effect of giving man the right to pursue natural science as a religious duty.

The adoption by Chalmers of the Baconian method was only a short term success. It is undeniable that Chalmers was an outstanding ecclesiastical statesman, who had an enormous impact upon Scotland and beyond. His work and influence were soon eclipsed by the popularity of the German school of Higher Criticism and the widespread acceptance of Darwin's evolutionary hypothesis. Within seven years of Chalmers death Darwin's *Origin* was published with immediate success. The popularisers of Darwin's hypothesis, namely Thomas Huxley and Herbert Spencer, soon made Darwin's name a household word. The Darwinists were claiming victory over Christian orthodoxy. For the naïve, it was a choice between science and religion.

During the early part of the nineteenth century, Chalmers would have been unaware of the pitfalls of the simplistic Baconian approach to science. The claim of David Hume that induction is circular because it employs the very kind of inductive argument, the validity of which is supposed to be in need of justification, would have been dismissed, on the grounds that science proceeded to great achievements under Robert Boyle and Isaac Newton. It is nevertheless true that Hume and Chalmers brought their assumptions to their respective epistemology. Hume's assumptions were antitheist whereas Chalmers assumptions were theistic. In the quoted passage below, there is a simplistic application of Baconian principles with no awareness of the role of the assumptions of the observer. Assumptions are value laden and they impact upon conclusions. In Chalmers the truth of Holy Scripture is assumed and his epistemic assumptions have the ring of the authority of reason.

> It is true that when Scripture criticism is carried to its full extent, the work of systematizing has already begun, for one of its objects is to ascertain the truth of a doctrine. But we might conceive one (i.e. A student of an observer) to go forth on Scripture (i.e. to study the Scripture) without one notion of systematic theology in his head, yet with the highest degree of that talent and preparation

which might enable him to estimate the import of words and phrases. We might suppose him incapable of deriving any guidance to the meaning of the passage from the analogy of the faith; and that therefore assigns its meaning to each passage on the pure principles of philology alone. He is like an observer going forth, innocent of all theory, on the field of nature. The scriptural observer can render accurately each separate word and sentence—just as the natural observer can describe accurately each individual object that lies within the domain over which he expatiates. The one, let us say, with his lexicon, and with all those lights which long practice and recollection in this walk of investigation can supply; the other perhaps, with his microscope, or his balance, or the busy use of his now well-exercised senses, and the benefit of all those habits which belong to him either as a diligent collector of individual facts, or as a scrupulously accurate describer of the properties of individual objects. The mere linguist is to Scripture what the mere observer is to science. The office of the one is to expound accurately all the separate sayings in the volume of God's Word. The office of the other is to expound accurately all the separate things in the volume of God's work, whether you (i.e. the reader of Chalmers' lecture) view them as objects, which is the light in which you regard them when you study contemporaneous nature, or view them as events, which is the light in which you regard them when you study successive nature.[45]

Chalmers is not completely neutral in his methodological approach. His voluminous works constantly adhere to his belief in God, the authority and inspiration of Scripture, creation is fiat creation *ex nihilo*, natural theology is incapable of resolving man's dilemmas and sinful nature.

The importance of Chalmers cannot be underestimated in Australian Presbyterianism. His Biblical theology, as well as his methodological apparatus, were firmly embedded in early Australian Church life.

The Princetonians Charles Hodge and B.B. Warfield had international fame as conservative theologians. While Chalmers had a direct impact upon the Australian Church in the early part of the nineteenth century, Hodge and Warfield had an indirect impact during the twentieth century. Although the impact may have been indirect, it nevertheless helped to sustain the scientific method in theological studies. During the past thirty years, the Banner of Truth Trust has republished the works of Warfield. During the 1970s any Presbyterian minister who had Warfield's works sitting on his library shelf, was declaring in some way his "Reformed orthodoxy", especially if they were accompanied by John Calvin's *Institutes* and other Puritan works. Andrew McGowan has ably argued that these Princetonian theologians held to an epistemology that was rooted in the scientific method. He quotes from Hodge's Systematic Theology:

> In every science there are two factors: facts and ideas; or, facts and the mind ... The Bible is no more a system of theology, than nature is a system of chemistry or mechanics. We find in nature the facts which the chemist or the

mechanical philosopher has to examine, and from them ascertain the laws by which they are determined. So the Bible contains the truths which the theologian has to collect, authenticate, arrange, and exhibit in their internal relation to each other. This constitutes the difference between biblical and systematic theology. The office of the former is to ascertain and state the facts of Scripture. The office of the latter is to take those facts, determine their relation to each other and to cognate truths, as well as to vindicate them and show their harmony and consistency.[46]

McGowan rightly points out that Hodge's method reduces Scripture to a set of facts or propositions which are then collected and arranged into a systematic theology.[47] This method of Hodge and Warfield was no different from that of Thomas Chalmers.

REPUBLISHING OF PURITAN WORKS

The popularity of the republished Puritan works during the late twentieth century occurred at a time when the Australian Presbyterians were in turmoil after the formation of the Uniting Church, and the search for an identity was paramount. The Puritan works, tending toward the scientific method, only helped to cement the methodology into the psyche of the Presbyterian ministry. This, argues McGowan, undermines the authority of Scripture. "We must insist that the Scriptures are the Word of the living God who uses them to address us, save us, challenge us, teach us, encourage us, feed us and much more. To reduce the Scriptures to a set of "facts" for the theologian, who must then "arrange and exhibit" them is to change the Scriptures from their true nature as the Word of God into something cold and clinical which we possess and which we manipulate".[48] This is of immense importance for the theory of "transformative subjugation". McGowan relies on Kevin Vanhoozer for his remarks on Hodge, but he is silent on the critical aspect of Hodge's methodology which "presupposes a subject–object dichotomy in which the interpreter's mind observes and analyses its object: the facts of the Bible"[49] The inductive method says Vanhoozer is that close observation allows the facts to emerge. But modern scholars insist that the received data is always theory laden. Hodge and Warfield's methodology lends itself to propositional teaching.

The theologian's reliance on this type of methodology is imbued with a rationalistic and reductionist spirit. Rationalism cannot supply all the explanations of one's epistemic structures. Hodge tries to overcome these nonconceptual issues by resorting to the work of the Holy Spirit, who authenticates the laws of belief, which God has impressed upon our nature. Supernatural revelation, says Hodge must therefore be addressed to the senses. If confidence in the laws of nature were abandoned, nothing in the area of faith and knowledge is possible; there can only be absolute scepticism.[50] These laws are not open to scientific and analytic scrutiny. Without this dimension in Hodge's work there is no possibility of faith knowledge. This illustrates the dilemma that exists when a purely secular empirical methodology is applied to religious material.

B. B. Warfield follows Hodge in accepting the Scriptures as the data of belief. He says, "Holy Scripture or the Word of God written". It is the root out of which all doctrine grows just because the Scriptures are the fountain from which all knowledge of God's saving purpose and plan.[51]

Warfield is at pains to argue the case for "inerrancy" of the original autographs, although there have been errors in transmission. Using a scientific paradigm, the Scriptures are geared for a propositional understanding of Christianity. Warfield uses this methodology in his treatment of the Westminster Confession of Faith. He argues that since the Scriptures are the "very Word of God" the Confession naturally proceeds to "exhibit the properties which flow from its divine origin". Among the properties discussed is the property in which "the confession adduces certain important corollaries from its whole doctrine of Scripture as to its uses".[52] Clearly, Warfield, resorts to rationalism and reductionism in his view of Scripture set forth in the Westminster Confession of Faith. Using this same methodology it is logical to argue that each section of the Confession of Faith contains propositional doctrinal statements that are the actual statements of truth of Holy Scripture and any serious deviation must by definition, be untrue. It is therefore no surprise to hear in private conversation that the theological propositions in the Confession of Faith are the distillation of the Word of God.

The use of reason in contemporary Biblical scholarship is still important but its use is somewhat different. Professor Tom Wright argues the importance of reason in the pursuit of a doctrine of Authority and Inspiration of Holy Scripture. Wright asserts that the authority of Scripture become operational as the Church goes about its work in the world, proclaiming the gospel of Jesus Christ. "The authority of Scripture makes sense within the work of God's kingdom, at every level from the cosmic and political through to the personal". Reason says Wright means giving up merely arbitrary or whimsical readings of the text and paying attention to lexical, contextual and historical considerations. It also means giving attention to and celebrating many of the great discoveries in biology, archaeology, physics, astronomy etc which shed light on God's world and the human condition.[53] Wrights view still preserves the authority and Inspiration of Scripture but his view is very different to the reasoning of Hodge and Warfield.

Chapter 6

POST ENLIGHTENMENT

McGowan sees that the world has moved on since the Enlightenment and the scientific paradigms that emerged from it have been seriously challenged. The old paradigms have given way to new ones, as Kantian dualism has relegated religion to the private domain where religion is seen only in terms of the noumenal world which is beyond scientific analysis. Confidence in Biblical truth claims, were lost as a result of Kantian philosophy, but even more so under the influence of Hume and the Logical Positivists. McGowan agrees with Allan Bloom's brilliant summation of the contemporary challenge to the ramifications of Enlightenment philosophy:

> There is one thing a professor can be absolutely certain of: almost every student entering the university believes, or says he believes, that truth is relative. If this belief is put to the test, one can count on the students' reaction: they will be uncomprehending. That anyone should regard the proposition as not self–evident astonishes them, as though he were calling into question 2+2 = 4. These are the things you don't think about. The students' backgrounds are as various as America can provide. Some are religious, some are atheists; some are to the Left, some are to the Right; some intended to be scientists, some humanists or professional businessmen; some poor, some rich. They are unified only in their relativism and in their allegiance to equality. And the two are related in a moral intention. The relativity of truth is not a theoretical insight but a moral postulate, the condition of a free society, or so they see it. They have all been equipped with this framework early on, and it is the moral replacement for the inalienable natural rights that used to be the traditional American grounds for a free society. That this is a moral issue for students is revealed by the character of their response when challenged – a combination of disbelief and indignation: "Are you an absolutist?" the only alternative they know, uttered in the same tone as "Are you a monarchist?" or "Do you believe in witches?" This latter leads into the indignation, for someone who believes in witches might well be a witch–hunter or a Salem judge. The danger they have been taught to fear from absolutism is not error but intolerance. Relativism is necessary to openness; and this is the virtue, the only virtue, which all primary education for more than fifty years has dedicated itself to inculcating. Openness—and the relativism that makes it the only plausible stance in the face of various claims to truth and various ways of life and kinds of human beings—is the great insight of our times. The true believer is the real danger. The study of history and of culture teaches that all the world was mad in the past; men always thought they were right, and that led to wars, persecutions, slavery, xenophobia, racism, and chauvinism. The point is not to correct the mistakes and really be right; rather it is not to think you are right at all".[54]

The discussion so far has shown the extent to which the epistemic foundations of the Enlightenment have penetrated society and educational institutions in particular. It is the acceptance of the Enlightenment's epistemic foundations that are divorced from the Creator that has given man the epistemic framework to develop an epistemology of power. The story of the Fall in Genesis chapters one to three is a story that shows the power of God in creation, and the usurping of that power by Adam. Adam expressed his autonomy by excluding God from his world and sought power over the society by trusting in and believing science and technology, which is symbolised in the sewing of the fig leaves in order to cover up the internal nakedness. This epistemology of Power has become so entrenched in the contemporary world that western culture, has lured generations of school children into the false belief that scientific knowledge and the technologies deriving from it are the ultimate tools of social and even personal salvation. The more we trust in the prelates of scientific knowledge, the more resources, both human and otherwise, we commit to the development of ever more powerful and controlling forms of technology.[55] Laura continues to argue that the defining characteristic of our age is, "our unbridled commitment to an implicit form of knowledge which shapes and defines the way in which we interact with nature. Given that science has become the primary vehicle for the expression of this form of knowledge, the teaching of science may, at the level of covert value agenda, be tantamount to the promulgation of an ideology of environmental destruction." This specific form of knowledge has recently been challenged by Diarmuid O'Murchu who sees that the pursuit of theology in its traditional epistemic bounds needs to change due to the development of the "quantum theory" in science. He argues that: "the quantum theory shows that we belong to a greater whole from which our very being and without which we have neither meaning, purpose, nor uniqueness, in the great cosmic drama. We discover our true uniqueness not in isolated competitive individualism but in convivial cooperation with the great evolutionary unfolding of our planet and our universe. Apart from the greater whole we are worth nothing". There are serious consequences for the Church and its theology and its notions of theological education so long as an implicit form of knowledge that shapes and defines the way we interact with nature is kept intact. O'Murchu argues: "in a quantum world orthodox theological dogmas serve as landmarks for guidance and certainty but in a quantum world they serve as pointers of a deeper truth".[56]

LITURGICAL MINIMISATION

It may well be asked, "What has all this philosophy got to do with liturgical minimisation?" In order to answer that it is helpful to recap what has been presented to this point. It has been argued that there is a strong connection between the process of liturgical minimisation and the Puritan movement. Prior to the formation of the Uniting Church in Australia in 1977 there was a revival of Puritanism within the Presbyterian Church. There are a number of factors that were operating at the time.

- During the 1960–1980 many of the old Puritan works were being republished by the *Banner of Truth*.
- The popularity of these republished works was enhanced when the editor of the *Banner of Truth*, the Rev. Iain Murray, was inducted into the pastoral charge of St Giles, Presbyterian Church, Hurstville, in Sydney.
- There was a growing popularity of Moore Theological College as a preferred place to study theology towards ordination. At the time the College was under the principalship of Dr Broughton Knox.

It was natural that young enthusiastic candidates for the ministry not only embraced Puritan Theology, but unwittingly embraced the epistemological methodology that was used to interpret the *Scriptures* and the *Westminster Confession of Faith*. The transmission of the scientific paradigm had come to the faith community in Australia via Thomas Chalmers, Charles Hodge, B. B. Warfield and of recent times through Dr Broughton Knox at Moore Theological College, who advocated Propositional Revelation, which assumed an epistemic framework of a Newtonian mechanistic world view. The focus of ministry which arose from this was a distinctive style of preaching/expounding of the Word of God. The patterns of worship that arose from this were adjusted to emphasise the exposition of the Word. All else is minimised. It is fundamentally the motivation of reformational reform. Within Presbyterian circles in Australia today the forms of worship are manipulated at will with the monotonous phrase, "so long as the Word of God is faithfully preached". The preached Word is propositional in character and conveys the notion of certainty and hope for an uncertain and confused world. Whilst this approach may appeals to many sincere Christian people, with beneficial results, the majority within society are imbued with the relativism of a postmodern world view. Allan Bloom in the quotation above notes that, men always thought that they were right, that led to wars, persecutions, slaves, Xenophobia, racism and chauvinism. The point he argues is, "not to correct the mistakes and really be right; rather it is not to think you are right at all". Whilst there is a fruitful advantage in preaching and teaching within a Newtonian and mechanistic framework in a thoroughgoing relativistic world where there is no certainty about anything it is generally thought that within the traditional constructs of worship services there is a need to minimise the liturgy, so as to attract the younger generation who are products of an educational system which promotes a specific form of knowledge that has a covert agenda. As a result the old liturgical structures are deemed to be irrelevant and worship services are restructured to satisfy the autonomous self. This is usually achieved with the technologies of light and sound, combined with the marketing techniques of a consumerist society. The sense of the Holy, Majesty and Awe of God that is essential for worship is lost and worship becomes synthetic. If James Watt's steam engine of 1787 became the symbol of the machine age, then it could be argued that the pop culture band and the technologies of light and sound are the symbols of postmodern worship practice. The "new" devotional popularity of contemporary worship symbols has led worship leaders to ignore the Calvinistic nature of worship characterised by solemn reverence and awe of God's holiness. This is the end product of the new ideas of the Doctrine of the Church with its Knoxian emphasis on fellowship and the acceptance of a methodology which gives man control of worship functions. It is in this way "transformative subjugation" is realised. Basic theological understanding of important doctrines is not spared in the process. Thomas Torrance, for example, poses the idea that Evangelical Protestantism has developed a way of preaching the Gospel which distorts and betrays it by introducing into it a subtle element of co-redemption. He argues this way: This happens whenever it is said that people will not be saved *unless* they make the work of Christ real for themselves by their own personal decision; or that they will be saved *only if* they repent and believe, for this is to make the effectiveness of the work of Christ conditional upon what the sinner does, and so at the crucial point it throws the ultimate responsibility for a man's salvation back upon himself.[57] Torrance argues that the New Testament says something quite different. The New Testament announces that God loves us, that He has given His only Son to be our Saviour, that Christ has died for us when we were yet sinners, and that his work is finished and *therefore* it calls for repentance and the obedience of faith. But never does it say: This is what God in Christ has done for you, and you can be saved on condition that you repent and believe. This type of thinking has developed says Torrance when there is the attempt to interpret Christ solely through His works. He argues that when "we start off from the saving work of Christ like that and from what he means to you in your experience, Christ tends to disappear behind His benefits, so that a doctrine of the person of Christ is determined by the value judgements you pass on Him".[58]

Many younger ministers have become enslaved by the symbolism of man's own creation. The realities of the symbolic form of worship that expressed the richness of Calvin's theology have become sterile, inert and dead. The unfortunate impact of some technologies in worship only helps people to avoid having to confront the realisation that real worship maximises the intimate personalisation between worshipper and God, and the intimate personalisation between worshipper and other worshippers. There is an essential connectivity between worshippers with each other and with God Himself. The overuse of technology only enhances man's individuality and separateness from each other. It has been concluded that, "we have essentially substituted the world of vital and living things for a predictable world of inert and dead things as the place in which we and the spirit of our humanity are forced to live".[59]

So long as there is a reliance upon a scientific-type epistemology and accompanying method, as found in a Newtonian paradigm, there will always be theological correctness, which tends to divide the Christian community between those who possess the truth and those who are misled and prevented from accepting the truth. A theological underclass is established within the Church. The Church will always struggle for unity and cohesion, so long as a dominant group, irrespective of its theological persuasion, seeks political control by subjugating the internal structures of Theological Education and the Church's administration.

DISENCHANTMENT

The Presbyterian Review is a journal which expresses the disenchantment of many within the Church as a result of the prevailing epistemology of power. Two examples from this journal illustrate this point. Ian A. Macdonald refers to the recent generation of ministers, trained at Moore College and the Presbyterian Theological Centre, refusing to baptise infants without the parents attending lessons. The level of disharmony can be felt when he cites an actual case in point: "This man with his anglicised piety, placed barriers and demands on the parents such that they made other arrangements for the baptism of their daughter and now want nothing to do with the Presbyterian Church. Is this man following the teachings of Jesus or Jensen?"[60] This comment is full of disappointment and vindictiveness.

In another letter to the same Journal the author refer to what he calls the emergence of pharisaical rigorism which he sees as a "function of the drift of Post–Modernism to its inevitable denouement: self-righteousness".[61]

The Rev. David Campbell, addressing the 2007 session of the General Assembly of Australia, in response to an overture from the Sydney South Presbytery seeking to limit the ordination to the eldership of men only, commented: "it is absolutely clear that there are two strongly held opposing views on the issue of ordaining women elders ... the question facing us today is how can we within our Church co-exist by holding on to both points of view? Unless we can somehow find a compromise position then we will continue to tear our Church apart".[62] So it becomes clear that there is a desperate need to develop a Christian Epistemology in which the Revelation of God's love for lost humanity becomes the dominative interpretive principle.

TOWARDS A CHRISTIAN EPISTEMOLOGY

Cornelius Van Til is a very innovative scholar in respect to the development of a distinctive Christian epistemology. John Frame, a sympathetic critic of Van Til, claims that Van Til's contribution to Christian thought is comparable in magnitude to that of Immanuel Kant in non-Christian philosophy. The foundation of Van Til's system, its most persuasive principle, is the rejection of the autonomy of man, since Christian thinking, like all of the Christian life, is subject to God's lordship. Van Til specifically rejects the traditional epistemic methodology as it is offered in Thomas Aquinas in its Catholic form and in Joseph Butler in its Protestant form, as it is based upon the assumption that man has some measure of autonomy, that in the space-time world is in some measure contingent and that man must create for himself his own epistemology in an ultimate sense.[63] In this method, man has the right and the ability to judge the claims of the authoritative Word of God. Van Til argues that by this method "the correctness of the natural man's problematics is endorsed". That is all he needs to reject the Christian faith. However Christian scholars have used this popular methodology arising out of the Enlightenment period, to interpret the realities of the Bible and applied the same principles to formulate various theologies. To make sense of reality, Van Til argues that one must presuppose the reality of the self-contained triune God and the self-attesting revelation of the Scriptures. From this basis the redeemed person then reasons analogically attempting to think God's thought after him. This means that humans may know reality truly (for God, in whose image they are created, knows it truly), but not exhaustively (for God is infinite and humans are finite). Van Til argues that the redeemed must demonstrate to the unregenerate that the presuppositions of chance occurrence in an impersonal universe, cannot account for any sort of order and rationality.[64] Greg Bahnsen sees the genius of Van Til's position to be his exposure of the inappropriateness of the intellectual attitude that "puts God in the dock".[65] He argues that a Christian epistemology should be elaborated and worked out in a way that is consistent with its own fundamental principles, lest it be incoherent and ineffective.

To present Van Til's argument in more detail, it is necessary to examine more closely the philosophical personalities that have previously been mentioned. Van Til asserts that Descartes not only stressed man's independence from the universe around him, but more importantly, emphasized man's independence from God.[66] He argues that the famous dictum, "*cogito ergo sum*", must not be thought of as a syllogism with the major premise "whatever thinks exists', rather, we must "think of man's present consciousness as the starting point from which he draws the general conclusion that whatever thinks exists'. Van Til sees Descartes' thesis as thoroughly antitheist, as the individual human consciousness is the ultimate starting point on which conclusions in respect to universal laws are to be based. He argues that both Empiricism and Rationalism are "developments of an aspect of Descartes' position". Ultimacy of the sense world is at the heart of Empiricism. The universe is independent of God as it is found in the work of Berkley and Hume. Universals in their scheme are entirely subjective, that is "they have nothing to do with objects beyond the human mind". The final outcome of Empiricism is the reduction to scepticism and absurdity.

Rationalism, argues Van Til, is also a derivative of Descartes' philosophy in that "certain universal principles hover somewhere in the universe and must be taken for granted" He links Rationalism with Platonic reasoning. Plato tried to interpret all reality in terms of certain *a priori* principles. But Rationalism could not escape the necessity of taking a position on the question of the relation of these general principles to the idea or principle of personality. Van Til concludes that eventually the principles rest in God as ultimate and self-sufficient personality or they reside in ultimate human personality.[67]

The philosophy of the Enlightenment is integral to understanding the development of theological Liberalism. Without going into the details of Van Til's argument on Kant, it is sufficient to say that Van Til sees Kant's philosophy as indicative of an antitheist position.

Van Til develops his epistemology by making a distinction in the way in which men reason. Non-Christian reasoning is called *univocal reason*, whereas Christian men reason *analogically*. He explains the distinction in this way:

> By this distinction we mean that every non-Christian theory of method takes for granted that time and eternity, are aspects of one another, and that God and man must be thought of as being on the same plane. God and man must be thought of as correlative to one another. God and man work under a system of logic that is higher than both, and that exists in independence of both. The law of contradiction is thought of as existing somehow in independence of God and man, or at least as operating in both God and man on the same level.
>
> In contrast to this, Christianity holds that God existed alone before any time existence was brought forth. He existed as the self-conscious and self-consistent being. The law of contradiction, therefore, as we know it, is but the expression on a created level of the internal coherence of God's nature. Christians should never appeal to the law of contradiction as something that, as such, determines what can or can not be true. Parmenides serves as a warning of what happens to history if the law of contradiction is in this fashion made the ultimate standard of appeal in human thought. Parmenides concluded that to understand anything historical, it would have to be reduced to an element in a timeless system of categories. He therefore denied the reality and significance of all historical plurality. In modern times it is customary to use the law of contradiction negatively rather than positively as Parmenides did. On the

surface this appears to leave room for historical factuality. But it does so only if this historical factuality be thought of as being unknowable or irrational.[68]

To reason analogically is to accept seriously the Christian doctrine of creation and *to make every thought captive to the obedience of Christ speaking in Scripture*. This type of reasoning does away with the Plutonic dualism of the sense world and the ideal world.[69]

Van Til goes back to the theology of Calvin because Calvin rather than Luther and other Reformers, had rid himself of the last vestiges of human independence or autonomy. Calvin:

- placed Holy Scripture with its formal principle of authority at the centre of his thinking whereas Luther emphasised the formal principle of Justification by Faith;
- emphasised the work of the Holy Spirit in the restoration of man to the true knowledge of God.

The authority of Scripture and the work of the Holy Spirit in Van Til's argument need to be understood in terms of man's sinfulness, in which the image of God in man has been shattered. Calvin distinguished between the image of God in man in a narrow and a wider sense, whereby man has lost the image of God in the narrow sense altogether, and retained only vestiges of God's image in the wider sense. Van Til argues his case this way:

> In the narrow sense, God's image in man is the true knowledge, the true righteousness and the true holiness that man possesses when created by God. In the wider sense, God's image in man is man's rationality and morality. Through sin man lost the image of God in the narrow sense altogether, and retained only vestiges of God's image in the wider sense. This means that man is spiritually blind but remains a rational nature, and as such is always confronted by the revelation of God about him and within his constitution. God does not deal with man as with a block in the way that Luther thought of it. We must think of man as spiritually blind without denying his personality. His spiritual blindness presupposes his being a covenantal personality. Accordingly, there was no occasion for the development of synergism in Calvinistic thought. There was no danger that man should be given any absolute originality in the field of soteriology. The "natural man" has in his idea changed God into something other than he is, and man cannot, unless the scales be removed from his eyes, know anything truly about God or about anything else. Similarly, Scripture is indispensable for the sinner in order to give to man spectacles through which he can truly see God in the facts round about him or in his own constitution.[70]

Van Til also argues that Calvin's view of revelation does away with the false scholastic distinction between natural and revealed theology. Nature can be read aright only by those who allow the light of Scripture to fall upon it. This distinctive conceptual framework of Van Til's sets him apart from most of the traditional protestant theologians.

THE IMPACT OF UNIVOCAL REASONING ON THE CHURCH'S WORSHIP PRACTICE

In terms of those, examined to date i.e. Thomas Chalmers, Charles Hodge and B.B. Warfield, it is clear that they all accepted the epistemology of the scientific world. That is they argued univocally instead of analogically. By doing so they inherited all the specific problems concerning natural and revealed religion, universals and logical determinism. To argue univocally would also have serious implications in respect to how sovereign is the work of the Holy Spirit, as it would be so easy to confuse the outcomes of man's manipulation of the facts, with the action of the Holy Spirit. In the conceptual framework of a scientific paradigm the work of the Holy Spirit must be limited in terms of man's rational understanding. If man's rationality is the prime reference point for determining truth then the mysterious work of the Holy Spirit can only be explained in terms of man's obedience. From a Reformed theological perspective this is unacceptable as it makes the work of the Holy Spirit conditional upon a doctrine of works. Salvation is no longer located in the Grace of God. Whilst saying this it needs to be understood that Chalmers, Hodge and Warfield were products of their age. In their time they were outstanding theological scholars, intellectual giants of the era. When Chalmers died in 1847 he was buried amid the tears of a nation and with more than kingly honours.[71]

The epistemology of Chalmers, Hodge and Warfield, though operating upon a different conceptual framework to Van Til, are nevertheless more open to what Laura argues as to be a form of indoctrination defined as: "a paralysis of intellectual imagination. The intellectual components of our individual autonomy are eroded by a narrowing of the mind's eye such that we only see those things which others want us to see".[72]

This discussion on epistemology is of great importance to the way we approach the discipline of theology. It is of critical importance to the central theme of this thesis, which is that of liturgical minimisation.

This book has pointed out that the whole development of the Church's liturgical perspective was grounded in Calvinism. The practice of worship was of primary importance to Calvin. It was in worship that one is confronted with the presence of the Almighty creator who is clothed in majesty and holiness. The publication of the new 1998 version of *Worship Book* was a radical change in the theological perspective. The rationale behind the change is suggestive of a modern paradigm that is Newtonian in character. The logical sequence has a consistent thread that can be easily seen:

- The first liturgy of Holy Communion that was used prior to the publication of the *Worship Book* was used during the liberal era of the Church.
- The use of the liturgy did not produce faithful committed people. They remained in their liberalism.
- The component parts of the liturgy form a ritual that is deemed unnecessary. It is at this point that an extreme use the "regulative principle" becomes operative.[73]
- Symbolism is unnecessary as the preached word is foundational.
- Aspects of the liturgy are suggestive of an outmoded pre reformational theology.
- Therefore we see that change is necessary.

This sequence is in itself reductionist. The reasoning model in Van Tilian terms is *univocal* and it follows the pattern of the powerful and influential theological ideologues Chalmers, Hodge, Warfield and Broughton Knox. This univocal approach has run counter to the fundamentals of Calvin's theology which emphasises the sovereign work of the Holy Spirit and the authority of the Holy Scriptures. These scholars would be greatly offended if it were suggested that they did not uphold the sovereign work of the Holy Spirit. Their epistemological method leads to the above conclusion. Van Til shook the foundations of the Reformed Faith by suggesting that Calvin's approach argued "analogically" because he had cast off the last vestiges of scholasticism and its epistemological method.

From Van Til's standpoint it is clearly demonstrated that the framers of the *1998 Worship Book* are caught in a time warp. While upholding a Reformed theology, they sought a reconstruction of the liturgy by arguing univocally. In doing so, they superimposed a secular epistemology upon the interpretation of the Scriptures. Their conclusions became highly reductionist.

The whole notion of worship in Calvin's scheme is wholly dependent, not on man and his manipulative control but upon the sovereign work of the Holy Spirit who leads man to be confronted with the authority and power of the Word in the Holy Scriptures. The pursuit of a Christian Epistemology is essential for the inner connectiveness of all the disciplines required to see the unified fabric of the created order. John Frame observes that Van Til's contribution to theology results in "a sense of the interconnectedness of the creation. God's plan is a wise one. He has not planned any one thing in creation without taking everything else into account. All elements of His plan dovetail with one another".[74] A Christian Epistemology would send the numerous philosophical ghosts to the graveyard as most have no resurrection powers except in the mind of autonomous man. The change of worship structure will not necessarily ensure that a worshipper will experience the divine. What is legitimate is to argue analogically and recognise the connection between purity of heart and worship in terms of Ps. 24: 4 and Matt. 5: 8.[75]

A broad application of the regulative principle governing worship is essential to preserving biblical requirements. The narrow and strict version of the principle which is used in the same way as those who use a scientific methodology can only become a manipulative tool to forcefully change and minimise a liturgy, so what was once a beautiful liturgy can become nothing more than a directory for public worship.

Unless theological educators provide specific courses in the epistemology of worship and the basic principles that lay behind the regulative principle, then a new generation of ministers will arise who are bereft of a knowledge of traditional liturgy and by adopting univocal reasoning, the conduct of and the content of worship will be controlled by the whims of the ministers' imagination. The insistence of a specific Liturgical Technology can only continue the process of "transformative subjugation" wherein the Church's mission will become moribund and irrelevant.

NOTES

1. R.S. Laura and M. Cotton, *Empathetic Education* (London: Falmer Press, 1999), 48–49.
2. R.S. Laura and A. Chapman, *The Paradigm Shift in Health* (Maryland: University Press of America 2009), 76–77.
3. Evelyn Underhill, *Worship* (London: Collins, 1962), 299.
4. Laura and Cotton, *Empathetic Education*, 74.
5. A.T.B. McGowan, *The Divine Spiration of Scripture* (Nottingham: Apollos Press, 2007), 23.
6. This part of the chapter may give the impression of a history of philosophy. We were tempted to exclude it altogether. It is retained in order to show the casual reader the long history and influence of the development of secular thought. Contemporary epistemological thought makes more sense with a historical background.
7. A. K. Rogers, *A Student's History of Philosophy* (New York: Macmillan, 1935), 89.
8. C. Van Til, *In Defence of the Faith. A survey of Christian Epistemology* (New Jersey: P&R Publishing, no date), Vol. 2, 44.
9. Van Til, *In Defence of the Faith,* 51.
10. D.W. Hamlyn, *The Encyclopedia of Philosophy* in Paul Edwards, ed. (New York: Macmillan, 1972), Vol, 1, 499.
11. Hamlyn, *Encyclopedia*, 240.
12. R. Descartes, *The Philosophical Writings of Descartes* (Cambridge: Cambridge University Press, 1985), Vol. 1, 10.
13. Descartes, *Philosophical Writings*, 10–15.
14. Descartes, *Philosophical Writings*, 15.
15. Bertrand Russell, *History of Western Philosophy* (London: Allen & Unwin, 1962), 623.
16. R. Laura and J. Ashton, *New Insights into Environmental Education.* (Adamstown: Insight Press, 2003), 32–33.
17. Laura and Ashton, *New Insights*, 34.
18. Rogers, *History of Philosophy*, 298.

19. John Locke, *Essay Concerning Human Understanding* (Oxford: Oxford University Press, 1960), Bk 2, Ch.11, Sec. 15, 91.
20. Locke, *Essay Concerning Human Understanding*.
21. Laura and Ashton, *New Insights*, 36.
22. J. Rifkin, *Entropy, A new World View* (New York: The Viking Press, 1980), 23–24.
23. T.S. Kuhn, *The Structure of Scientific Revolutions* (Chicago: University of Chicago 1970, 121.
24. R. Wollheim, *Hume on Religion* (London: Collins, 1963), 226.
25. David Hume, *The Natural History of Religion and Dialogues Concerning Natural Religion* (Oxford: Colver & Price, 1976), 261.
26. McGowan, *Divine Spiration*, 53.
27. David F. Wells, *Above All Earthly Powers* (Grand Rapids: Eerdmans, 2006), 30–31.
28. McGowan, *Divine Spiration*, 117.
29. T. Payne, *D. Broughton Knox, Selected Works* (Kingsford NSW: Matthias Media, 2000), Vol. 1, 307.
30. Payne, *Broughton Knox*, 308–09. Knox argues that his claim to propositional revelation can be established in two ways, first by considering how the Bible describes revelation, and secondly by examining biblical revelation to see its nature. After a lengthy discussion he concludes Revelation is essentially propositional. For an event to be revelational it must be interpreted by God himself. This and not merely some human reflection on the occurrence is the real differentiating factor.
31. Ronald S. Laura, "Philosophical Foundations of Religious Education" in *Educational Theory*, 28 (1978):
32. McGowan, *Divine Spiration*, 117.
33. Wells, *Above all Earthly Powers*, 25.
34. McGowan *Divine Spiration*, 117.
35. K.J. Vanhoozer, "The Atonement in Post-modernity" in *The Glory of the Atonement* (Illinois: Intervarsity Press, 2004), 369, eds. C. Hill and F. Thomas. For a concise statement on the impact of Enlightenment thinking in the theological area see P.E. Moore, *Can a Bishop be Wrong*? (Harrisburg: Morehouse Publishing, 1998), 116–19.
36. Vanhoozer, *Atonement*, 370, 404.
37. S. Piggin *The St. Andrews Seven* (Edinburgh: Banner of Truth .1985), xi
38. W. Hanna, *Memoirs of Thomas Chalmers* (London: Thomas Constable & Co, 1854), Vol 1, 27. The relationship between science and theology that Chalmers argues for is methodological. For this part of our argument we draw on a previous work; see J. Webster, *Science and the Scottish Evangelical Movement*, MA(Hons) thesis, University of Wollongong, 1989, Ch. 6.
39. Thomas Chalmers, *Institutes of Theology* (Edinburgh: Sutherland & Knox, 1849), Vol 1. xi–xii.
40. Thomas Chalmers, *Prelections on Butler's Analogy, Paley, Hill* (Edinburgh: Sutherland & Knox, 1849), Posthumous Works, Vol. ix, 438.
41. Chalmers, *Prelections*, 442.
42. Chalmers, *Institutes*, 329–30.
43. Chalmers, *Institutes*, 332–33.
44. Chalmers, *Institutes*, 336.
45. Chalmers, *Institutes*, Vol. 1, 330.
46. Charles Hodge, *Systematic Theology* (London: James Clarke, 1960), Vol. 1, 1–2.
47. McGowan, *Divine Spiration*, 137.
48. McGowan, *Divine Spiration*.
49. Kevin J. Vanhoozer, "On the Very Idea of a Theological System", in *Always Reforming*, ed. A. McGowan (Leicester: IVP, 2006), 137.
50. Charles Hodge, *Systematic Theology* (London: James Clarke, 1960), Vol. 1, 60.
51. B.B. Warfield, *Selected Shorter Writings* (Nutley: P&R Publishing, 1973), 561.
52. B. Warfield, *Selected Shorter Writings*, 566–68.
53. Tom Wright, *Scripture and the Authority of God* (London: SPCK, 2013), 2nd Edition, 116–22.

54. Allan Bloom, *The Closing of the American Mind* (New York: Simon & Schuster, 1987), 25–26.
55. Laura and Cotton, *Empathetic Education*, 3.
56. Diarmuid O'Murchu, *Quantum Theology* (N.Y.: Crossroads Publishing, 2013), 64, 89.
57. Thomas F. Torrance, *God and Rationality* (London: Oxford University Press, 1971), 58.
58. Torrance, *God & Rationality*, 58–63.
59. R.S. Laura and T. Marchant, *Surviving the High Tech Depersonalisation Crisis* (Sydney: Insight Press, 2002), 203.
60. *Presbyterian Review*, March 206, 8.
61. *Presbyterian Review*, May 2006, 10.
62. *Presbyterian Review*, November 2007, 12.
63. C. Van Til, "My Credo", in *Jerusalem and Athens*, (US: Presbyterian and Reformed Publishing 1980), 10–11.
64. D. Kelly has provided this simplistic summary of Van Til's position; see *New Dictionary of Theology* (Illinois: IVP, 1988), 704.
65. Greg L. Bahnsen, *Van Til's Apologetic* (New Jersey: P&R Publishing, 1998), 3.
66. C. Van Til, *In Defence of the Faith. A Survey of Christian Epistemology* (Philipsburg: Presbyterian & Reformed Publishing,), Vol. 2, 103.
67. Van Til, *In Defence of the* Faith, 103–107.
68. C. Van Til, *In Defence of the Faith. An Introduction to Systematic Theology* (Philipsburg: Presbyterian & Reformed Publishing, 1974), Vol. 5, 11.
69. Van Til, *A Survey of Christian Epistemology*, 65–66.
70. Van Til, *A Survey of Christian Epistemology*, 94–96.
71. Iain Murray, *Letters of Thomas Chalmers* (Edinburgh: Banner of Truth Trust, 2007), vi.
72. Laura and Cotton, *Empathetic Education*, 74.
73. J.I. Packer argues that the first generation of Reformers were generally agreed in the defining of the principles of worship. They were agreed that Christian worship must express man's reception of, and response to, evangelical truth, and they were substantially in agreement as to what that truth was. They agreed in analysing worship as an exercise of mind and heart in praise, thanksgiving, prayer, confession of sin, trust in God's promises, and the hearing of God's Word, read and preached. They all agreed that each Church had the liberty to arrange its worship in the way best adapted to edify its own worshippers. "The idea that direct biblical warrant, in the form of precept or precedent, is required to sanction every substantive item included in the public worship of God was in fact a Puritan innovation, which crystallised out in the course of the prolonged debates that followed the Elizabethan settlement. See J. I. Packer, *A Quest for Godliness* (Wheaton: Crossway Books, 1990), 246–47. John M. Frame argues for the limitation of the regulative principle to official worship services. It is not a doctrine about Church power and officially sanctioned worship services. It is about all forms of worship. Limiting the doctrine to officially sanctioned worship robs it of its biblical force. It is rather "a charter of freedom, not a burden of bondage". See. John M. Frame, *Worship* (Phillipsburg: P &R Publishing, 1996), 44–45.
74. John Frame, *Van Til the Theologian* (Chattanooga: Pilgrim Publishing, 1976), 29.
75. The prerequisite is a "pure heart" and a right relationship with the Lord. These are required for true worship in these two passages. The Psalmist writes: "Who may ascend the hill of the Lord? Who may stand in his Holy place? He who has clean hands and a pure heart, who does not lift up his soul to an idol or swear by what is false", Ps. 24:3–4. The Matthew passage says the same: "Blessed are the pure in heart for they will see God", Matt 5: 8.

Chapter Seven

Towards a Reconstruction of Theological Education

In the previous chapter we outlined the importance of the link between Liturgical Minimisation and the scientific methodology which arose out of the Enlightenment period. The ensuing epistemology was characterised as an epistemology of power, in the theological sense that it located the loci of science, firmly in the grip of human autonomy and the final authority of reason.

In this chapter we will argue that Theological Education needs to be reconstructed in a way in which the conceptual framework is based upon a *Christian Epistemology*, engendering the Lordship of Christ, and encouraging a spirit of transformative love and connectedness.

It is only in this context that the theology of worship and the beauty and usefulness of liturgical forms can be appreciated. Without a reconstruction of theological education with within the Presbyterian Church in New South Wales and indeed the other centres, Melbourne and Brisbane, the dangers of Liturgical Minimisation will never be realised.

1. THERE IS A NEED FOR RECONSTRUCTION

In previous chapters we have argued that there is a specific link between Puritan theology and the scientific method. We have traced the transmission of this construct onto Australian soil, particularly within the Presbyterian Church.

Adopting a scientific methodology in the discipline of theology creates two basic problems: the first is the fragmentation of theological studies into more and more discrete specialities. With such fragmentation there is no unifying factor. The second problem, Farley describes as "surfeiting". He writes:

> In disciplines whose subject matter is more or less fixed—for example, an ancient text and in disciplines where there has been a surfeit of investigation, there is still a moving horizon of enquiry, but the focus is always on new methods to interpret that more or less fixed material. A book of an ancient canon or a famous literary figure from the past can be psychoanalysed, deconstructed, psychohistoricised, structuralised and phenomenologized. But the neomethodologies give scope only to a kind of artificial ingenuity whose subtilities grow more implausible with each new analysis.[1]

At the New South Wales General Assembly meeting of the Presbyterian Church in June 2008, the Theological Education Committee distributed a paper entitled "Educational Philosophy of the P.T.C." This paper sought to outline the educational philosophy of the Theological College. The paper serves only to endorse the problems that Farley describes. The lack of a unifying epistemology only enhances the Enlightenment paradigm of man's autonomy and the final authority of reason. The paper states the College's policy is: It is consistent with the Calvinist Reformational heritage that emphasises both the authority of the Scriptures and the responsibility of every Christian to read and interpret the Scriptures. The P.T.C. acknowledges the Lordship of Christ over every area of life and thought and encourages its students to foster an approach to teaching and learning that places Christ at the centre of all knowledge.[2]

The paper clearly assumes a scientific methodology in the pursuit of theological truth.

In the fourth paragraph of the document, the P.T.C. indicates that it has accepted this position, by saying that it accepts the development of cognitive knowledge in terms of a scientific method; Apprehending, assess, synthesise, analyse and critique existing knowledge or by experimentation with new areas of knowledge. This statement is a more detailed analysis of the claim in the second paragraph: "the PTC also accepts that through . . . an understanding of the world owes much to observation, analysis and deduction . . . although all such understanding is to be judged in the light of Scripture". It is here that a paradox is revealed. On the one hand, a commitment to a scientific methodology which has been passed down from Thomas Chalmers in the nineteenth century into the modern Church in Australia through the powerful, influence of B.B. Warfield and Broughton Knox, in the twentieth century, through this process truth tends to be propositional in character. Propositional statements of truth imply an acceptance of an empirical approach. On the other hand there is an inner inconsistency within the paper. In the second paragraph reference is made to the Lordship of Christ: "The P.T.C. recognises the Lordship of Christ over every area of life and thought". This statement implies a different epistemology than the previous one. It has all the markings of a concept out of the work of Cornelius Van Til. As we have previously argued, a statement such as this can only be achieved through the development of a specific Christian epistemology. Reference to "Calvinist Reformational heritage", which is expressed in the puritan Westminster Confession of Faith, and on the other hand, reference to a scientific methodology confirms the argument of Edmund Farley of fragmentation and surfeiting. The P.T.C. paper shows evidence of theological fragmentation when it argues that it is through fragmentation that students are taught to think theologically. This is implemented through Biblical studies, Exegetical skills, Historical Theology, Systematic Theology, Church History and Ethics and Practical Ministry.

Edward Farley has argued that that the four basic theological disciplines of Bible, Systematic Theology, Church history and Practical Theology were a development of theological education arising out of the Enlightenment. This fourfold pattern was anticipated as early as Hyperius (1556) "actually originated with the theological encyclopaedic movement in Germany in the second half of the eighteenth century".[3] Farley shows that it was the establishment of the modern universities during the seventeenth century that moved theology from being a "cognitive *habitus* of the soul" to a science along with law, medicine, and humanities (including philosophy). He writes: "With the Enlightenment and the modern university came the ideal of autonomous science, of scholarship, proceeding under no other canons than proper evidence".[4] It was a deliberate and methodical undertaking whose end was knowledge. Promoted by Thomas Aquinas and the Schoolmen, theology in this sense became a discipline. Jeffrey K. Jue in a penetrating article *Theologia Naturalis*[5] claims that scholasticism under the influence of Greek philosophy in the medieval and post reformation period produced a theological school that prioritized the use of reason. He quotes Brian Armstrong,

> While it produced profound alterations in some of Calvin's doctrinal teachings, perhaps the most significant result was a change in methodology . . . No longer was the primary approach the analytic and inductive, but rather the synthetic and deductive . . . This was, then, primarily interested in the logical explanation of the source of theology.

This then, gives explanation to the discontinuity in the development of Reformed theology from the early sixteenth Reformers such as Calvin to the Protestant scholastics of the late sixteenth and seventeenth centuries. The reason for this discontinuity is clearly the acceptance and appropriation of uncritical Aristotelian logic. This fourfold pattern of theological education as developed in Germany has continued into the twenty-first century despite the fact that science and the scientific method has been challenged by quantum mechanics. Nevertheless, the Church and its theological institutions have held on to the old Newtonian paradigm. The result is that we have come to understand and verify only that which we can construct and shape for ourselves. It is none other than the *me only* form of knowledge. As Thomas F. Torrance argued " this is the attitude of mind that has come to permeate our Western culture, not least the human and social sciences, and of course the technological society within which they function, but also within which the Christian Church is bound to communicate its message and interpret it to the contemporary world. Here an insidious sociology of knowledge tends to replace epistemology and a social ideology substitutes for theology".[6] The sociology of knowledge and social ideology are contained within the methodological structures of the autonomy of man's reasoning powers. Furthermore, the statement in the *Philosophy of Theological Education* does not stand up to historical scrutiny. Stuart Piggin claims that it is the study of philosophy that teaches man how to think. It was this discipline that enabled the Scottish Universities to transcend the English Universities. He writes, "In Oxford emphasis was placed on the classics; in Cambridge on mathematics; but in Scotland philosophy was given pride of place. Philosophy taught students to categorise, scrutinise, and criticise data, to ask questions, and to develop judicious interpretations. In short, it taught students how to think. Stuart Piggin's comment only seeks to explain the value of philosophy as a discipline in Scottish theological education, it cannot be construed that Cambridge and Oxford did not value nor teach philosophy.

The transference of the scientific methods to theology and the ever increasing fragmentation of the discipline, theological knowledge with its component parts, become more predictable in their outcomes and are therefore more readily controlled. Ronald Laura argues that knowledge is a form of power as it becomes a form of control. It is through the knowledge of the things of nature that predictability can be acquired and this is more readily controlled. He writes,

> Because knowledge is a form of power, knowledge becomes a form of control, and the more control we have, the more secure we become, or so Bacon and his followers supposed. Bacon's cherished hope was that knowledge provided power through the acquisition of predictability. The more readily the behaviour of the things of nature could be predicted, the more readily they could be controlled. Technologies born out of this value-laden form of knowledge as power will themselves replicate through their own interventions in nature the obsession of our culture with dominion and subjugation.[7]

Although Laura writes in terms of power in the world of nature, the principles espoused are just as relevant for theology and the Church. The acquisition of predictability is true for theological systems and the technologies born out of the value-laden forms of knowledge are those devises that secure the entrenchment of a particular theological system to the exclusion of all others. Andrew McGowan acknowledges that science became the model for the theological enterprise. He writes, "Science soon became the model for all academic work, and scientific accuracy became the standard against which all other truth claims was judged".[8] The detail and accuracy of a historical and systematic theology gives evidence of this claim. The technologies of science are used to support a particular theological perspective. For example, the sale of "predictable" theological works and the practice of a "predictable" form of "expository preaching", as well as the more common technologies of light and sound and multimedia presentations are used to support and control a distinctive type of worship service. Other means that are used to control worship though not distinctively "scientific" in character, may well fall into the category of "technology". These are the use of "multi gifted leaders with a great vision", "functional building structures", and "inspirational services" that can be described as fun.[9] "Inspirational services" are contingent upon charismatic leaders who have powerful personalities, and who are able to communicate effectively in the prevailing culture with powerful oratorical skills. Human control is entrenched within all these "technologies". It is clear, that priority is given to scientific knowledge and it is this form of knowledge which we value, as a culture for the purposes of power and control. This particular form of knowledge has been institutionalised in our educational institutions. "It is our insatiable appetite for power that drives us to a form of knowledge which covertly stipulates that the only knowledge worth having is that which allows us to reorder the world and our relationships to each other in ways that suit our own ends and presumed interests, no matter how selfish or destructive those ends and interests are."[10] Such is the influence of this epistemology of power. Laura concludes that it has become an elemental facet of our physical existence.

The present difficulties with the philosophy of Theological Education within the P.T.C. were matters of considerable debate within the Presbyterian Church in Australia in 1981. After the formation of the Uniting Church, students for the ongoing Presbyterian ministry were trained at Moore Theological College, Sydney. The Theological Education Committee of the General Assembly in New South Wales called for, and published, submissions for the "establishment of a Theological Hall".[11] The Rev. Jon Boyall claimed that there were two ways of "thinking theology" and these were termed "conservative" and "progressive" (see Table 7.1).

Jon Boyall sees these two interpretations are comprehensive in scope but mutually incompatible. The progressive view is further defined as a perspective that arose in the nineteenth century and came to be known as "liberalism" and "neo-Calvinism and neo Thomism in the twentieth century.[12]

The re-establishment of the college was not without serious debate between the "conservatives" and the "progressives". The conservative notions

Table 7.1.

Conservative:	Progressive:
Straight line	spiral
Antithetical	synthetical, dialectical
Absolutist	relativitist
Akin to "scientific"	akin to "arts"
Confrontation in encounter	accommodation and dialogue in encounter
Centred on divine directives	centred on man's perspectives
Mediate infallibility possible (and necessary)	mediate infallibility impossible
Counter to cultural world view	consistent with cultural world view

of "antithetical", "absolutist" and "akin to science" and "divine directives" were notions that were perfectly consistent with Puritan theology and the Westminster standards, specifically due to the perceived doctrine of the "authority and inspiration of Holy Scripture". It was this conservative view that won the day, but not before a fight. Dr. Hugh Cairns, Principal of St. Andrews College, University of Sydney, claimed that the "Verbal Inspirationists" had already gained control of the Church; "the future will be fundamentalist", says Cairns.[13] Hugh Cairns argued in his submission against a connection between Church and Bible College. He claimed that in Bible Colleges there is a lack of acceptance of modern human knowledge – both scientific and within humanities, which prevent the teaching of sound learning to budding ministers. In a pertinent statement he argues:

> for all their good, there is no openness to data and theory, no adjusting and changing towards deeper truths from within human knowledge and the human community which surround Bible College and church. The Bible College is not a place of search in which being open to the data may mean adjusting or discarding views and accepting data and theories from else where: they are places of commitment to the certainty of one particular view only—the verbal Inspiration of Scripture and the Evangelical interpretation of Scripture and Gospel in the Fundamentalist way which this entails. So the Bible College is not a place of the maturing intellect, the development of intelligent personality: it is the place of faith, fellowship and enthusiasm—not education.

The history of the Presbyterian Church, claims Cairns, reveals a history of "living in the real world and in the world of human knowledge in which there has been a zest for new understanding, for sharpened perception and deeper knowledge to be culled out of every area of modern scholarship, so the integrity of the Church could be fuller and the doctrine of the Church more integrated".

Although the Church in practice approved Jon Boyall's outline by adopting the great theological divide in what he called "theological thinking", this move has subsequently had serious consequences for the academic basis of theological education. Professor Crawford Miller at the time cogently pointed out that the placement of the "great divide" is located in the wrong place.[14] He argues that to locate it in "theological thinking" is to adopt the method used by theologians. Miller then argues that these are human matters determined by personality the cultural and historical background of the theologian and as such cannot be the ground of basic theological divisions. *The great divide is located in Christology.* The central question, says Miller must be, *in what sense was God present in Christ reconciling the world to himself?* He argues that the Church Fathers clearly saw the big theological divide was and always will remain the gulf fixed between those who confess that Christ is true God as well as being true man, and those who are satisfied with some lesser and more qualified mode of the Divine presence. The former confess the catholic faith essentially worked out in the dogmas of the Trinity and the person of Christ.[15] Rejecting Boyall's "straight line" and "absolutist" and "akin to scientific" on the basis that theology deals with "mystery", Miller argues that:

> any theology necessarily embodies itself in the language and thought forms of a particular cultural and historical time. So in a sense theology is inevitably "synthetical and dialectical"! . . . All living theology is necessarily both conservative, as looking back to God's once for all saving act in Christ, and progressive as constantly reinterpreting the Gospel so that it may be understood within the dynamic process of human history, a process the dynamic character of which has been notably increased by the impact upon it of the Gospel! When people self-consciously and deliberately go in for a theology of confrontation what tends to result is the confrontation of the contemporary world by the theology of yesterday, an encounter which is not necessarily the same thing as confrontation by the truth of God in mercy and in judgement.[16]

2. A REPLACEMENT EPISTEMOLOGY

In a meaningful reconstruction of Theological Education a unifying epistemology is not only desirable but a necessity. We would argue that there is a real need for the teaching and development of a "Christian Epistemology", as it is only in this specific type of epistemology that the popularity of the common epistemologies of power will give way to an epistemology of love and empathy. So long as there is a commitment to human autonomy and the final authority of reason, there will always be the fruit of an epistemology of power. It is now pertinent to suggest that it is necessary to consider a Christian Epistemology for any reconstruction of theological education. We suggest it is through this radical approach, that it will be possible for the Church to experience unity and cohesion in realistic Biblical terms as well as the restoration of profound scholarship and meaningful liturgy.

Cornelius Van Til is one scholar who has written with this in mind. Foundational to Van Til's system is the rejection of the autonomy of man, since Christian thinking, like all of Christian life is subject to God's lordship. We have argued in the previous chapter that Van Til's work offers great possibilities for a realistic way ahead for Biblical scholarship which hitherto has been stuck in the proverbial methodological mud. We put forward three symbols as a way to understand a Van Tilian approach to a theological reconstruction.

THE FIRST SYMBOL OF A SPECIFIC EPISTEMOLOGY IS THE TREE OF KNOWLEDGE

The story of the creation of the heavens and the earth is the essential prerequisite to an epistemic perspective. Genesis 1: 26–31 and 3: 1–23 are of pivotal importance to the foundations of faith and an epistemology of love and empathy.

It has been argued by Sidlow Baxter that the opening sentence of Genesis chapter one contains the denial of all the principal false philosophies which have been taught by man. The opening paragraph reads: In the beginning God created the heavens and the earth.

In this passage Baxter, along with all other Christian theologians assumes that God is personal and relational. He then claims:

> In the beginning *God*—that denies Atheism with its doctrine of *no* God.
> In the beginning *God*—that denies Polytheism with its doctrine of *many* gods.
> In the beginning *God created*—that denies Fatalism with its doctrine of *chance*.
> In the beginning *God created*—that denies Evolution with its doctrine of infinite *becoming*.
> God created *heaven and earth*— that denies Pantheism which makes God and the universe identical.
> God created *heaven and earth*—that denies Materialism which asserts the eternity of matter.[17]

Baxter's presupposition is a belief in a personal God who has created all things out of nothing, *creation ex nihilo,* and the acceptance that the creation was *good.* He contrasts this profound passage with the principal antitheistic movements that have captured the attention of man over 2000 plus years of history. To deny this theistic interpretation of Genesis creates two fundamental problems. The first is there is no real explanation for the fact that the external world not only exists but has a specific form. Francis Schaeffer puts it this way, "as I look at the Being which is the external universe, it is obviously not just a handful of pebbles thrown out there. What is there has form. If we assert the existence of the impersonal as the beginning of the universe, we simply have no explanation for this kind of situation"[18] The second major problem that arises with an impersonal universe is that there is no explanation of personality. As Schaeffer explains there is no explanation for modern man's question, Who am I? The assumption of an impersonal beginning "can never adequately explain the personal beings we see around us, and when we try to explain man on the basis of an original impersonal, man soon disappears." The impersonal gives no basis for understanding human relationships, building just societies or engaging in any kind of cultural effort.[19]

Alan Richardson using the documentary hypothesis to exegete Genesis, argues that the creation of man, in Genesis chapter one, denotes mankind as document P in verse 27, does not speak of the creation of a pair of individuals, a man and a woman (as does J) but speaks of human species.[20] Man's creation was in the image of God. It is this which differentiates man from the animal kingdom. The command of verse 28 to "subdue the earth and to multiply", is a God-given responsibility in which he is to listen to the voice of God and to respond to the divine word, as Richardson says, man is akin to God in respect, that he knows God's word: as we say, "like speaks to like".[21] To man alone is given the responsibility of conscious choice; man of all the created things is free to disobey the Creator's will.

The P source, claims Richardson, posits the creation of man and woman at the same time and is equally important and complementary to each other. There was no gender superiority in God's design. The modern notions of male monotheism and the theistic presumptions of male superiority is the direct result of the "Fall". It was the "fall", says Van Til that man "tried to interpret all his relationships in an exclusively immanentistic fashion . . . he tried to draw conclusions about himself and especially about his future from the laws of nature".[22] Being no longer in union with God, man exercised his autonomy and authority as there was no possibility of "union" with God which is a prerequisite for empathy and connectedness. We would argue that patriarchy is a direct outcome of an epistemology of power, despite the traditional interpretation by the Church of the Genesis passages. Kevin Giles argues that the patriarchal interpretation of Genesis is in fact only secondary. He argues:

> In Genesis chapter one, the teaching of Jesus and the Pauline "magna carta" of Galatians 3:28 the ideal is given. Men and women are to be regarded as equals. This is the primary message of the Bible. The subordinating passages are to be dismissed because they reflect a past, patriarchal culture and a limited appreci-

ation of the mind of Christ; the egalitarian teaching is to be endorsed because it accurately reflects the mind of Christ.[23]

For Richardson the creation's original intention is re-established in Christ where there is no distinction of male and female. It is explicit in P that the division of mankind into two sexes is not a result of the Fall; it is part of God's original plan which he saw creation as "very good".[24]

The difference in the creation of man and woman in chapter two is seen more in terms of a parable. It is reliant on the J source which personifies mankind under the figure of a single male. Richardson claims that it is only the form of the teaching in which J differs from P; J's Adam is a poetic personification rather than an actual historical individual. To imagine that J intended his parable to be taken "*a pied de la lettre*" is a purely gratuitous assumption and almost certainly false.[25]

The "tree of life" in chapter 2 verse nine represents man's unbroken communion with God. It is a most powerful symbol which is foundational to an epistemology of love and empathy. Richardson interprets the fruit of the "tree of life" is synonymous with "all knowledge", both "good and bad". It does not necessarily mean or imply moral good. He concludes that "the tree of the knowledge of good and evil is a symbol denoting human experience in its entirety."[26]

Interpreting Genesis chapters one to three from an entirely different theological perspective, Edward J Young, a well-known conservative Old Testament scholar, rejects the documentary hypothesis used by Richardson. Young interprets Genesis chapters one to three being about fiat creation and is to be seen as a coherent whole. He divides Genesis up into two divisions. The first is Gen. 1: 1–2: 3, which deals with creation. The second is Gen. 2: 4 – 50:26, which Young describes as "the genealogies".[27] Genesis 2:4 is treated as a superscription and not a subscription, he writes;

> The phrase, "These are the generations of the heavens and the earth", is a superscription and not a subscription. In other words, it does not bring to a close what has just gone before. It is rather an introduction to what follows. This phrase occurs some ten or eleven times in the book of Genesis, and it is clear that in every one of its occurrences that is the way in which the phrase is used. It is always a superscription.[28]

The relationship between Adam and Eve is interpreted by Young in terms of their creation in the image of God. Young points to the New Testament teaching that the relationship is in terms of that which exists between Christ and the Church. Both man and woman have their God-given responsibilities, but the relationship is dependent upon "love", of the same quality as the love that Christ had for the Church. That love demands sacrifice. The relationship in other words is complementary and loving.[29]

This Biblical story is foundational to the development of an epistemology of love and empathy. Man and woman is in perfect harmony with God the creator, accepting responsibility in the whole experience of life, fulfilling the design of God. Nature and man are harmonious man listens to God and obeys God. Earth is a paradise where all things are intimately connected to each other, thereby expressing a wholeness and purpose. The basis of knowledge is harmonious between God, man (including woman) and nature.

Cornelius Van Til sees this as being foundational, as the Christian man assumes the plan of God, with the facts of creation, have a divine order. So the task of the Christian in science is to uncover the God – ordained structure of the world, as man and the world so that the rational abilities of man are applicable to the world, as man seeks to "subdue the earth".[30] Van Til therefore argues for the epistemological importance of Adam and Eve in their pre fallen state:

1. The Adamic consciousness, or, the reason of man as it existed before the fall of man. This reason was derivative. Its knowledge was, in the nature of the case, true, though not exhaustive. This reason was in covenant with God, instead of at enmity against God. It recognised the fact that its function was that of the interpretation of God's revelation. In paradise Adam had a true conception of the relation of the particulars to the universals of knowledge with respect to the created universe. He named the animals "according to their nature", that is, in accordance with the place God had given them in his universe. Then, too, Adam could converse truly about the meaning of the universe in general and about their own life in particular with Eve. Thus the object—object relationship was normal. In paradise man's knowledge was self – consciously analogical; man wanted to know the facts of the universe in order to fulfil his task as a covenant—keeper.[31]

The situation after the Fall is radically different and has far reaching consequences for epistemology.

Richardson argues that J clearly teaches in Genesis chapter three that pride is the root and essence of all human sinfulness. He argues in this way: the serpent suggests to the woman that God did not forbid the eating of the tree of knowledge out of any concern for the human well-being, rather God wished to preserve his divinity for himself. Therefore, argues Richardson, God pretended that there was a penalty attached to the eating of the fruit, namely death. The real truth notes Richardson is that to eat of the tree of knowledge is to confer the power to be AS GOD. This is the fatal weakness of human nature: "man's desire to give glory to himself and not to the creator, to usurp the place of God and put himself at the centre of the universe, to set himself up in the position which belongs to God alone".[32] In the

New Testament language it is the lust of the flesh, the lust of the eyes and the pride of life.[33]

The epistemological explanation is well expressed by Van Til who sees the Fall in terms of man's autonomy and the supreme authority of reason. The Fall is seen as *unregenerate consciousness . . . the natural man wants to be something that he cannot be*. The non-regenerate man takes for granted that the meaning of the space–time world is immanent in itself and that man is the ultimate interpreter of the world, instead of a humble re-interpreter. The natural man wants to be creatively constructive instead of receptively reconstructive.[34] Elsewhere Van Til argues that the non-Christian constantly attempts the impossible by demanding a coherence that originates with himself. It is here there is a negative and positive aspect. Negatively, claims Van Til, man must assume that reality is not divinely created and controlled in accordance with God's plan at all, and that the Christian story therefore cannot be true. The world of facts springs from "Chaos and Old Night" – ultimate chance.

Positively, man must assume that reality is after all rationally constituted and that it answers exhaustively to his logical manipulations. If the world were not rational or uniform then there could be no science. Any cosmic mind, or God, must therefore be able to be manipulated by man –made categories. Any God not reducible to logical or empirical categories, and therefore completely understandable, is a false God.[35]

Van Til continues to argue that both Christian and non–Christian claim that their position is in accord with the facts of experience. But, says Van Til, there is a difference:

a) the Christian claims this because he interprets the facts and his experience of them in terms of his presupposition. The "uniformity of nature" and his knowledge of that uniformity both rest for him upon the plan of God. The coherence which he sees in his experience he takes to be analogical to, and indeed, the result of, the absolute coherence of God.

b) the non Christian also interprets the facts in terms of his presuppositions. On the one hand is the presupposition of ultimate non –rationality. On such a basis, any fact would be different in all respects from other facts. There could be no "uniformity", the foundation of all science. Here is "Chaos and Old Night" with a vengeance. On the other hand, says Van Til, is the presupposition that all reality is rational in terms of the reach of logic as manipulated by man. On such a basis the nature of any fact would be identical with the nature of every other fact, or, in short, only one big universal fact. Then Van Til argues there could be no experience, because there could be no change. All would be static unity. The non–Christian tries somehow to balance these contradictions.[36]

The contribution of Ronald Laura at this point is profound and similar to that of Van Til. Laura's "epistemology of power" coincides with Van Til's notion of "unregenerate consciousness" and man being "the ultimate interpreter of the created order". Laura, however, advances this concept by introducing a God substitute, namely "technology". Since man in his Fallen state is living independent of God, technology hides his nakedness before God. That is the message of Adam and Eve sewing the fig leaves together to hide their inner nakedness after they ate of the tree of knowledge. Technology therefore becomes the symbol of man's autonomy and belief in the power of rationality. From this foundation Laura argues that technology is the tool that provides for an epistemology of power and subjugation as educational institutions inculcate the belief that scientific knowledge and the derivative technologies are the ultimate tools of social and personal salvation.[37] Using an empirical methodology, nature is divided into component parts, then analysed in terms of mathematical formulations and so the machine of nature becomes reductionistic. Such a methodology leads man to subdue and to control nature for his own selfish benefit. The epistemology is one of power, to subjugate and to control.[38] There is a common perception that the Biblical account of creation provides validation for this perception, as it specifies that man should "subdue the earth", and have "dominion" over it. We have already shown from two scholars, Richardson and Young, this point of view cannot be validated in the wider interpretation of the whole Genesis record in chapters one to three. However it is very difficult to change public perception. It needs to be recognised that an epistemology of power and subjugation is driven by fallen man who claims autonomy from God, and it is this that has destroyed the spiritual bond between man, God and nature.

In keeping with the above, Francis Schaeffer advocates a Biblical interpretation of the creation story in which he sees the idea of stewardship of the created order rather than one of exploitation. He sees support for a Biblical idea of holistic interaction between man and nature. Schaeffer is highly critical of the perceived orthodox Christian view which promotes limitless exploitation. The popularity of the epistemology of power, based partly as it is on an inadequate exegesis of Genesis will not solve any ecological problems, as it will ultimately resort to a pantheism which reduces man to a value of "no more than grass".[39] "Christians of all people, should not be the destroyers. We should treat nature with an overwhelming respect".[40]

Ashton and Laura advance some examples of human responsibility in the care of the environment:

a. Fields were to be left fallow every seventh year. Food which grew of its own accord was not to be harvested (Leviticus 25: 3–5, 20–22).
b. When an orchard was planted, the fruit from the first three years of bearing were not to be harvested (Leviticus 19: 23–25).
c. Not all the grain in a field or all the fruit trees or vines were to be harvested (Leviticus 23: 22; Deut.20: 19–20).

    d. In war and when conquering lands, trees were not to be chopped down. In particular fruit trees were not to be destroyed. Leviticus 23:28; Deut. 22: 6–7.
    e. Nature was to be presented as a resource to be protected and looked after, not exploited.[41]

The discussion so far may seem somewhat confluent, but it is of critical importance to the understanding of an epistemology of power which is a clear expression of the autonomy of man and the ultimate authority of reason.

It is also of critical importance to an understanding of a more Christian perception of a Christian Epistemology which would have important ramifications in education, especially theological education. A failure to understand the importance of a Christian epistemology in theological education is a failure of the Church's mission.

In summary, it is essential to understand that Genesis, chapters one to three, provides a coherent understanding that both Adam and Eve were created in the image of God, and this creation was designated the creation of man. Man and woman was a creation of equality and unity with designated partner responsibilities. There is no suggestion of modern day patriarchy. Before the "Fall" both Adam and Eve were in captivity to God the creator and life was characterised by love and empathy. From an epistemic perspective, to use Van Til's idiom they thought "analogically".

THE SECOND SYMBOL FOR A SPECIFIC CHRISTIAN EPISTEMOLOGY: NOAH AND THE ARK

Whereas the story of creation in Genesis provides a basis for a Christian Epistemology before the Fall Noah and the flood story on the other hand provides a symbol for a Christian Epistemology after the "Fall". The principles of coherence, love and empathy between God and man is still relevant.

Genesis 6: 5 says: "The Lord saw how great man's wickedness on earth had become and that every inclination of the thoughts of his heart was evil all the time. . . . Noah was, a righteous man blameless among the people of his time, and he walked with God".[42] In this narrative Noah had an intimate relationship with God. God spoke and Noah listened and responded. The famous Old Testament scholar Gerhard von Rad comments that Noah completed the building of the Ark without knowing God's intentions; he had only the command which drove him to blind obedience.[43] The New Testament confirms this "faith" and oneness with God in the epistle to the Hebrews 11: 7; "By faith Noah being warned by God concerning events unseen, took heed and constructed an ark for the saving of his household." Noah's oneness with God, or in terms of the Epistle to the Romans in the New Testament, "union" with God is described in the Genesis record as "righteousness". In Van Tilian terms Noah was self- consciously analogical, whereby Noah wanted to know the facts in order to fulfil his task as a covenant keeper, "and Noah did all that the Lord commanded him".[44] Von Rad argues that it is unfortunate that there is no satisfactory English word for this theologically significant Hebrew word "*saddiq*". This word in the Old Testament says von Rad "does justice to a relationship in which he (Noah) stands". If God abides by his covenant acts according to the covenant then he is "righteous". Righteousness in this sense is not a juridical term of relation, but rather a theological one."[45] The wickedness of men in the community in contrast was so extensive that evil pervaded the depth of man's whole being all the time. Philosophically Noah's world view was diametrically opposed to that of the community conscience which was governed by an autonomous outlook that rejected any notion of non-empirical reasoning. Van Til would deem this as sinful or unregenerate consciousness.[46] Man sets himself up as the ideal of comprehensive knowledge. The non –regenerate man takes for granted that the meaning of the space-time world is immanent in itself and that man is the ultimate interpreter of the world instead of its humble re-interpreter. The natural man wants to be creatively constructive instead of receptively reconstructive. This is a far better explanation than the cryptic argument offered by Von Rad, who considers the act of destroying the wickedness of men was not made by God, in terms of being "unconcerned and cold indifference. The destruction was necessary to "save" mankind. Immediately after the flood "the first human work that the liberated earth, which is again restored to man sees, is an altar for God the Lord. Verse twenty one, says von Rad, has the character of a sacrifice of reconciliation.

John Calvin says something very similar in a less philosophical manner. He argues that the destruction of man by the flood was not an idle decision on God's part. Men willingly rejected the Grace of God in favour of what Calvin calls "extreme disorder". If God had created man in his own image, then the actions of men were obliterating that image from his thinking. This is none other than men assuming a God-like status and authority. It is the preservation of God's image and the sacred recognition of God in worship that necessitated the judgement of the flood. The rains came only after God considered his censure on an excessive and incurable obstinacy.[47] Calvin sees the Flood in terms of preserving the dignity of a divinely created Church of God.[48] He also posits the view that the covenant God establishes with Noah should "quicken us and inspire each of our members with vigour to yield obedience to God". Calvin then refers his readers to the testimony of St Paul in Colossians 1: 5 in which he argues: "love flourishes in the saints on account of the hope laid up for them in heaven". It is necessary that the faithful should be confirmed by the word of God, lest they faint in the midst of their course. This is Calvin's interpretation of Noah and the Flood.[49]

Therefore the saving of the world through the Ark can only mean that the Adamic consciousness is "restored and supplemented". When God reasons with us and changes our minds, points out Van Til, our "every thought is brought into captivity to the obedience of Christ, we must use our minds, our intellect our reason, our consciousness, in order to receive and reinterpret the revelation of God has given of himself in Scripture. That is the proper place of reason in theology".[50]

The destruction of society and the saving of the few within the Ark, conveys the message that God's love and empathy is with the created order and he gives to man a second chance to receive the gift of life and to think analogically.

The whole story cogently conveys the idea that God the Creator is passionate in his love for mankind and provides the means of escape from the coming destruction by flood. It is unfortunate that at this point the Presbyterian Church has not been consistent. There have been prominent theologians such as Warfield and Hodge who have held to a strong Biblical faith in the all sufficiency of Christ, but who seek to defend it with a methodology that denies the very theology that they espouse. That is to say they lack a distinctive and profound Christian Epistemology. The focus of the method used by these theologians is based upon the assumption that the space–time world is in some measure contingent and that man must create for himself his own epistemology in an ultimate sense. Previous theologians proceeded upon the same assumption. Thomas Aquinas is a case in point in the catholic form, and Joseph Butler's work is the protestant form.[51]

Embedded in the symbolism of Noah and the Flood is an epistemology of love that seeks the good of man. Only within this type of epistemology the natural world will be spared of the carnage at the hands of men who are possessed with an epistemology of power. In Noah's day the constant rejection of God's love towards the environment and mankind in favour of a world view placed man in a God-like position in which he acted as the final interpretative reference point resulted in abuse and power. It was this which resulted in judgement. In a similar way today judgement is falling upon modern society in terms of the environment and mankind. Nature is being pillaged in the name of progress and profit and the result is pollution on a grand scale. For example, BHP-Billiton dumped 80,000 tons of tailings containing copper, zinc, cadmium and lead directly into the Fly and Ok Tedi Rivers over a period of two decades. This has ruined the lands of thousands of subsistence farmers, poisoned some 2000 square miles of forest, polluted the Ok Tedi and contaminated a section of the Fly River, PNG's second biggest river system, severely depleting fish stocks. For many years, successive PNG governments have colluded with BHP to cover up the mine's environmental damage and suppress compensation claims.

Mankind suffers through political decision making at governmental and corporate level of society which results in genocide and the curtailments of religious freedom. The judgement on the environment and mankind is a direct imposition of an epistemology of power and greed, demonstrating the autonomy of man and the ultimacy of human authority.

GOD'S LOVE IS FOUNDATIONAL FOR A CHRISTIAN EPISTEMOLOGY IS THE THIRD SYMBOL

The idea of love in the above two symbols within the Genesis record, is the principal theme of the whole of the Biblical record. D.A. Carson in a study of love in the Scriptures offers three brief reflections which show the importance of this love theme:

1) The love of God for his people is sometimes likened to the love of a parent for the child (e.g., Heb 12: 4–11; cf. Prov. 4: 20). The Lord disciplines those he loves. We must never forget that we are held responsible to keep ourselves in the love of God (Jude 21), remembering that God is loving and merciful "to those who love him and who keep his commandments" (Exod. 20: 6).

2) The love of God is not merely to be analysed, understood, and adopted into holistic categories of integrated theological thought. It is to be received, to be absorbed, to be felt. Meditate long and frequently on Paul's prayer in Ephesians 3: 14–21. The relevant section finds the apostle praying for the believers in these terms: "I pray you, being rooted and established in love, may have power, together with all the saints, to grasp how wide and long and high and deep is the love of Christ, and to know this love that surpasses knowledge—that you may be filled to the measure of all the fullness of God".

3) Never underestimate the power of the love of God to break down and transform the most amazingly hard individuals. One of the most powerful affirmations of this truth in a context far removed from our Church buildings is the worldwide showings of the musical version of *Les Miserables*, Victor Hugo's magnificent novel. Sentenced to a nineteen–year term of hard labour for stealing bread, Jean Valjean becomes a hard and bitter man. No-one could break him; everyone feared him. Released from prison, Valjean finds it difficult to survive, as innkeepers will not welcome him and work is scarce. Then a kind bishop welcomes him into his home. But Valjean betrays the trust. During the night he creeps off into the darkness, stealing some of the family silver.

But Valjean is brought back next morning to the bishop's door by three policemen. They had arrested him and found the stolen silver on him. A word from the bishop, and the wretch would be incarcerated for life. But the bishop instantly exclaims, "So here you are! I'm delighted to see you. Had you forgotten that I gave you the candlesticks as well? There're silver like the rest, and worth a good 200 francs. Did you forget to take them?" Jean Valjean is released, and he is transformed. When the gendarmes withdrew, the bishop insists on giving the candlesticks to his speechless, mortified, thankful guest. The bishop admonishes: "Do not ever forget that you promised me to use the money to make yourself an honest man". Throughout Hugo's story Javert the police inspector pursues Valjean. Javert, is consumed by the letter of the law but knows nothing of forgiveness or compassion. He crumbles psychologically when his black and white categories of justice fail to cope with grace that goes against every instinct for revenge and retribution. Valjean is transformed but Javert jumps off a bridge, committing suicide by drowning in the Seine.[52]

From a Christian perspective, love is truly transformative and is powerful; yet it is puzzling that theologians have continued to accept and use a methodology that is reflective of an epistemology of power that reveals itself in exploitation and control rather than developing a Christian epistemology that is reflective of love, compassion and empathy.

3. TOWARDS THE RECONSTRUCTION

An understanding of the theory of transformative subjugation provides essential clues for future pathways of education from within a modern educational context,[53] but as we have already suggested that there are many areas in which Laura's thought coincides with the work of Cornelius Van Til, and as such, it makes for an educational theory suitable for theological education, which utilizes Van Til's notion of a Christian epistemology.

The older epistemology of power which was used by the scientific community to great effect, and then applied to theological studies has been seriously challenged in recent years by developments in the philosophy of science and quantum mechanics. The more we attempt to define the world in terms of its fundamental constituents and to isolate those fundamental constituents, the more we discover that they can only be explained by reference to each other. Quantum mechanics forces us to admit that the world is one seamless indivisible unity. The component parts only gain their integrity and identity by virtue of being related to each other.[54] With this discovery it is more apt to develop an epistemology of participation, empathy and connectivity that reflects the degree of that seamless indivisible unity, rather than to hold on to the epistemology of power that has been so prevalent in the scientific enterprise and in educational and theological institutions.

The classical view of physical reality is in essence fragmented. To discover the truth of reality requires the reduction of matter into its smallest component parts, in the reductionist hope of reaching absolutely simple building blocks of which everything else is made and can be understood. The objective of classical physics is therefore to show how all the parts work together and to reveal patterns of organisation. In contrast to this, quantum physics shows something very different. The secrets of reality are not determined by reducing matter into smallest component parts at all. Rather, the primitive component parts turn out to be so inextricably related that their coherent description depends upon a world of seamless unity and indivisible wholeness.[55] The conclusion is, *not to exploit human consciousness to achieve control but rather to achieve connection, relationship and balance through consciousness.* Empathetic knowing involves seeing the fundamental interrelationships which express the character of the whole. We must learn to discern how our participation in the dynamical process of indivisible unity represents an investment in the future rather than an extractive lien on the past.[56]

There are two essential steps which must be taken to affirm a new epistemological paradigm, because the great need of education today, including theological education, is "to reconstruct an epistemic framework which eschews reductionist methodologies of environment degradation".

The First Step: The reconceptualisation of knowledge is the means to "empathetic connectivity", whereby the role of education is to "educate the sensibilities of moral conscience to recognise the value and the point of moral responsibility".[57] Instead of "controlling" there is the idea of "connecting". This is the first cognitional step. The whole notion of theological education is therefore to provide strategies for students to connect not only with the sovereign creator and His salvic love for humanity, but to comprehend the scope of the epistemological interconnections of historical theology. To adhere to methodologies which enhance separateness and create a critical platform in order to critique and suppress every other theological point of view is to fail the ideals of an epistemology of love and empathy. The anti-catholic debates of the past and the defrocking of theologians who disagree with an accepted denominational point of view,[58] are evidence of how an empirical/reductionist methodology is less than helpful for the peace and unity of the Church. The New Testament as well as the history of Scottish Presbyterianism, already provides the teaching in respect to the importance of connectedness. St. Paul's teaching in his epistle to the Romans teaches the necessity of our "union with Christ". It is from the ontological union with Christ that man experiences renewal and transformation.[59]

T.F. Torrance argues that John Calvin in his *Institutes* treats "our regeneration in Christ" before dealing with the doctrine of "Justification" because "our union with Christ" belongs to the inner content of Justification.[60] For Torrance, Justification is not merely a judicial or forensic event but the imputation to us of Christ's own divine/human righteousness which we receive through "union with him". There is connectedness in terms of Pauline theology. "Apart from Christ's incarnational union with us and our union with Christ on that ontological basis, justification degenerates into only an empty moral relation."[61] The Scots Confession preserved the Pauline teaching but the Westminster Confession did not as it reversed the order and relied on notion of justice of God. Torrance notes that the order of Justification is as follows in the Confession of faith: "we are justified through a judicial act, then through an infusion of grace we live through a sanctified life, and grow into Christ". The effect of this, says Torrance, gave rise to an evangelical approach to the saving work of Christ in which the atonement is divorced from incarnation, substitution from representation and the sacraments are detached from union with Christ.' Justification, as a result began to be interpreted subjectively.

Once the ontological relationship with Christ disappears, man is in control of doctrine and the pathway of salvation, as he imposes conditions. Hence, the notion of conditional grace. In other words, the autonomy of man has taken control, the essential ingredient of an epistemology of power.

The Second Step is recognising the conventional way of knowing encourages the learner to seek separation and detachment from the world of nature so that nature can, through transformative subjugations of technology, be manipulated without conscience, harnessed for commercial exploitation and mindlessly consumed.[62] The revelation of quantum interconnectivity means that we can no longer detach ourselves in the name of objectivity. This is equally true in the pursuit of theological science. The idea of detachment in theology only serves to enforce an epistemic power which encourages separateness, and at times harsh judgements, and superior claims of correctness. For example, Episcopalian Churches that insist on re-ordaining clerics from non Episcopalian traditions: The Roman Catholic demands that its clergy should not participate in the Eucharist of another Christian Church; the insistence of some Presbyterian Church's complete detachment from Roman Catholicism; the idea of "fencing the Table" at Holy Communion, so as to preserve the purity of a particular view of the sacrament. Within some of the newer "non-traditional Churches", Gospel faithfulness is linked with "speaking in tongues" as an essential requirement for a true Church; in terms of the overall theme of this book the rejection of historical liturgies of the Church in favour of a *minimised liturgy* suggests manipulation and control to preserve a peculiar view of liturgy.

When educational knowledge is motivated by our faith in the virtue of connectivity of God's love then our participatory role ought to be one of interaction and appreciation with the whole history of theological themes. The Calvinist view of worship is to *connect* the worshipper with the Holy, awesome God, so that our participatory mode is one of interaction with the worship of Jesus Christ. His worship, becomes our worship. The practical outcome of this worship is that all true worshippers are related to each other as they express their common unity with Christ. Denominationalism has in the past acted in a private capacity when it comes to the theological education of its candidates for the priesthood/ministry. Each seeks to educate with a specific methodology so as to preserve its own theological identity, be it Roman Catholic, High Anglican, Low Anglican, Presbyterian, or Pentecostal. This attitude towards theological education is typical of the need to preserve the reduction-mechanistic methodologies. L. Heshusius[63] notes if we are to leave the old paradigm of thinking we need to foster a participatory mode of consciousness. This will involve a "somatic", "non–verbal" reordering of our understanding of the relationship between the self and other where the focus of attention is away from the self. There is according to Heshusius, a "procedural" anxiety faced by educators which is a result of their trying either to be as objective as possible in their methodologies, or as rigorous as possible in their management of the subjective. This result says, Heshusius suggests, in an alienated mode of consciousness.[64] Theological education needs to be more open and a greater awareness of the holistic approach to the development of various theologies, with a genuine understanding of their epistemological starting points and the implications they have on the broad spectrum of doctrine.

To adopt a new methodology which expresses an epistemology of empathy and love will require specific courses of study in the history of epistemology and philosophy. It is essential that an epistemological framework be provided in the study of philosophy and the history of theological themes.

At this point, the work of Professor Crawford Miller is of critical importance, as it fits well, with the Laura, Cotton thesis. Central to the Laura/Cotton thesis is that the secrets of reality are not determined by reducing matter into the smallest component parts, so as to reveal patterns of organisation. Rather the secrets of reality are determined by, *primitive components that are so inextricably related that their coherent description depends upon a world of seamless unity and indivisible wholeness.* This theory is at the heart of Miller's view of "doing theology". For Miller, Theological Education is not a matter of students learning a collection of facts and assertions. It is rather a process of initiating people into ongoing reflective activity. This claim is based on the assumption that "theology is not God's truth in an unqualified sense but a historical and culturally conditioned human attempt to grasp and express the truth of God.[65] Miller therefore argues that there are three types of "reflective thinking" which coincides with the "seamless unity and indivisible wholeness":

   a. There is the reflective thinking of philosophy. Miller posits the notion that theology as an intellectual discipline began in the patristic period, with the marriage of philosophical reflection with Christian proclamation. The process involved the borrowing of some philosophical concepts but more importantly it involved the use of philosophical techniques of reflection.

b. There is reflective thinking as a result of the techniques of historical investigation. Miller sees the importance of history goes along with the recognition that human beings are creatures of history—made what they are in part by processes of cultural and social change.

c. There is the reflective thinking of more recent times too, both the natural and social sciences which increasingly make an impact upon theology. "On the one hand science reveals a universe vastly greater in space and time and vastly more complex in its structure than anything which entered into the thoughts of the Biblical writers. On the other hand psychological and sociological investigations are relevant to the theological understanding of man, and clearly are important for the pastoral praxis of the Church". This single point alone is in perfect harmony with the Laura and Cotton thesis.

Miller continues to argue that while theology operates in dialogue with these other disciplines it is nevertheless is a discipline *sui generis* which has four aspects. As Biblical theology, it is concerned with the interpretation of Scripture as setting forth the Scriptural witness to the Word and Revelation of God who is in Jesus Christ. As Systematic theology, it is concerned critically to construct that balanced and integrated structure of proclamation of the Gospel committed to it. As philosophical theology, it is concerned with the relations in which, this specifically Christian truth stands to the other forms of truth by which people live. As practical theology, it is concerned with the implications of this truth of Christ for the Church's praxis, its action in the widest sense of that term.[66]

Miller's contribution to what Theological Education is, and his notion of "doing theology" has long been forgotten in the Presbyterian Church. The document on *Submissions for a Theological Hall* have long been buried in the archives of the Ferguson Library Sydney; besides there are only two full time pastoral ministers left in the New South Wales Presbyterian Church who had the privilege of having Miller as lecturer.

A new generation has arisen and taken control of the Church. Whilst this may be the case there is a strange sense of similarity in what Miller was saying in 1981 and what the modern Reformed scholar, Professor Andrew McGowan,[67] is saying in respect to the place of theology in a modern university context. In a lecture at the University of Newcastle in 2008, McGowan argued that theology, as a discipline, has a rightful place in a modern university in which its claims are subjected to the accreditation, validation and scrutiny as in any other discipline. McGowan argued that theology had pride of place in the ancient universities of Oxford, Cambridge, St. Andrews and

Glasgow. In more recent times, says McGowan, Cardinal John Henry Newman argued that theology, based as it is in revelation from God, is real knowledge and so deserves its place within the university. Newman says: "A university, I should lay down, by its very name professes to teach universal knowledge: how then is it possible for it to profess all branches of knowledge, and yet exclude from the subjects of its teaching one which, to say the least, is as important and as large as any of them? I do not see that either premise of this argument is open to exception".[68] Had the Church at the time embraced the ideals of Theological Education put forward by Professor Miller, the Church may be a different Church from what it is today.

STEPS TAKEN

The Presbyterian Theological College has taken a step in the right direction in that there are two compulsory philosophical units to be studied. The first is *Introduction to Philosophy*; the other is a *Christian World View*.

The *Introduction to Philosophy* course is a thirteen week course which covers pre-Socratic philosophy, Plato, Aristotle, Hellenistic philosophy, Early Christian philosophy and Neo-Platonism, Medieval philosophy, Renaissance and Reformation, The Age of Reason, The Enlightenment, 19th century Philosophy, 20th century: Phenomenology, Existentialism and 20th century: Post-modernity. The stated aim of this compulsory unit is clear:

1. To be able to outline the major concerns of significant thinkers in the Western tradition;
2. To be able to explain and discuss the philosophical problems associated with the nature of knowledge, reality and morality.
3. To be able to discuss the mutual influence of theology and philosophy through Western history.
4. To be able to offer a critical assessment of the role of philosophy in theological thought;
5. To have developed a basic competency in reading and assessing philosophical texts.

The second compulsory unit is *Christian World View*. The aim of which is to develop an understanding of world views and in particular the Christian world view. It examines the nature and functions of a world view and the history of reflection on worldviews. This is also a thirteen week course covering:

1. What is a world view
2. The history of "world view" reflection

3. Developing a Christian world view
4. Christian world view and apologetics
5. Christian world view and the arts
6. Christian world view and politics
7. Christian world view and history
8. Christian world view and science[69]

Although these courses are useful in their own right they are wholly inadequate in terms of this book. They need to be developed from the introductory stage into a series of connected course subjects to form a full major strategy. In the present situation, these subjects, even though they are compulsory are left up in the air with nothing to follow. It is all but impossible to come to grips with all the basic themes in thirteen weeks. The coverage of both courses is only a bird's eye view which cannot provide any real content for meaningful analysis and reflection. The content covered suggests that a meaningful approach for serious reflection should be over three full years.

The content of the courses, although offering the possibility of an epistemological approach, fails to provide an effective epistemology. Without an effective epistemological framework these courses, though interesting, become an academic exercise which students must endure. Such introductions may develop negative attitude in some students.

The worldview course without an epistemology runs the perilous danger of becoming aspects of ideology. David Wells comments that ideology is a worldview with attitude and has the intent to control![70]

Serious consideration should be given to the study of a History of Epistemology.[71] George Pappas discusses: What is knowledge, the extent of our knowledge and about what sort of things is knowledge actually held? What are the sources of knowledge and how is it acquired? and, is there any genuine knowledge? Pappas provides a useful starting point. In terms of Reformed Theology an epistemological understanding of the discontinuity between the early Reformers and the later Reformers in the sixteenth and seventeenth centuries is a necessity as this deals with the important issues of natural theology and scholasticism.[72] Unless such a study is pursued, most students will naturally use a scientific methodology as a default position, which will only encourage the notion that Scripture can be reduced to a set of propositional truths, which imply that all other views are inadequate or false statements of truth.

In order for students to be engaged in "doing theology", which is open to accreditation, validation and scrutiny, as in any other discipline, We would argue that the Presbyterian Church Theological College needs to embrace the idea of theological education as put forward by Crawford Miller and strongly suggested by the modern Reformed theologian, Andrew McGowan.

NOTES

1. E. Farley *Theologia: The Fragmentation and Unity of Theological Education* (Philadelphia: Fortress Press, 1983), 49.
2. 2 This "Paper" was a handout to members of the General Assembly.
3. Farely, *Theologia*, 49.
4. Farley, *Theologia*, 41.
5. Jeffery K. Jue, "Theologia Naturalis", in *Revelation and Reason*, ed. K. Scott Oliphant and L.G. Tipton (New Jersey: P&R Publishing, 2007), 168–73.
6. Thomas F. Torrance, *Transformation & Convergence in the Frame of Knowledge*, (Michigan: Eerdmans, 1984), 246–47.
7. Laura and Cotton, *Empathetic Education*, 48.
8. McGowan, *The Divine Spiration*, 117.
9. See C.A. Schwartz, *The ABC's of Natural Church Development* (Carol Stream: Church Smart Resources, 1998).
10. R. Laura, T. Marchant and S. Smith, *The New Social Disease* (Maryland: University Press of America, 2008), 6–7.
11. Theological Education Committee, *Submissions on the Establishment of a Presbyterian Theological Hall* (Sydney: Theological Education Committee, 1981).
12. Jon Boyall, *Submissions*, 56.
13. Dr Hugh Cairns, *Submissions*, 52–54.
14. The Rev. Professor Crawford Miller (1913–2001) was appointed in 1958 as professor of Systematic Theology in the Theological Hall of the Presbyterian Church in New South Wales which was attached to the St Andrew's College, University of Sydney. In his obituary in the *Sydney Morning Herald*, Dr Richard Campbell wrote: "Miller was never sufficiently satisfied with his own thinking to write out the major book of philosophical theology that was always brewing within him. But with his passing, Australia has lost the most unswerving, and the most powerful, religious thinker to have graced our shores". "When the Presbyterian Church resolved to unite with the Methodists and the Congregationalists to form the Uniting Church of Australia in 1977, Miller was one of those who chose to remain Presbyterian. He wrote trenchant critiques of the two drafts of the Basis of Union of the new Church, arguing that they expressed excessively an amalgam of theological liberalism and pietism". Central to his theological thought was the contention of Karl Barth that "those who start theologising with Descartes ended with Feuerbach"; Richard Campbell, *Sydney Morning Herald*, 16 July 2001, 40.
15. *Submissions*, 60.
16. Miller, *Submissions*, 61.
17. J. Sidlow Baxter, *Explore the Book* (London: Marshall, Morgan & Scott, 1956), Vol. 1, 34.
18. Francis Schaeffer, *Genesis in Space and Time* (London: Hodder & Stroughton, 1973), 20.
19. Schaeffer, *Genesis in Space and Time*, 21.
20. Alan Richardson, *Genesis 1–11* (London: SCM Press, 1963), 53. While exegeting in this way Richardson acknowledges that J, E, D, P may never have been "documents" at all, rather they may have been "streams of oral tradition". It is furthermore acknowledged that those sources cannot be confined to any specific period of time. See Genesis, 15.
21. Richardson, *Genesis*, 54.
22. Cornelius Van Til, *In Defence of the Faith* (New Jersey: P&R Publishing, 1974), 86.
23. Kevin Giles, *Created Woman* (Canberra: Acorn Press 1985), 1–2.
24. Richardson, *Genesis*, 56.
25. Richardson, Genesis, 59.
26. Richardson, *Genesis*, 64–66.
27. Edward J. Young, *In the Beginning* (Edinburgh: Banner of Truth Trust, 1976), 63.
28. Young, *In the Beginning*, 61–63.
29. Young, *In the Beginning*, 77.
30. Cornelius Van Til, *The Reformed Pastor and Modern Thought* (New Jersey: P&R Publishing, 1980), 28.

31. Cornelius Van Til *In Defence of the Faith* (New Jersey: P&R Publishing, 1974), Vol.5, 25.
32. Richardson, *Genesis*, 72.
33. See *Holy Bible*, I John 2:16.
34. Van Til, *In Defence of the Faith*, Vol. 5, 26.
35. Cornelius Van Til, *The Reformed Pastor and Modern Thought* (New Jersey: P&R Publishing, 1974), 28.
36. Van Til, *In Defence of the Faith*, Vol. 5, 28.
37. Laura and Cotton, *Empathetic Education*, 3.
38. J. Ashton and R.S. Laura, *New Insights in Environmental Education* (Adamstown: Insight Press, 2003), 32–33.
39. Francis Schaeffer, *Pollution & the Death of Man* (Illinois: Tyndale Press, 1979), 12–14.
40. Schaeffer, *Pollution & the Death*, 74.
41. Ashton and Laura, *New Insights*, 97.
42. *Holy Bible*, Genesis 6: 5–9.
43. Gerhard von Rad, *Genesis* (London: SCM Press, 1970), 116.
44. Genesis 7:5.
45. von Rad, *Genesis*, 116.
46. Cornelius Van Til, *Defence of the Faith. Introduction to Systematic* Theology (New Jersey: P&R Publishing,1974), Vol. 5, 26.
47. John Calvin, Commentaries, *Genesis* (Michigan: Baker Book House Reprint, 1979), Vol. 1, 242.
48. Calvin, *Genesis*, 238.
49. Calvin, *Genesis*, 258–59.
50. Van Til, *In Defence of the Faith*, Vol. 5, 30.
51. E.R. Geehan, ed., *Jerusalem & Athens* (New Jersey: P&R Publishing, 1980), 10–11.
52. D.A. Carson, *The Difficult Doctrine of the Love of God.* (Leicester: IVP, 2000), 92. Carson also writes in the same work, on our love to God. He considers that sooner or later one cannot adequately grasp the love of God in Scripture without reflecting on the ways in which God's love *elicts* our love.
53. Ronald S. Laura is Professor of Education at Newcastle University, Australia.
54. Laura and Cotton, *Empathetic Education*, 137.
55. Laura and Cotton, *Empathetic Education*, 138. In this section of Laura and Cotton's book reference is made to the works of Bohr and Heisenberg. A detailed discussion is also given to Bell's theorem. See 138–45.
56. Laura and Cotton, *Empathetic Education*, 144.
57. Laura and Cotton, *Empathetic Education*, 162–63.
58. The trial of Rev. Macleod Campbell in the Church of Scotland is a case in point. Campbell raised serious questions in respect to the "penal substitutionary" theory of the Atonement, which at the time was regarded as the teaching of the Westminster Confession of Faith.
59. The same Pauline idea is expressed in the second letter to the Corinthians 5:17: "if anyone is in Christ, he is a new creation; the old has gone, the new has come!"
60. T.F. Torrance, *God and Rationality* (London: Oxford University Press, 1971), 64–65.
61. Torrance, *God and Rationality*,65.
62. Torrance, *God and Rationality*,164.
63. L. Heshusius, "Freeing ourselves from objectivity", *Educational Researcher* (April 1994).
64. Heshusius, "Freeing ourselves",169–70.
65. Professor Crawford Miller, *Submissions*, 57.
66. Miller, *Submissions*, 58.
67. Andrew McGowan, "Is there a Place for Theology in a Modern University?" Lecture, The University of Newcastle, 25 August 2008.
68. John Henry Newman, *The Idea of a University* (London: Longmans, Green & Co, 1931), 19–20.
69. The details of these courses in Philosophy and Worldviews are taken from the 2007 syllabus outlines provided by the College.

70. David Wells, *Above all Earthly Powers* (Michigan: Eerdmans, 2005), 25.
71. George Pappas has an outstanding article on the History of Epistemology, complete with an invaluable reading list. This would be a worthwhile starting point. See E. Craig, ed. *Routledge Encyclopedia of Philosophy* (London: Routledge, 1998).
72. See the important contribution of a number of Reformed scholars, in K. Scott and L.G. Tipton, eds, *Revelation & Reason* (New Jersey: P&R Publishing, 2007). For an in-depth appraisal of the importance of epistemology in theological disciplines, see John Frame, *The Doctrine of the Knowledge of God* (New Jersey: P&R Publishing, 1987).

Conclusion

This book on Liturgical Minimisation within the Presbyterian Church in Australia, has demonstrated that the minimisation process is the outcome of a monumental crisis within the professional development of its clergy, which has impacted upon the life of the Church and its institutional politics. There has been a radical departure from Calvin's notion of worship in which recognition is given to 'God's unspeakable Majesty and Otherness, and the nothingness and simplicity of man.' In the service of worship, the worshipper is confronted with the divine transcendence on the awestruck soul. Calvin's paradigm has given way to a new and disturbing paradigm whereby worship has capitulated to the desires and whims of a culture that is imbued with a postmodern philosophy. This paradigm shift with its unfortunate outcomes is explained in this book, by incorporating two fundamental themes, one of which is minor, the other constituting the major theme of the book.

It is only after an understanding of the nature of the paradigm shift that we offer a way forward to resolve the crisis of worship confronting the Church.

The first is the minor theme, in which Liturgical Minimisation is placed into the historical context of Australian Presbyterianism. In this it was shown that the founding of the Presbyterian Church, particularly in New South Wales under the direction of Rev. John Dunmore Lang M.A., D.D. was so turbulent in the harsh political, social and economic environment, that a pattern of conflict emerged within the Presbyterian Church, which has characteristically resurfaced from time to time in the history of the Church, to the present day.

Lang fought many battles with government officialdom over funding, marriage licences, education and immigration. Many of these issues were bound up with what Lang called Anglican hegemony. Education, for example became the issue which caused a serious rift between Dr Lang and Archdeacon Broughton, who viewed each other with suspicion and distrust. This was a sad outcome as the two denominations were in the main unified in doctrine. Although the two denominations held to either the Westminster Confession of Faith in the case of the Presbyterians or the Thirty Nine Articles in the case of the Church of England, they were both Calvinistic documents. Unfortunately both denominations in Great Britain were national Churches, in England or Scotland. It was, therefore, always going to be difficult to have common recognition by an English appointed administration in the colony of New South Wales. The twin difficulties of ineptitude and a destructive oratory on Lang's part are clearly evident in the saga of the establishment of the Scots Church and the founding of the first school.

Lang also fought battles with his fellow clergy. On one occasion he accused the Presbytery of being a synagogue of Satan. He was excommunicated only to be readmitted to the fold some time later. Despite his argumentative nature he became a prominent figure in the politics of the Colony and exerted a powerful influence in many areas of public life.

This pattern of conflict continued in the life of the Church. Conflict disturbed the peace and quiet of the Church on more than one occasion during the twentieth century, in the heresy trials of Professor Samuel Angus and Dr. Peter Cameron. There were also the debates and division over the Church Union proposal which was consummated in 1977, causing a disruption in the Church. After the Church union disaster, the Church became embroiled in the debates concerning the ordination of female ministers. This unsettling matter has spilt over into the twenty-first century in further debates on the ordination of women elders. This issue has the potential to cause further division in the Church.

It is in this context of a 'pattern of conflict', that we have examined the notion of Liturgical Minimisation, the major theme of this book. I have defined liturgical minimisation in chapter four as, *"the process of removing from a liturgy anything that is theologically unacceptable or anything that is indifferent which has no direct command in Holy Scripture."* The latter aspect of this definition is of particular interest as it relates more to the radical religious reformers. For example, the sixteenth century protestant reformers declared that transubstantiation was an unacceptable doctrine as it was the foundation building block of the Roman Mass. This meant that in the eyes of the protestant reformers, all references to this doctrine had to be removed from the liturgy, and thus the liturgy was minimized. According to some of the more radical of the reforming party, especially some of the English and Scottish Puritans, other parts of the liturgy may also be removed if there was no definitive Biblical command. This became known as the Regulative Principle. The development of worship practice according to this principle led to the formulation of the bare outlines of worship of the Westminster Directory of Public Worship.

It was the 1991 General Assembly of Australia that replaced the committee that was revising the *Book of Common Order*. This Committee was responsible for the radical change in the Church's liturgical direction. The 1998 *Book of Common Order* gave expression to a minimised liturgy in which all the symbolism, artistic beauty and other component parts of the historical liturgy were removed. The consequences of this minimisation have resulted in the widespread neglect of liturgical forms. This radical change has caused great hurt among many of the Church's senior members and older clergy.

In order to understand the Liturgical tradition of the Presbyterian Church an overview of what liturgy means within the Reformed tradition has been provided. This overview provides the contrast between what used to be, and what now is. The contrast provided, illustrates the destructiveness of Liturgical Minimisation. The Strasbourg and Geneva liturgies of John Calvin have been compared and shown that Calvin never wished to replace sacramental worship by a preaching service. His aim was to restore the Eucharist in its primitive simplicity, as a weekly celebration and communion and to restore the Holy Scriptures to their authoritative place.

The Calvinistic liturgical outlook was well expressed by the Rev. Alan Dougan in the New South Wales Church. Dougan exerted a powerful influence in the Church but was opposed by many who desired a minimised liturgy. The debates of that era in the Church's journal indicate that there was disdain and ridicule of anything liturgical.

From a theological perspective the debates on liturgy and especially the current minimised versions of worship are a serious matter. Duncan Forrester has rightly argued in his book *Encounter with God* worship is concerned with the search for meaning, with renewing, affirming, re-ordering our view of reality, of God, the world, and our relations with our neighbours. Worship is necessary for the sustaining and proclamation of the Christian vision, because it is an encounter with God that is Reality. And that is why the crisis of worship has to be taken with the most profound seriousness.

The minimisation process has reached its pinnacle in the *Metro Papers*. These papers discourage any liturgical approach, or the use of liturgical forms, so that the sacramental character of Calvin's liturgy is replaced by a preaching service. Not only is this suggested approach not in accord with the theology of John Calvin, but also the idea that there is a choice between form and no form is a false antithesis. In recent years popular worship has become a time for outreach and evangelism. D.G. Hart and John Muether have argued that this has been achieved by worship committees which seek to reach the unchurched so that growth in numbers replaces the spiritual growth of believers as the goal of worship. All members are encouraged to exercise a ministry for the purpose of evangelism. Hart and Muether sees this as being detrimental to the ministry and health of the Church, as the same principle cannot be applied to other areas of life such as investment portfolios and medical practice. The implementation of worship leaders has been at the cost of undermining the office of ordination, as the underlying premise is that all members have a valid ministry based on the priesthood of all believers.

The comment of William Maxwell has long been forgotten by the contemporary generation, he said that, the purpose of all form in worship is to provide a body for the spirit, and as far as possible to ensure that the worshippers offer in the right spirit, and not just according to their own desires, devices or fancies. Worship must be consonant with God's will and offered to His glory and honour.

It is an essential feature of this theme on Liturgical Minimisation, to recognise that it operates upon a faulty epistemology. In chapter six we have traced the development of the philosophy behind the scientific method and its application to theology. This section within chapter six may appear to be too long but I deemed it necessary to have a comprehensive, though brief, understanding of the issues involved, for the purpose of a greater epistemological understanding for theology. Professor Ronald Laura argues that priority is given to scientific knowledge in the modern educational system, and it is this form of knowledge which we value, as a culture for the purposes of power and control. This particular form of knowledge says Laura, has been institutionalised in our educational institutions. 'It is our insatiable appetite for power that drives us to a form of knowledge which covertly stipulates that the only knowledge worth having is that which allows us to re-order the world and our relationships to each other in ways that suit our own ends and presumed interests, no matter how selfish or destructive those ends and interests are.' Such is the influence of this epistemology of power that 'it has become an elemental facet of our physical existence'. It is this insight of Laura's that is extremely useful in theological studies and in the theology of worship in particular. There has been a significant impact of a scientific epistemology in theology. To that end we have traced the transmission of the influence of a scientific methodology into Australia from Thomas Chalmers, Charles Hodge and B.B. Warfield, and have shown that it has been used effectively in the contemporary era through the influence of Principal Broughton Knox of Moore Theological College, Sydney. The use of this type of epistemology preserves the autonomy of man, in that man retains the control of a specific theology of worship.

There is a great need for a specific Christian Epistemology as the scientific model is inappropriate, as it becomes mere Christianised scientism. The fundamental difference been the two models is one epistemology is an epistemology of power and control, whereas the other is an epistemology of love and connectedness. The work of Cornelius Van Til is critical at this point as shown in chapter six. Van Til's contribution to Christian thought is comparable in magnitude to that of Immanuel Kant in non-Christian philosophy. The foundation of Van Til's system is the rejection of the autonomy of man, since Christian thinking, like all of the Christian life, is subject to God's lordship. Van Til specifically rejects the traditional epistemic methodology as it is offered in Thomas Aquinas in its Catholic form, and in Joseph Butler in its protestant form, as it is based upon the assumption that man has some measure of autonomy, that in the space-time world is in some measure 'contingent' and that man must create for himself his own epistemology in an ultimate sense. In this method, man has the right and the ability to judge the claims of the authoritative Word of God. Van Til argues that by this method the correctness of the natural man's problematics is endorsed. That is all he needs to reject the Christian faith. However Christian scholars have used this popular methodology arising out of the Enlightenment period, to interpret the realities of the Bible and applied the same principles to formulate various theologies. To make sense of reality, Van Til argues that one must presuppose the reality of the self-contained triune God and the self-attesting revelation of the Scriptures.

It is significant that Van Til goes back to the theology of John Calvin rather than Luther and other Reformers because he had rid himself of the last vestiges of human independence and autonomy. This is of importance to the theology of worship, as Calvin's theology of Worship was Trinitarian rather than Unitarian. James B. Torrance argues that Trinitarian worship is the gift of participating through the Spirit in the incarnate Son's communion with the Father.

Liturgical minimization has effectively destroyed the practice and use of the Church's historical liturgy and its forms, and reduced worship to a preaching service.

The crisis confronting the Church in Australia, especially in New South Wales, has reached the point that it is now necessary to look back to the Church's historical and Calvinistic heritage to redirect the Church's focus to Trinitarian worship so as to save the Church's worship from chaos and mayhem. To do so will require a serious reappraisal of the content of theological education. Chapter seven is therefore devoted to the reconstruction of theological education. Following Ronald Laura, we have argued that the first step is what he calls, the reconceptualization of knowledge.

Laura argues that the reconceptualization of knowledge is the means to empathetic connectivity, whereby the role of education is to educate the sensibilities of moral conscience to recognise the value and the point of moral responsibility. Instead of controlling there is the idea of connecting. This is the first step of recognition. Cornelius Van Til in a similar way advocates the development of a specific Christian Epistemology for theological studies in which love is the ontological focus point. The Gospel of John chapter 15, Jesus tells his disciples 'I call you my friends', 'I no longer call you slaves, because the slave does not know what the master is doing'. The slave in the mind of Jesus is not a slave because of the conditions of his labour, underpaid and overworked, but because he is denied intimacy with the master. There is no relation of caring, no vulnerability of emotions, no sharing of feelings. The slave and the master are always at arms length. Our culture, for the reasons that Ronald Laura has spelt out makes the sharing of deep intimacies difficult. Unfortunately we approach others as objects and we calculate success in terms of things, possessing them and manipulating them for our personal benefit. Both Laura and Van Til are complementary to each other as both advocate an epistemology of love that makes for meaningful 'connections' with God and nature. The whole notion of theological education is, therefore, to provide strategies for students to connect not only with the sovereign creator and His redeeming love for humanity, but to comprehend the scope of the epistemological interconnections of historical theology. To adhere to methodologies which enhance separateness and create a critical platform to critique, and to suppress every other theological point of view is to fail the ideals of an epistemology of love and empathy. The anti-catholic debates of the past and the defrocking of theologians, who disagree with a perceived denominational point of view, are evidence of how an empirical/ reductionist methodology is less than helpful for the peace and unity of the Church.

Unless there is a reconstruction in theological education whereby students are not only schooled in the history and development of scientific epistemology but also, out of necessity, trained to imbibe the foundations of a specific Christian epistemology and to understand the impact that various epistemologies have had upon theological disciplines, the Church will continue to be bound to popular cultural thought. Until the Church returns to the epistemic and theological foundations of its heritage, the 'pattern of conflict' will continue to be a major destabilising factor.

Bibliography

Armstrong, John. ed. *Reformation and Revival.* Illinois: Carol Stream: Vol. 10, No 3.
Ashton, J. and R. Laura. *New Insights in Environmental Education.* Adamstown: Insight Press, 2003.
Atkinson, Nigel. *Richard Hooker, Authority of Scripture Tradition and Reason,* London: Paternoster, 1997.
Australian Dictionary of Bibliography, Vol. 1. Melbourne: Melbourne University Press, 1983.
Australian Church Quarterley, September 1972.
Australian Presbyterian Life, March 2007, April 2006, December 2007.
Bacon, Francis. *The New Organon and Related Writings.* New York: Bobbs Merril, 1960.
Bahnsen, Greg L. *Van Til's Apologetic.* N.J.: P&R Publishing, 1998.
Baillie, D. M. *The Theology of the Sacraments.* London: Faber & Faber, 1965.
Baillie, J. *Natural Science and Spiritual Life.* London: Geoffrey Cumberlege 1951.
Baird, C. W. *The Presbyterian Liturgies.* Grand Rapids: Baker Books, 1957.
Baker, D.W. A. *Days of Wrath.* Melbourne: Melbourne University Press, 1985.
———. *Preacher, Politician, Patriot.* Melbourne: Melbourne University Press, 1998.
Banks, Robert J. "The Theology of D. B. Knox", in *God Who is Rich in Mercy* edited by P. O'Brien and D. Peterson, 395-397. Homebush West: Lancer Books 1986
Barcan, Alan. *Two Centuries of Education in New South Wales.* Sydney: NSW University Press, 1988.
Barclay, A. *A Protestant Doctrine of the Lord's Supper.* Glasgow: Jackson, Wylie & Co, 1927.
Barkley, John. *Presbyterianism.* Belfast: Presbyterian Church of Ireland, 1966.
Barna, George. *Marketing the Church.* Colarado: Nav Press, 1988.
Barnes, Peter. *A Rich History.* Australian Presbyterian, December 2011.
Bathurst National Advocate 28 February 1952.
Baxter, J. Sidlow. *Explore the Book,* Vol. 1. London: Marshall, Morgan & Scott, 1956.
Berkhof, L. *Systematic Theology.* London: Banner of Truth Trust, 1949.
Best, Harold. "Contemporary Music-Driven Worship", in *Exploring the Worship Spectrum,* ed. by P. Engle and P. Basden, 123, Grand Rapids: Zondervan, 2004.
Betterson, H. ed. *Documents of the Christian Church.* London: Oxford University Press, 1964.
Blainey, Geoffrey. *A Short History of Christianity.* Camberwell: Penguin Group. Australia, 2011.
Bloom, Alan. *The Closing of the American Mind.* New York: Simon and Schuster, 1987.
Border, R. *Church and State in Australia 1788 – 1872.* London: SPCK, 1962.
Bridges, Barry. and R. Ward. *Ministers and Licentiates and Catechists Biographical Register,* Melbourne: R. Ward, 1989.

Bridges, Barry. *Ministry in Scotland in the First Half of the Nineteenth Century.* Paper located in Ferguson Memorial Library, Sydney.
The Briefing. Sydney: St. Matthias Press, Nov.1993.
Budde, M. and R. Brimlow. eds. *The Church as Countercultur.* New York:State University of NY Press, 2000.
Bullock, J. *The Kirk in Scotland.* Edinburgh: St. Andrews Press, 1960.
Burton, Brian K. *Anatomy of Heresy.* Sydney: Books and Writers Network, 2003.
Calderwood, *History of the Church of Scotland.* Vol. 4. Edinburgh: Wodrow Society, 1842.
Calvin, John. *Institutes of the Christian Religion.* London: James Clark, 1962.
———. *Commentaries Genesis*, Vol. 1. Michigan: Baker Book House, 1979.
———. *Commentrary on Ephesians*, Vol. 21. Grand Rapids: Baker Book House, 1979.
———. *Commentaries*, Vol. 22. Michigan: Baker Book House, 1979.
Culhane, Elizabeth. *Slamming the Door Shut,* BA(Hons) Thesis, University of Melbourne, 2011.
Cameron, Rev. James. *Centenary History of the Presbyterian Church in NSW.* Sydney: Angus & Robertson, 1905.
Cameron, Peter. "Rev. A.A.Dougan", *The St. Andrew's College Magazine*, 1974.
Carey, Hilary. *God's Empire.* Cambridge: Cambridge University Press, 2011.
Carnley, P. *Reflections in Glass.* Sydney: Harper Collins, 2004.
Carson, D. A, *The Difficult Doctrine of the Love of God.* Leicester: IVP, 2000.
Chapell, Bryan, *Christ Centered Worship.* Grand Rapids: Baker Academic, 2009.
Chalmers, Thomas, *Prelections on Butlers Analogy & Hill*, Posthumous Works,(Edinburgh: Thomas Constable, 1849.
———. *Institutes of Theology* Vol. 7. New York: Harper, 1857.
Chung, Y. *Growth Consolidation and Revolution. Journal of Oxford University History Society*, 2005.
Clark, Neville. *Call to Worship.* London: SCM Press, 1960.
Clarke, L, *Constitutional Church Government*, 1924.
Colson, Charles. *Burden of Truth.* Illinois: Tyndale House, 1997.
Craig, E. ed. *Encyclopedia of Philosophy.* London: Routledge, 1998.
Cross, F.L. ed. *Oxford Dictionary of the Christian Church.* London: Oxford University Press, 1958.
Davies, J. *Dictionary of Liturgical Worship.* London: SCM, 1972.
———. *Australian Anglicans and their Constitution.* Canberra: Acoin Press, 1993.
Descartes, R. *The Philosophical Writings of Descartes*, Vol. 1. Cambridge: Cambridge University Press, 1985.
Dewey, J. *The Quest for Certainty.* London: Allen & Unwin, 1930.
Dickens, A. *Documents of Modern History.* New York: St. Martins Press, 1977.
Dickinson, W. *John Knox's History of the Reformation in Scotland.* London: Thomas Nelson, 1949.
Donaldson, Gordon. *The Making of the Scottish Prayer Book of 1637.* Edinburgh: University Press 1954.
Duba, Arlo D. *Recapturing the Liturgical Essence of the Reformed Tradition.* Association for Reformed and Liturgical Worship, 2009.
Due, Noel. *Created for Worship.* Glasgow: Mentor Press, 2005.
Dyck, John T. *Calvin and Worship* WRS Journal, 16:1 February 2009.
Ebenezer Church Newsletter, No 17, November 2014.
Educational Theory, Vol. 28, Fall 1978. No 4.
Emilson. Susan. A *Whiff of Heresy: Samuel Angus & the Presbyterian Church in New South Wales.* Sydney: N.S.W. University Press, 1991.
Engle, P. and P. Basden. eds. *Exploring the Worship Spectrum.* Michigan: Zondervan, 2004.
Farely, Edward. *Theologia.* Philadelphia: Fortress Press, 1983.
Ferguson, S., Wright. D. Packer. J. I. eds. *New Dictionary of Theology.* Illinois: VPS, 1988.
Fishburn, Janet. "Theological Education: A Reformed Imperative." In Sienkewicz, T. and Betts, J. eds. *Festschrift in Honour of Charles Speel.* Illinois: Monmouth College, 1997.

Forrester, D. and D. Murray. *Studies in the History of Worship in Scotland.* Edinburgh: T&T Clark, 1996.
Forrester, D. and J. McDonald. *Encounter With God.* Edinburgh: T&T Clark, 1983.
Geehan, E. R. ed. *Jerusalem and Athens.* New York: P&R Publishing, 1980.
Gilchrist, A. *J.D. Lang Contemporary Documents*, Vol. 1. Melbourne: Jedgarm Publishing, 1951.
Gilchrist, A. and G. Powell. *John Dunmore Lang, Pioneer Republican.* Melbourne: New Melbourne Press, 1999.
Giles, Kevin. *What on Earth is the Church?* Blackburne: Dove Australia, 1995.
———. "Created Woman", *Sydney Morning Herald*, 6 March 2015.
Dix, Dom Gregory. *The Shape of the Liturgy.* Westminster: Dacra Press, 1949.
Geisler, Norman L. *Is Man the Measure.* Michigan: Baker Book House, 1983.
Gore, R. J. *Covenantal Worship.* Phillipsburg: P & R Publishing, 2002.
Grantham, Ted. ed. *The Presbyterian Review.* Sydney: Scots Church, March, May 2006, November 2007.
Hamlyn, D.W. *The Encyclopedia of Philosophy*, Vol.1. New York: Macmillan, 1972.
Hanna, W. *Memoirs of Thomas Chalmers*, Vol. 2. London: Thomas Constable & Co, 1854.
Hart, D.G. and Muther. J.R. *With Reverence and Awe.* Phillipsburg: P&R Publishing, 2002.
Hart, D.G. *Mother Kirk.* Grand Rapids: Baker Academic, 2003.
———. *Calvinism: A History.* New York: Yale University Press, 2013.
———. *John Williamson Nevin: High Church Calvinist.* New Jersey: P&R Publishing, 2005.
Herman, A. *The Scottish Enlightenment.* London: Fourth Estate, 2003.
Heshusius, L. "Freeing ourselves from objectivity", *Educational Researcher*, April 1994.
Hill, C. and F.,Thomas F. *The Glory of the Atonement.* Illinois Intervarsity Press, 2004.
Hill, George. *Theological Institutes.* Edinburgh: Bell and Bradfute, 1803.
Hislop, D.H. *Our Heritage in Public Worship.* Edinburgh: T&T Clark, 1935.
Hodge, Charles. *Systematic Theology*, Vol.1. London: James Clarke, reprint 1960.
Holy Bible, New International Version. London: Hodder & Stoughton, 1984.
Hooykaas, R. *Scientific Progress and Religious Dissent.* Open University Press, 1975.
Horton, M. *A Better Way.* Michigan: Baker Books, 2002.
Hume, David. *The Natural History of Religion and Dialogues Concerning Natural Religion.* Oxford: Colver & Price, 1976.
Hustad, D.P. *Church Music in the Evangelical Tradition.* Illinois: Hope Publishing, 1981.
Hutchinson, M., *Iron in Our Blood.* Sydney: Ferguson Publications, 2001.
Institute of Australian Culture, 24 September 2012.
Jones, C. *The Study of Liturgy.* London: SPCK, 1983.
Journal Royal Australian Historical Society, Vol. 69, June 1883; Vol. 74, October 1988.
Judd, S. and Cable. K. *Sydney Anglicans.* Sydney: Anglican Information Office, 2000.
Jue, H. K. *Theologia Naturalis,* in Oliphant and Tipton, *Revelation and Reason.* New Jersey: P&R Publishing, 2007.
Knox, Broughton D. *Selected Works,* Vol. 1. Sydney: Matthias Media, 2000.
Kuhn, T.S. *The Structure of Scientific Revolutions.* Chicago: University of Chicago, 1970.
Kuyper, Abraham. *Lectures on Calvinism.* Grand Rapids: Eerdmans Press, 1975.
Laing, A. *John Knox and the Reformation.* London: Longmans Green, 1905.
Lang, J. D. *Historical & Statistical Account of New South Wales*, Vol. 2. Sydney: 1834.
———. *Vol 16 Letter, Broughton to Lang*, 16 January 1830.
———. *The Dead Fly in the Apothecary's Ointment.* Sydney: 1861.
———. *Lord John Russell.* 1840.
———. *Rt Honourable H. Labouchere*, July 1839.
———. *Reminiscences of My Life and Times.* Melbourne: Heinemann, 1992.
Laura, R., and M. Cotton. *Empathic Education.* Philadelphia: Falmer Press, 1999.
Laura, R., and J. Ashton. *New Insights into Environmental Education.* Adamstown: Insight Press, 2003.
Laura, R., and T. Marchant. *Surviving the High Tech Depersonalisation Crisis.* Adamstown: Insight Press, 2002.

Laura, R., T. Marchant, and S. Smith. *The New Social Disease,*. Maryland: University Press of America, 2008.
Laura, R., and A. Chapman. *The Paradigm Shift in Health*. Maryland: University Press of America, 2009.
Leishman, T. *Ritual of the Church of Scotland Past and Present*, Edit., Story, R.H.. London: William Mackenzie, 1890.
Lloyd Jones, D.M. *The Puritans*. Edinburgh: Banner of Truth Trust, 1987.
Locke, John. *Essay Concerning Human Understanding.* Oxford: Oxford University Press, 1960.
Mackintosh, H.R. *The Person of Jesus Christ*. Edinburgh: T&T Clark, 1956.
Matthews, H.S. and Harrison, B. eds. *Oxford Dictionary of National Biography*, Vol. 32. Oxford: Oxford University Press, 2004.
Maxwell, William. *Concerning Worship.* London: Oxford University Press, 1948.
Maxwell, W.D., *Outline of Christian Worship*. London: Oxford University Press, 1963.
———. *The Genevan Service Book 1556*. Westminster: Faith Press, 1965.
May, P.R., *Richard Baxter in Education*, British Journal of Education, 1967.
McGibbon, J. *The Duty of the Church*. Sydney: Fredrick White, 1864.
McGowan, A.T.B. *The Divine Spiration of Scripture*. Nottingham: Apollos Press, 2007.
———. *Always Reforming.* Leicester: IVP, 2006.
———. *Conference Paper,* in *Australian Presbyterian Life*, April 2006.
McIntyre, J. *Theology After the Storm*. Michigan: W. Eerdmans, 1997.
McLeod, Donald. *Presbyterian Worship Its Meaning and Method.* Richmond: John Knox Press, 1965.
McNeill, John T. *History and Character of Calvinism*. London: Oxford University Press, 1954.
McSkimming, Josie. *The Sydney Morning Herald*, 6 March 2015.
Macquarie University Law School, *Decisions of the Superior Courts of New South Wales. 1788-1899*, Sydney.
Medical Journal of Australia, 13 December 1966.
Moffatt, J. *The Presbyterian Churches*, London: 1928.
Mooney, C.G. "The Teaching of Latin and Greek in the County of Cumberland New South Wales, Prior to the Foundation of the University of Sydney", Ph.D. Thesis, University of Newcastle, 1995.
Minutes, *Commission of N.S.W. General Assembly 20th November 2013.*
Moore, Peter. *Can a Bishop be Wrong?*, Harrisburg: Morehouse Publishing, 1998.
Moore, L.J. "Sing to the Lord a New Song: A study of changing musical practices in the Presbyterian Church of Victoria 1861-1901", M.Mus Thesis, Australian Catholic University.
Morgenthaler, Sally. "Emerging Worship." In *Exploring the Worship*, edited by P. Engle and P. Basden, 223 Grand Rapids: Zondervan, 2004.
Murray, Iain. *Australian Christian Life*. Edinburgh: Banner of Truth Trust, 1988.
———. *Letters of Thomas Chalmers*. Edinburgh: Banner of Truth Trust, 2007.
Muether, John R. *Cornelius Van Til*. New Jersey: P&R Publishing, 2008.
Muller, Richard A. *Post-Reformation Reformed Dogmatics*, Vol. 2. Grand Rapids: Baker Books, 1993.
New South Wales Government Parliamentary Service >http://www.parliament.nsw.gov.au<.
New South Wales Presbyterian, July, December 1937, September, November, December 1944, January 1945, May 1956, April 2006.
Nolan, Randall. "A Mediating Tradition: The Anglican Vocation in Australian Society", PhD thesis, Griffith University. May 2007.
O'Brien, P. and D. Peterson, ed. *God Who is Rich in Mercy.* Homebush West: Lancer Books, 1986.
Oliphant, K. Scott and L. G. Tipton, eds. *Revelation and Reason*. New Jersey: P&R Publishing, 2007.
O'Murchu, Diarmuid. *Quantum Theology*. New York: The Crossroads Publishing, 2013.
Orr, James. *The Christian View of God and the World*. 1891). Grand Rapids: Kregel Publishing, Reprint, 1989.

Oswalt, John N. *Crises in American Theological Education* >http// www.hiswayministries.org/ fdcrisis<, October 2008.
Packer, J. *A Quest for Godliness*. Illinois: Crossways Books, 1990.
Payne, Jon D. *In the Splendour of Holiness*. Tolle Lege Press, 2008.
Piggin, S. *The St. Andrew Seven*. Edinburgh: Banner of Truth, 1985.
Porter, M. *The New Puritans*. Clayton: Melbourne University Press, 2006.
Potter, G.U. *Zwingli*. London: Historical Association, 1977.
Prentis, Malcom D. *The Scots in Australia*. Sydney: Sydney University Press, 1983.
Presbyterian Church, General Assembly of Australia, *White Book*. Sydney. 1994, 2000.
Presbyterian Church, General Assembly of Australia, *Blue Book*. Sydney. 1991, 1997.
Presbyterian Church of Australia, *Directory of Public Worship of God*. Sydney: Angus & Robertson, 1892.
Presbyterian Church of Australia, *Basic Documents of Presbyterian Polity*. Board of Christian Education, S. Laing Blackburn, 1961.
Presbyterian Church of Australia, *Blue Book*, 1918, 1930.
Presbyterian Church of Australia, *Constitution Procedure and Practice*. Melbourne: Board of Religious Education, 1950.
Presbyterian Church in New South Wales, *The Code*. The General Assembly, Sydney 1994
Presbyterian Youth NSW, *Ministry Papers*, Sydney: 2006
Procter, F. ed. *Treasury of Quotations*. Michigan: Kregel Publishing, 1977.
R.S. Ward, *Rev. Dr. John Dunmore Lang 1799-1878 Turbulent Presbyterian Leader*, www.knoxpcea.org.au/index.php?view,retrieved 14 January 2016
R.S. Ward, *A Short History of the Church of Scotland*. Melbourne: New Melbourne Press, 2015.
Ramsland, J. and C. Mooney. "The Teaching of Classics in a Remote Pioneering Colony: Dr Laurence Halloran in a Penal Settlement of New South Wales, 1819–1831", in Hager, Fritz-Peter et al., eds. *Aspects of Antiquity in the History of Education*. Hannover: Bildung und Wissenschaft, 1992.
Rayburn, Robert G. *O Come Let us Worship*. Grand Rapids: Baker Book House, 1980.
Reformed Theological Review, December 2001, December 2002.
Reid, G.R.S. *The History of Ebenezer*. Windsor: Hawksbury Press, 4th Edition, 1953.
Reid, J.R. *Marcus L. Loane* . Brunswick East: Acorn Press, 2004.
Richardson, Alan. *Genesis 1–11*. London: SCM Press, 1963.
Riddell, P. and P. Cotterell, P. *Islam in Context*. Grand Rapids: Baker Academic, 2003.
Rifkin, J. *Declaration of a Heretic*. New York: Routlege Kegan Paul, 1985.
Rifkin, J. and T. Howard, *Entropy A New World View*. New York: Viking Press, 1980.
Rogers, A.K. *A Students History of Philosophy*. New York: Macmillan, 1935.
Ross, J.M. *Four Centuries of Scottish Worship*. Edinburgh: St. Andrew Press, 1972.
Russell, Bertrand *History of Western Philosophy*. London: Allen & Unwin, 1962.
Ryken, P.G. ed. *Give Praise to God*. New Jersey: P&R Publishing, 2003.
Sefton, A. N. Cheng, and I. Thong, *The Centenary Book of the Sydney University Medical Society*. Sydney: Hale & Iremonger, 1992.
Scott, K. and L. G. Tipton, eds. *Revelation & Reason*. New York: P&R Publishing, 2007.
Schaeffer, Francis. *Genesis in Space and Time*. London: Hodder & Stroughton, 1973.
———. *Pollution & the Death of Man*. Illinois: Tyndale Press, 1979.
Sprott, G. and T. Lushman, *The Book of Common Order* . Edinburgh: William Blackwood & Sons, 1868.
Stafford, T.A. *Christian Symbolism*. New York: Abington- Cokesbury, 1942.
Story, R.H. *Life and Remains of Robert Lee D.D.*, London: Hurst and Blackett, 1870.
Sydney Gazette, 8 August 1878.
Sydney Morning Herald, 8, 9 August 1878.
Sydney Morning Herald, 21 November, 19 December 1831.
Supplementary Report, *Sydney Diocesan Doctrine Commission*, 2008.
Tacey, David. *The Spirituality Revolution*. Sydney: Harper Collins,
Tillich, P. *Systematic Theology*, Vol. 1, 1951.
Torrance, James. *Worship, Community and the Triune God*. Intervarsity Press, 1966.

———. *Worship, Community and the Triune God of Grace*. Carlisle: Paternoster, 1996.
Torrance, T.F. ed. *John Calvin's Tracts and Treatises*. Michigan: Eerdmans, 1958.
———. *Theological Science*. London: Oxford University Press, 1969.
———. *God and Rationality*. London: Oxford University Press, 1971.
———. *Transformation & Convergence in the Frame of Knowledge*. Michigan: Eerdmans, 1984.
Underhill, Evelyn. *Worship*. London: Collins, 1936.
Van Til, C. *In Defence of the Faith Vol.2 A Survey of Christian Epistemology*. New Jersey: P& R Publishing, no date.
———. *Jerusalem and Athens*, E.R.Geehan, Edit.. Presbyterian & Reformed Publishing, 1980.
———. *In Defence of the Faith Vol.5 An Introduction to Systematic Theology*. Presbyterian and Reformed Publishing, 1974.
———. *The Reformed Pastor and Modern Thought*. New York: P&R Publishing, 1980.
von Rad, Gerhard. *Genesis*. London: SCM Press, 1970.
Warfield, B.B., *Calvin and Augustine*. Philadelphia: P&R Publishing, 1956.
———. *Selected Shorter Writings*. New Jersey: P&R Publishing, 1973.
Webber, Robert E., *Ancient Future Faith*. Grand Rapids: Baker Books, 1999.
———. *The Younger Evangelicals*. Michigan: Baker Books, 2002.
Webster J. "Science and Religion in Thomas Chalmers", MA(Hons) Thesis, University of Wollongong. 1989.
Wells, David. *Above All Earthly Powers*. Grand Rapids: Eerdmans, 2006.
Western Times, 11 July 1944, 2 June, 18 August, 27 October 1945.
Willson, Robert. *Life and Times of Alan Dougan*, An Address at the Annual Meeting of the Friends of the Ferguson Library, Sydney, 19 March 2005.
Wisdom, John. *Paradox and Discovery*. Oxford: Basil Blackwell, 1965.
———. *Philosophy and Psycho – Analysis*. Oxford: Basil Blackwell, 1957.
Wollheim, R. *Hume on Religion*. London: Collins, 1963.
Presbyterian Church of Australia, *Worship*. Maryborough, Victoria: 1990, 1998.
Wright, Tom. *Scripture & the Authority of God*. SPCK, 2nd edition, 2013.
Young, Edward J. *In the Beginning*. Edinburgh: Banner of Truth Trust, 1976.
Zwingli, U. *Commentary on True and False Religion*, Edit., S. Jackson. North Carolina: Labyrinth Press, 1981.

About the Authors

REV. JOHN E. WEBSTER PH.D

Dr. John E. Webster was born in the Riverina city of Wagga Wagga, N.S.W. Australia. He qualified as a Fitter and Turner, working with Caterpiller earth moving machinary and machine tools. He studied for the ministry of the Presbyterian Church. Ordained in 1971 he served the Church in several cities in both N.S.W., and Victoria. Whilst in Victoria he was the minister of the historic gold mining city of Bendigo. He served for nine years on the Victorian Theological Education Committee and was elected the Convenor of the Business Committee of the General Assembly.

Returning to N.S.W. he was elected the State Moderator of the General Assembly in 1999 while he was minister of Scots Kirk, Hamilton.

During the years in pastoral ministry the appetite for academic pusuits came to the fore. He graduated form the University of Wollongong with a BA and MA(Hons) majoring in the History and Philosophy of Science. More recently a Ph.D. from the University of Newcastle in the School of Education.

In his spare time Dr. Webster grows orchids.

PROFESSOR RONALD S. LAURA, D.PHIL. (OXON)

Educated at the Universities of Harvard, Cambridge and Oxford,where he completed his Doctoral Studies. Dr.Ronald Laura is Professor in Education at the University of Newcastle, Australia. In addition to publishing in excess of 300 scholarly artices, he has also published over 40 books including Empathetic Education (1999), and the New Social Disease: From High Tech Depersonalization to Survival of the Soul (2008), The Paradigm Shift in Health:

Towards a Quantum Understanding of the role of Consciousness in Health Promotion and Education. (2009) He teaches in both the faculty of Education and Arts, offering subjects in the Philosophy of Education, Leadership Education and Health and Fitness Education. He is the creator of the now world renowned exercise system called, Matrix Quick Fit (MQF).

www.ingramcontent.com/pod-product-compliance
Lightning Source LLC
Chambersburg PA
CBHW022011300426
44117CB00005B/140